THE SCARECROW AUTHOR BIBLIOGRAPHIES

1. John Steinbeck (Tetsumaro Hayashi). 1973. *See also no. 64.*
2. Joseph Conrad (Theodore G. Ehrsam). 1969.
3. Arthur Miller (Tetsumaro Hayashi). 2nd ed., 1976.
4. Katherine Anne Porter (Waldrip & Bauer). 1969.
5. Philip Freneau (Philip M. Marsh). 1970.
6. Robert Greene (Tetsumaro Hayashi). 1971.
7. Benjamin Disraeli (R.W. Stewart). 1972.
8. John Berryman (Richard W. Kelly). 1972.
9. William Dean Howells (Vito J. Brenni). 1973.
10. Jean Anouilh (Kathleen W. Kelly). 1973.
11. E.M. Forster (Alfred Borrello). 1973.
12. The Marquis de Sade (E. Pierre Chanover). 1973.
13. Alain Robbe-Grillet (Dale W. Frazier). 1973.
14. Northrop Frye (Robert D. Denham). 1974.
15. Federico Garcia Lorca (Laurenti & Siracusa). 1974.
16. Ben Jonson (Brock & Welsh). 1974.
17. Four French Dramatists: Eugène Brieux, François de Curel, Emile Fabre, Paul Hervieu (Edmund F. Santa Vicca). 1974.
18. Ralph Waldo Ellison (Jacqueline Covo). 1974.
19. Philip Roth (Bernard F. Rodgers, Jr.). 2nd ed., 1984.
20. Norman Mailer (Laura Adams). 1974.
21. Sir John Betjeman (Margaret Stapleton). 1974.
22. Elie Wiesel (Molly Abramowitz). 1974.
23. Paul Laurence Dunbar (Eugene W. Metcalf, Jr.). 1975.
24. Henry James (Beatrice Ricks). 1975.
25. Robert Frost (Lentricchia & Lentricchia). 1976.
26. Sherwood Anderson (Douglas G. Rogers). 1976.
27. Iris Murdoch and Muriel Spark (Tominaga & Schneidermeyer). 1976.
28. John Ruskin (Kirk H. Beetz). 1976.
29. Georges Simenon (Trudee Young). 1976.
30. George Gordon, Lord Byron (Oscar José Santucho). 1977.
31. John Barth (Richard Vine). 1977.
32. John Hawkes (Carol A. Hryciw). 1977.
33. William Everson (Bartlett & Campo). 1977.
34. May Sarton (Lenora Blouin). 1978.
35. Wilkie Collins (Kirk H. Beetz). 1978.
36. Sylvia Plath (Lane & Stevens). 1978.
37. E.B. White (A.J. Anderson). 1978.
38. Henry Miller (Lawrence J. Shifreen). 1979.

Robinson Jeffers and the Critics, 1912-1983:

A Bibliography of Secondary Sources with Selective Annotations

by
JEANETTA BOSWELL

Scarecrow Author Bibliographies, No. 77

The Scarecrow Press, Inc.
Metuchen, N.J., & London
1986

Library of Congress Cataloging-in-Publication Data

Boswell, Jeanetta, 1922–
    Robinson Jeffers and the critics, 1912–1983.

    (Scarecrow author bibliographies ; no. 77)
    Includes indexes.
    1. Jeffers, Robinson, 1887–1962––Bibliography.
I. Title. II. Series.
Z8451.5.B67 1986 ⌊PS3519.E27⌋ 016.811'52   86–17862
ISBN 0–8108–1914–7

Once more, with love and
fond remembrance, to Fred,
Sister, and all the dear
lately departed ones. . .
in this year of Halley's Comet

CONTENTS

ABOUT ROBINSON JEFFERS

Robinson Jeffers was born in Pittsburgh, Pennsylvania, in 1887. He studied at private schools in Geneva, Lausanne, Zurich, and Leipzig, returning to Los Angeles in 1903 (where his parents had moved) and enrolling at Occidental College. He graduated in 1905, at the age of eighteen, and subsequently enrolled at the University of Southern California. Here he met Mrs. Una Call Kuster, separated but not divorced from her husband, and developed an attachment that ulti- mately resulted in her divorce and their marriage in 1913. From that point on, Jeffers' life was largely free from outward incidents, and his years were punctuated with the publications of his volumes of drama and verse. He and his wife Una lived in the village of Carmel on the California coast in a huge stone edifice called "Tor House." Later Jeffers built, with his own hands, Hawk Tower, with rocks which he gathered and dug from the surrounding area. The bleak coast, the seabirds, the isolation suited his temperament. Jeffers died in 1962.

Although he never attracted much popular acclaim, and hardly more critical accord, he nonetheless had his following, and it was an enthusiastic audience, especially in the American 1920's when the temper of life hovered near the edge of despair and nearly came to believe in utter and total oblivion and annihilation. Jeffers' outlook is the ultimate statement in a dark, negative philosophy, but his es- timate of the human condition falls short of tragedy since he does not affirm the essential greatness of Man. For him man is cursed with consciousness but achieves Nothing. There is no one like Jeffers in American poetry. He cannot be read without sacrificing ease and peace of mind. He may never be loved, but he will never be for- gotten.

ABOUT THE BIBLIOGRAPHY

At the conclusion of each bibliography which I have compiled, I have always felt that I learned more perhaps than anyone who may consult it in the future. This is nowhere truer than in the case of Robinson

Jeffers. I came to Jeffers with little knowledge and less appreciation. I stayed, and lived to regret the years I taught American literature and did little or nothing with Jeffers. Like the poor soul of the cliché, I came to scorn and stayed to pray. I could blame the text-books, they are wretched when it comes to representing Jeffers, or I could blame this or that. The truth is that I neglected Jeffers because I did not know he was a major poet. My head was always so full of Whitman, Emerson, and Thoreau; Jeffers was their brother of the twentieth century, at another time and in another place but arriving at many of the same conclusions, albeit by different routes and seemingly opposite means. I have learned this from reading Jeffers and from reading the many excellent pieces of biography and criticism that have been written about him.

As to the critics, Jeffers has not fared too badly on the American scene. Given his propensity to lead many readers down mistaken avenues of ideas, it is not surprising that Jeffers has never been popular, popular in the way that Robert Frost was popular, popular as was Sandburg, but still somehow he has succeeded in appealing to the uncommon reader and at the same time never sacrificing one jot of his artistic integrity. Admittedly one cannot run up an account of three thousand critical and biographical items (as is the case with Melville and Whitman) and still be incomplete, but give him time! In some ways, however, Jeffers is more fortunate than some of the nineteenth-century figures: there is perhaps less trivia in his criticism than in some of theirs. Most of his critics and biographers have been men and women of sound persuasion and have said excellent things about him, although sometimes in a negative vein. One measurement by which an author may be judged is in the number of doctoral and masters theses which he attracts, and in this respect Jeffers has done well.

All bibliographical studies are built upon those which have gone before, and mine is no exception. Of particular interest are some of the following: Sydney Alberts' Bibliography of the Writings of Robinson Jeffers (1933, reprinted 1968), important for its careful scholarship and the fact that it came first; A. A. Vardamis' The Critical Reputation of Robinson Jeffers (1972) which grew out of his doctoral dissertation of 1970; two articles are interesting for the overall insight they provide of Jeffers--Vernon Young's "Jeffers Revisited" (1977) and William Nolte's "Robinson Jeffers Redivivus" (1978), both written on the occasion of the reissue of three important Jeffers volumes by Norton in 1977. The Robinson Jeffers Newsletter is now in its third decade, having been initiated by Mabel Bennett in 1963, and, since her death, edited by Dr. Robert Brophy. This publication has been the source of several valuable checklists: Covington Rodgers' checklist of Jeffers poetical writings since 1934 (1977); Robert Brophy's lists of doctoral and masters theses (1969, 1970); and finally a series of survey articles on library holdings of Robinson Jeffers. His papers, letters, manuscripts, etc. are scattered far and wide in American libraries, and this survey should be greatly appreciated by future students interested in primary source material.

All of these items and others are listed in the bibliography, indexed under the subject-heading of "Bibliography."

Finally, I have the great pleasure of thanking those who have helped in the compiling this work: my assistant, Tanya Simmons; friends who gave moral support and believed in the work; my brother who kept up with the library books and did not allow a single one to become overdue; and the library staff itself, especially the Inter-Library Loan division, bringing in books from libraries far and wide. I have little love for the age of computers, but I must revise my thinking as regards the computers which enable librarians to put books beyond the imagination into the hands of students and teachers.

Jeanetta Boswell
Arlington, Texas
April 7, 1986

THE BIBLIOGRAPHY

1 ANONYMOUS (listed chronologically). "Review of Californians."
  Overland Monthly, 68 (December, 1916), 570.

2 "Comment on 'He Has Fallen in Love with the Mountains.'" Literary Digest, 53 (December 2, 1916), 1484.

3 "Review of Californians." Springfield [Mass.] Republican, January 18, 1917.

4 "Pacific Headlands: Review of Tamar and Other Poems." Time,
  5 (March 30, 1925), 12+.

5 "Publication of Poems by Jeffers Creates Strong Demand for More."
  Salt Lake Telegram, November 29, 1925.
      Review of Roan Stallion, Tamar, and Other Poems.

6 "Jeffers' Poetry Vivid and Bold...." Nashville Tennessean, December 27, 1925.
      Review of Roan Stallion, Tamar, etc.

7 "Review of Roan Stallion, Tamar, etc." Brooklyn Times, December 27, 1925.

8 "Robinson Jeffers in the Fury of His Passage." Brooklyn Citizen,
  December 27, 1925.
      Review of Roan Stallion, Tamar, etc.

9 "Review of Roan Stallion, Tamar, etc." University of Chicago
  English Journal, 15 (January, 1926), 86.

10 "Pagan Horror from Carmel-by-the-Sea," an editorial. The Monitor (San Francisco), 67 (January 9, 1926), 8.
       Answers the review which called Jeffers a great poet--that
   California has produced a great poet. Calls Jeffers "intrin-
   sically terrible" and accuses him of being a genuine pagan,
   shamelessly being read in Christian homes throughout America.

11 "Review of Roan Stallion, Tamar, etc." New York Evening Post,
   January 11, 1926.

12 "Review of Roan Stallion, Tamar, etc." Boston Evening Transcript,
    January 13, 1926.
        Says Jeffers' style is more prosaic than poetical, and that
    often he uses a word order which tends to confuse the sense
    of the passage. With the exception of a few lines which
    achieve grandeur, he is an extreme realist. He does have a
    remarkable power to portray character.

13 "Review of Roan Stallion, Tamar, etc." Omaha [Nebraska] World-
    Herald, January 24, 1926.

14 "Review of Roan Stallion, Tamar, etc." Booklist (Chicago), 22
    (February, 1926), 201.

15 "Review of Roan Stallion, Tamar, etc." Dial, 80 (February, 1926),
    161.
        Says Jeffers' poems are "informed with the terror and the
    violent beauty of man fulfilling his destiny, over against cold-
    ness and the tenor of a stone tranquility; slow life, the growth
    of trees and verse." In fertility and in primitive strength his
    poetry strikes a new and necessary chord in the chorus of
    contemporary American song.

16 "Review of Roan Stallion, Tamar, etc." The Argonaut (San Fran-
    cisco), 98 (February 27, 1926), 9.

17 "Portrait of Robinson Jeffers: Author of Roan Stallion, etc."
    Arts and Decoration, 24 (March, 1926), 63.

18 "The Poetry of Robinson Jeffers." The Argonaut (San Francisco),
    98 (March 13, 1926), 8.

19 "August Contributors." Overland Monthly, 84 (August, 1926),
    241.

20 "Comment on 'Noon' by Robinson Jeffers." New Republic, 45
    (July 21, 1926), 38. Reprinted in Literary Digest, 90 (August
    7, 1926), 32.

21 "A Little Poetry." Nation, 123 (October 20, 1926), 391-392.

22 "Portrait of Robinson Jeffers and George Sterling in front of Tor
    House, with Text." San Francisco Examiner, November 14,
    1926.

23 "Review of Roan Stallion, Tamar, etc." Chicago Schools Journal,
    9 (April, 1927), 317-318.

24 "A New Chant of Despair by Robinson Jeffers." New York Eve-
    ning Sun, July 1, 1927.
        Review of Women at Point Sur.

25 "A Note on Robinson Jeffers' Poetry." Saturday Review of Literature, 3 (July 9, 1927), 968.

26 "Robinson Jeffers Has New Poem." Davenport [Iowa] Daily Times, July 9, 1927.
        Refers to Women at Point Sur.

27 "Hysterics." St. Louis Post Dispatch, July 9, 1927.
        Review of Women at Point Sur.

28 "Happily Not Many Will Read 'The Women at Point Sur.'" Syracuse Post-Standard, July 13, 1927.

29 "Jeffers' New Book." Argonaut (San Francisco), 102 (July 23, 1927), 9.

30 "A Rising American Poet." Omaha World-Herald, July 24, 1927.
        Review of The Women at Point Sur.

31 "Again, Jeffers." Time, 10 (August 1, 1927), 31-32.
        Review of The Women at Point Sur.

32 "Grand and Otherwise." Nashville Tennessean, August 7, 1927.
        Review of The Women at Point Sur.

33 "Eliot and Crane Give Poetry Grand Style." Miami Daily News, August 7, 1927.
        Review of The Women at Point Sur.

34 "Jeffers in Tragic Song." San Jose Herald, August 21, 1927.
        Review of The Women at Point Sur.

35 "Jeffers Poem." San Francisco Bulletin, August 27, 1927.
        Review of The Women at Point Sur.

36 "Review of The Women at Point Sur." Chicago Step Ladder, 13 (October, 1927), 273.

37 "Review of The Women at Point Sur." Independent, 119 (October 15, 1927), 389.
        Believes Jeffers is sincere, serious, and powerful but has not discovered the dividing line between poetry and a burlesque of poetry.

38 "Review of The Women at Point Sur." University of Chicago English Journal, 16 (November, 1927), 749.

39 "Critical Comment on Roan Stallion and The Women at Point Sur." New Orleans Times-Picayune, November 20, 1927.

40 "Review of Three Poems." Poetry, 32 (January, 1928), 1. Also in San Francisco Examiner, January 8, 1928.

41   "Violent Verse of Robinson Jeffers." Springfield [Mass.] Republican, February 5, 1928.

42   "Review of A Miscellany of American Poetry: 1927." New Republic, 53 (February 8, 1928), 330.

43   "Not Wanted: A Poet Laureate." Editorial. The Argonaut, 104 (September 15, 1928), 2-3.

44   "Robinson Jeffers' Poem." Boston Evening Transcript, December 15, 1928.
        Review of Cawdor and Other Poems. Says this poem is more incoherent than the earlier ones and just as unpleasant. The characters have no relation to life, neither beauty nor honesty. The shorter poems in the volume, on the other hand, have a distinct merit.

45   "The Poet of Terror." Omaha World-Herald, December 23, 1928.
        Review of Cawdor and Other Poems.

46   "Review of Cawdor and Other Poems." Argonaut, 105 (January 12, 1929), 12.

47   "Review of Cawdor and Other Poems." Springfield [Mass.] Republican, February 3, 1929.

48   "Walt Whitman Finds Hellas." New Statesman (London), 32 (February 9, 1929), 572-574.
        Review of Roan Stallion, etc.

49   "Review of Cawdor and Other Poems." American Mercury, 16 (March, 1929), 46.

50   "Review of Cawdor and Other Poems." The Booklist, 25 (March, 1929), 241.
        Remarks that the theme is one of bitter tragedy, but is lacking "much of the alleviating beauty of his other narrative poems." As to the plot it is one based on a love triangle, that of a son and father over a woman, passionate and unscrupulous.

51   "Recommended Books." Yale Daily News Literary Supplement, 3 (May 25, 1929), 3.
        Includes Cawdor and Other Poems.

52   "The Author of Dear Judas and Other Poems." Boston Evening Transcript, September 14, 1929.

53   "New Books to Appear." Daily Oklahoman, Sepember 22, 1929.
        Review of Dear Judas and Other Poems.

54 "Notice of Dear Judas...." Bookman, 70 (October, 1929) 188-
    190.

55 "The Battle Continues." Nation and Athenaeum, 46 (November
    23, 1929), 294.
        Review of Cawdor, etc.

56 "Tragedian." Time, 14 (December 9, 1929), 72.
        Review of Dear Judas, etc.

57 "Review of Dear Judas, etc." American Mercury, 19 (March,
    1930), 24-26.

58 "Forty Notable Books of 1929." Publishers' Weekly, 117 (April
    26, 1930), 2209.
        Includes Dear Judas.

59 "Review of Dear Judas." University of Chicago English Journal,
    19 (September, 1930), 593.

60 "Robinson Jeffers: Bard." Magazine of Sigma Chi, 50 (May-
    June, 1931), 292-296.

61 "Robinson Jeffers' Dramatic Poem of Spiritual Tragedy." New
    York Times Book Review, April 3, 1932.
        Compares Thurso's Landing with earlier poems and finds
    that this one "seems more pertinent to life." On the other
    hand, it lacks the peculiar and exceptional beauty as passages
    to be found in previous works. While not Jeffers' most
    striking narrative, it is his crowning achievement to date.

62 "Cover Photo," with inside story. Time, 19 (April 4, 1932),
    63-64.
        Begins with a summary commentary of Jeffers' latest publi-
    cation, Thurso's Landing, emphasizing the violence and ab-
    normal behavior of the characters. Remainder of article is a
    review of Jeffers' life, his marriage, the building of Tor House
    and Hawk Tower, etc. In conclusion, the reviewer returns
    to Thurso's Landing, calling it the most native American, the
    least "Greekish" tragedy.

63 "A Poet's Son Turns Critic." New York Evening Post, April 22,
    1932.
        Review of Thurso's Landing, etc.

64 "Review of Thurso's Landing and Other Poems." Washington
    Daily News, April 23, 1932.

65 "Review of Thurso's Landing." University of Chicago English
    Journal, 21 (June, 1932), 512.

66 "Poet Turns to Tragedy: 'Thurso's Landing' is Jeffers at Best."
    Detroit Free Press, June 5, 1932.

67 "Review of Thurso's Landing, etc." The Forum, 88 (July,
    1932), 7.
        Calls this work the most human, the one which has the
    best chance of finding a popular audience. "It is as grim
    and somber as Cawdor or The Women at Point Sur,, as full
    of tragic grandeur, but abnormal passions are for once sub-
    ordinated."

68 The English Association, eds. The Modern Muse: British and
    American Poems of Today. New York: Oxford University
    Press, 1933. Robinson Jeffers, pp. 78-92.

69 "Review of Give Your Heart to the Hawks and Other Poems."
    Boston Transcript, November 18, 1933.
        Does not find much that he thinks matters in this volume.
    The characters--wretched, weak, tormented--struggle on the
    verge of madness and do not succeed in gaining any knowledge
    of themselves, their lives, or of life in general. The verse
    is typical Jeffers, "surging like the earth, through storms of
    cosmic sunlight as if forever."

70 "Los Angeles Occidental College: Robinson Jeffers, 1905-1935,
    an Exhibition Commemorating the 30th Anniversary of Gradu-
    ation from Occidental College." 1935.

71 "Review of Solstice and Other Poems." New York Times, October
    20, 1935.
        Says the verse of Robinson Jeffers is like that of Whitman,
    it must be read aloud, again and again. Fears that the minor
    poems may be neglected, but Jeffers has never been impressive
    in his short pieces. In "At the Birth of an Age" Jeffers ven-
    tures into a new conception and has plunged deeper than
    heretofore.

72 "Review of Such Counsels You Gave to Me and Other Poems."
    Time, 30 (October 18, 1937), 86.
        Does not think the book reveals anything new about the
    "parts of Jeffers' hybrid nature, but rather a wearied divi-
    sion between them." It does reveal, however, an ageing
    prophet still hell-bent on emitting clouds of sulphur and
    smoke, and the poet simultaneously becoming more and more
    corner-loving and "mealy-eyed."

73 "Review of Medea." Kirkus, 14 (February 1, 1946), 56.
        Thinks this version of the Greek play will be read by
    followers of Jeffers and poetry readers in general but will
    not appeal to a general public. Does not think this play is
    as effective as some of Jeffers' pseudo-Greek tragedies set
    in his native California.

74 "Review of The Double Axe and Other Poems." Kirkus, 16
    (June 15, 1948), 276.
        Quotes a good deal from Jeffers' Preface to his book, his
    first volume of poetry since 1941. It is in this Preface that
    Jeffers gives a relevant explanation of his theory of Inhu-
    manism: "In this, as in some previous work of mine, the
    objective has been to present a certain philosophical attitude,
    which might be called Inhumanism, a shifting of emphasis and
    significance from man to not-man; the rejection of human
    solipsism and recognition of the trans-human magnificance...."

75 "Review of The Beginning and the End and Other Poems." Time,
    81 (May 3, 1963), 114.
        This book is made up of 48 poems representing the last
    work of Robinson Jeffers. They were collected from hand-
    written manuscripts by his sons and secretary after Jeffers'
    death in 1962. Reviewer does not think these poems comparable
    in value to earlier works. In these he most frequently appears
    to be merely "sour, displaying the eccentric crankiness of a
    75 year old man who could never learn to live with other
    people." These poems are lacking in the beauty of language
    and poetic attributes which his best early work displayed.

76 ACKERMAN, Diane. "Robinson Jeffers: The Beauty of Trans-
    human Things." The American Poetry Review, 12 (March-
    April, 1983), 16-18.
        Unworldly, unconniving, at odds with society both as he
    found it and foresaw it, he fits an apocryphally definitive
    idea of the American mind: close to nature, to the universe,
    closer to them than to fellow-humans, and inclined to prize in
    himself elements held in common with galaxies, rocks, stallions,
    or cormorants. He takes the big-sky idyll to an extreme and
    he achieves an empathy writ so large that in the end the only
    quality that pulls some readers into his poems is the manner
    and tone. He is a born explainer, even going so far as to
    prefer definitions of words to words themselves. His poems
    feel illustrated, although there are no pictures in the margins,
    and the reader feels seduced by the visuals, half-persuaded
    by the straight-forward that doesn't hesitate to repeat itself.

77 ADAMIC, Louis. Robinson Jeffers: A Portrait. Seattle: Uni-
    versity of Washington Bookstore, 1929. 35 pp. Reprinted
    Folcroft, Penn.: Library Editions, 1973. Also reprinted in
    a limited edition, signed by Garth Jeffers (son) with an
    essay of reminiscence by Garth, and a collection of sixteen
    photographs of the family never before published: Covelo,
    Calif.: Yolla Bolly Press, 1983.

78 _____. "Robinson Jeffers and Una: A Portrait of a Great
    American Poet and His Wife." San Franciscan, 3 (March,
    1929), 16 & 29.

79 ADAMS, Ansel; Morley Baer; Wynn Bullock; et al., photographers.
     Not Man Apart: Lines from Robinson Jeffers. San Francisco:
     Sierra Club, 1965. Reprinted San Francisco: Sierra Club/
     Ballantine Books, 1969. Paperback edition.

80 ADAMS, John Howard. "The Poetry of Robinson Jeffers: A
     Reinterpretation and Re-evaluation." Ph.D. diss., University
     of Denver, 1967. DA, 28 (1967), 1423A.
         Jeffers the inhumanist emerged after World War I, strongly
     influenced by the bleak quarter-century which began with the
     disillusion of Stephen Crane and saw not only the continuing
     despair of E. A. Robinson but Spengler, Cubism, Dada,
     Eliot, and, preeminently, the war. But Jeffers the inhuman-
     ist kept within him always traces of the idealistic, pre-war
     humanist who grew up on Shelley and Emerson. The ever-
     present tension/between these two visions informs all Jeffers'
     mature poetry.

81 ADLER, Elmer. Breaking into Print. New York: Simon &
     Schuster, 1937. Reprinted Freeport, N.Y.: Books for Li-
     braries Press, 1968. Robinson Jeffers, pp. 85-92.
         Article entitled "First Book" appeared in Part 10, The
     Colophon, May 1932. Jeffers summarizes the details of finding
     a printer for his first little book of poems, 500 copies of
     which he would pay for. Title is derived from the "Song of
     Songs": "Stay me with flagons, confort me with apples, for
     I am sick of love." So the small book was called Flagons and
     Apples (1912), a title much too big for it. Later Jeffers
     wrote Tamar which was generously received and made the
     author's name well known.

82 AIKEN, Conrad. "Unpacking Hearts with Words: A Review of
     Cawdor and Other Poems." Bookman, 68 (January, 1929),
     576-577.
         Calls the work "an impressive thing, for all its monstrosi-
     ties and absurdities and excessive use of symbolism, his
     wounded eagles and shot lions." Aiken speculates that if
     Jeffers would learn to control himself a little, "be a shade
     less drastically and humorlessly melodramatic" he might create
     something really astonishing.

83 ALBERTS, Sydney. "Jeffers' Trip to Ireland." Carmelite, 5
     (October 20, 1932), 7.
         Review of Descent to the Dead.

84 _____. A Bibliography of the Works of Robinson Jeffers.
     New York: Random House, 1933. Reprinted New York:
     Burt Franklin, 1968. 262 pages.

85 ALEXANDER, John R. "Conflict in the Narrative Poetry of
     Robinson Jeffers." Sewanee Review, 80 (Winter, 1972), 85-99.

At the heart of any debate over the achievement of
Robinson Jeffers lies a fundamental conflict between two
competing loyalties on the poet's part. The first of these
is his lifelong philosophical preoccupation, the stoic "doctrine
of Inhumanism." Jeffers articulated this complex doctrine as
only a bleak personal alternative to continued participation in
what he felt was a corrupt and dying civilization. At the
same time he subscribed to a second and equally strong conviction that poetry should seek to reclaim the narrative real-
ism which he felt had been abandoned in the Imagist movement.
For Jeffers, this desire manifested itself in a return to the
traditional narrative form of poetry complete with plot development, setting, and characters.

86 ALLEN, Don Cameron, ed. The Moment in Poetry. Baltimore:
     Johns Hopkins University Press, 1962. Jeffers, passim.
          Jeffers not discussed; referred to briefly in chapter
     "Surroundings and Illuminations," by John Holmes, pp. 4-24.

87 ALLRED, Jared R. "The Western Inhumanism of Robinson
     Jeffers." Masters Thesis, University of Utah, 1971.

88 _____. "Robinson Jeffers and the Problem of Western Vio-
     lence." The Possible Sack, 3 (October, 1972), 6-13.
          ... violence in the Western is a deeper problem than
     simply a bowing to convention. California poet Robinson
     Jeffers, a very different sort of Western writer, was never
     hampered by the demands of Western convention. His poetry
     is charged with more violence than any tales of cow-town
     vigilantism or Indian massacre; yet he was no more success-
     ful in justifying the significance of the extreme violence in
     his poetry than have been those who relied on the wild situ-
     ations of conventional Western violence. The misuse of vio-
     lence in Western fiction, including Jeffers' poetry, emerges
     as a problem of an overabundance of the type of violence that
     carries an overriding symbolic significance; it has too little
     relationship or meaning to the characters. The constant
     repetition of violent actions produces a kind of emotional
     numbness in a reader, the effect of which is to negate much
     of the significance of the acts.

89 ANDERSON, Judith. "Judith Anderson Letters and Memorabilia:
     Tor House, Carmel." Robinson Jeffers Newsletter, 56 (1980),
     45-47.
          A detailed listing of items which Miss Anderson contributed
     to the Tor House Foundation in 1979 toward a center for
     Jeffers studies at Tor House. The materials focus chiefly on
     the writing and production of Medea. The categories are
     Letters of Robinson Jeffers; Photographs and portrait; Letters
     of other correspondents; and Miscellaneous clippings, bro-
     chures, etc.

90 ANGOFF, Charles. "Three Towering Figures: Robert Frost,
    Robinson Jeffers, William Carlos Williams." Literary Review
    6 (1963), 423-429.
       Reflections have been generated by the deaths within one
    year of Robert Frost, Robinson Jeffers, and William Carlos
    Williams. "These towering figures represent something large
    and melodic and profound and joyous in American poetry.
    They belonged to all time, but they were also deeply committed
    to America...." The death of Jeffers caught the American
    reading public by surprise. Many of them had thought he had
    died long before. He had scolded America for so long and had
    scorned human life even longer that people thought his yearning
    for "self-destructive" love had many years before driven him to
    natural extinction or some form of self-destruction. He de-
    scended from the Greek tragic writers. He knew the bitter
    mockery of the flesh; what havoc it raises with the spirit that
    is trapped within it. He knew the vulgarity of human history,
    and the horror of the human animal with all its spiritual pre-
    tensions.

91 ANTONINUS, Brother (William W. Everson). "A Tribute to Rob-
    inson Jeffers." Critic, 20 (June-July, 1962), 14-16.
       Jeffers died in January, 1962, having just turned seventy-
    five. His death does not mark the end of an era, and at this
    date many of his earlier admirers have fallen away. He went
    almost unhonored among poets, "and he cared not a damn."
    This critic concludes by saying: "So now he is gone, an
    aged eagle that long outlived his mate, and had no wish to live.
    The decade of bitterness preceding his death is hardly sur-
    prising, given his attitude, given the temper of his mind, the
    tenor of his soul. These obsequies, could he have read them,
    would hardly have interested him. In substance all that had
    been uttered decades ago, and no one found anything very
    original to say...."
       Concludes his tribute by reprinting a poem by Tim Reynolds,
    "The Stone-Mason," which first appeared in Poetry magazine.
    Poem is free-form prose and is distinguished by its imagery of
    rocks, cliffs, mountains, towers. The poet says: "The stone-
    mason seeketh for work in all manner of hard stone. When he
    hath finished it his arms are destroyed, and he is weary."

92 _____. Robinson Jeffers: Fragments of an Older Fury.
    Berkeley, Calif.: Oyez, 1968.
       (Note: other works are discussed under Everson, William).
    This work consists of 173 pages arranged in seven essays.
    Much earlier Brother Antoninus had aspired to write a full-
    length study and evaluation of Jeffers, mostly defensive, but
    as the years went by hostility to Jeffers was largely becoming
    outmoded, and so the work was not written. The essays in
    this volume were written at various times and were published
    here and there. The essays are titled as follows:

"Not Without Wisdom" (published in Critic, 1962)
"The Giant Hand"
"Post Mortem: The Uses of Imprecision"
"The Beauty of God" (review of The Beginning and
    the End, published in Ramparts, 1963)
"Hellenistics"
"The Far-Cast Spear"
"The Poet is Dead," with an elegy.

93 ARMS, George. " 'Fire on the Hills,' an Analysis." Explicator,
    1 (May, 1943), item 59.
        Thinks the problem of the poet in this work is the secur-
    ing of the reader's acceptance of his own violent reaction to
    what he has seen. In this Jeffers uses three major means:
    1) he leads up to his final statement by the anticipation in
    line 4 which interprets the fire esthetically not ethically;
    2) in the handling of his images the poet dulls the violence
    of the scene; 3) the metrical pattern is chosen to confine the
    barbarity of his metaphor and statement. The tension created
    especially by this means and by the form of the statement
    increases the power of the poem greatly.

94 ARVIN, Newton. "The Paradox of Jeffers." New Freeman, 1
    (May 17, 1930), 230-232.

95 ASHELMAN, Margaret. "Ethical Fiber of Robinson Jeffers'
    Poetry." Masters Thesis, Swarthmore College, 1938.

96 AUSLANDER, Joseph. "Dark Fire, Black Music." The Measure,
    61 (March, 1926), 14-15.
        Review of Roan Stallion, Tamar, etc.

97 _____. "Review of Roan Stallion, etc." New York World,
    January 3, 1926.

98 _____, and Frank E. Hill. The Winged Horse. Garden City:
    Doubleday, Page, 1927. Jeffers, p. 411.

99 AUSTIN, Mary. Earth Horizon. Boston: Houghton Mifflin,
    1932. Robinson Jeffers, p. 354.
        Does not discuss Jeffers but refers to him in chapter
    "The Land of Journey's Ending," in which she visits a friend
    in Taos, New Mexico, where she met, among others, Robinson
    Jeffers, "a person of interest and distinction."

100 B., H. "Books on Our Table." New York Evening Post, De-
    cember 8, 1925.
        Review of Roan Stallion, etc.

101 BADOSA, Enrique. "Robinson Jeffers." Atlántico, 8 (1957),
     75-84.

102 BANCROFT, Caroline. "Literary Lolly Pops." Denver Post,
     April 10, 1932.
          Review of Thurso's Landing.

103 BARKAN, Phoebe. "The Jeffers Family As I knew Them."
     Robinson Jeffers Newsletter, 53 (1979), 26-30.
          1964 Memoir; is based entirely on a personal relationship
     with the Jefferses', not on literary considerations. Ms. Barkan
     recalls details of Una's housekeeping, the Jeffers twins, the
     trees which Jeffers planted around his property, the death of
     Una in 1950, and its devastating effect on Jeffers. Article
     is interesting for the insight and affection it sheds on the
     Jeffers' relationship. Author was recipient of many letters,
     especially from Una.

104 BARONE, Amico J. "The Audacious Mr. Jeffers." Springfield
     [Mass.] Union, August 12, 1927.
          Review of Women at Point Sur.

105 BARSCHI, Jack. "The Sexual Imagery in Robinson Jeffers'
     Narrative Poetry." Ph. D. diss., New York University,
     1969. DA, 30 (1969), 2519A.
          The purpose of this study is to increase the understanding
     of Jeffers' narrative poetry by examining its imagery. This
     poet's uniqueness does not lie in his ideas but in the psycho-
     logical ramifications of his poetry and in his dramatization of
     the suffering that comes from erotic desire. A textual ap-
     proach is used in the first three chapters to determine the
     predominant images, the patterns these images fall into,
     their relationship to each other, and the manner in which they
     reveal the meaning of the poems. Jeffers' imagery is essen-
     tially sexual, and his characters can therefore be classified
     according to whether they desire sex, are repelled by it, or
     are ambivalent towards the object of their erotic desires.
     Thus the characters in all of the narratives relate to each
     other sexually, and insight into their relationships is implicit
     in the imagery. The images which reveal these characters to
     be similar are discussed in the last three chapters.

106 BASSETT, W. K. "Wherein One Poet Talks Not And Another
     Shoots Squirrels." Carmel Cymbal, 1 (June 15, 1926), 3,
     11. Also in San Francisco Review, February and March,
     1926.

107 BATES, E. S. "Criticism in 1930." New York Herald Tribune
     Books, January 24, 1932.

108 BEACH, Joseph Warren. Concept of Nature in Nineteenth-

English Poetry. New York: Macmillan, 1936. "Victorian
Afterglow," pp. 522-546. Jeffers, passim.
   In Jeffers, nature comes back in all her romantic splendor
and sublimity but accompanied by such a ruthless nihilism,
so far as man is concerned, that she would be quite unrec-
ognizable to Wordsworth and other poets of that order.
Jeffers is the most completely realistic of all nature poets.
In him, Man is not so much made noble by his participation
in nonhuman nature as shown in contrast to it, futile and
mean, and eaten up with fevers of thought that destroy him.

109 BECK, Clyde. "The American Lyre: Some Varied Strains."
      Detroit News, August 21, 1927.
         Review of The Women at Point Sur.

110 _____. "Lofty Beauty of Two Poets." Detroit News, Decem-
      ber 29, 1929.
         Review of Dear Judas, etc.

111 BECKER, Edward Lindley. "The Moment of Vision in William
      Butler Yeats, Wallace Stevens, T. S. Eliot, and Robinson
      Jeffers." Ph. D. diss., University of California (Berkeley),
      1980. DA, 41 (1981), 3101A.
         In this dissertation Becker makes a running comparison of
      the works of the four poets in terms of their depiction of
      what he calls the moment of vision, the momentary experience
      of unitary consciousness, of unification of the opposites.
      Most of the concerns of each can ultimately be seen as a
      constellation, with this experience at its center. It is the
      particular emphases of each poet that provide the comparisons
      which can increase our understanding of each, in terms of
      both style and basic philosophy.

112 BEDNAR, Kamil. "Jeffers in Czechoslovakia." Robinson Jeffers
      Newsletter, 27 (November, 1970), 8-9. Earlier version of
      article appeared in Newsletter, 13 (February, 1966), 2-3.
         Reviews his activities in translating Jeffers since 1950,
      revealing that he has derived much happiness from the work.
      In addition Bednar reviews Jeffers' success in Czechoslovakia
      and says it "is something of a mystery." Among reasons for
      this success:

         1) Jeffers seems to have a great spiritual power.
         2) The country which creates the scenery of Jeffers'
             poems has enormous charm for Czech reader.
         3) Jeffers' return to nature and his criticism of
             contemporary civilization have an immense impact.

113 BEERS, Terry. "Robinson Jeffers: His Imagery and Symbol-
      ism." Masters Thesis, California State University (North-
      ridge), 1982.

114 BEILKE, Marlan. "God and Man in the Works of Robinson Jeffers." Masters Thesis, University of Tasmania (Australia), 1972.

115 _____. Shining Clarity: God and Man in the Works of Robinson Jeffers. Illustrated by Kenneth Jack and Lumir Sendelar. Amador City, Calif.: Quintessence Publishers, 1977. Distributed by Blue Oak Press, Auburn, Calif.
     Consists of 294 pages with Index. Also complete index to poems cited. Book is a handsome tribute to Jeffers: contains commentary, quotation of many poems, and excerpts from many other poems. Also contains valuable photographs and other pictures which have been glued into the text. Arranged in chronological order, it is not, or intended to be, more than a loving tribute to the poet, but it is accurate, in good taste, and reflects knowledge of Jeffers.

116 _____. "Robinson Jeffers." Second Spring, 6 (June-July, 1980), 12-13.

117 BELITT, B. "Jeffers' Work Not His Best." Lynchburg [West Virginia] News, April 10, 1932.
     Review of Thurso's Landing.

118 _____. "Cataclysmic Disaster and HIgh Emotion." Richmond Times-Despatch, April 10, 1932.
     Review of Thurso's Landing.

119 _____. "Review of Thurso's Landing, etc." Roanoke Times, April 10, 1932.

120 _____. "Review of Thurso's Landing, etc." Staunton News-Leader, April 10, 1932.

121 BELL, Lisle. "Review of Medea." Weekly Book Review, April 21, 1946. P. 19.
     Praises Jeffers because he "does not call for modern dress. Still less does he lower the terrible story to the level of surrealism and Freudian fantasy, as Cocteau did with the Oedipus legend. He seems chiefly to have desired to make Euripides' drama fit the frame of the modern theater, and be reasonably clear to a modern audience. Doubtless his personal predilection for strong meat was amply satisfied by the original story...." The reader of this version will not sense the operatic nature of Greek tragedy, but he will feel without question its tremendous dramatic impact."

122 BENET, William Rose. "From Pieria to Mediocria." Outlook, 141 (December 30, 1925), 674.
     Review of Roan Stallion.

Book contains evidence of creative power of the first order.
If Jeffers goes his own way, we cannot predict how far he
will go.

123 _____. "Jeffers' Latest Work: A Review of Thurso's Landing."
Saturday Review of Literature, 8 (April 2, 1932), 638. Reprinted in Designed for Reading. Pp. 234-238.
"I admire greatly his pictorial eye, whether in the descrip-
tions of the physical appearance of his characters or their
scenic background. The people grow into roundness, the
rock, earth, trees, flowers, and animals of his country are
alive. He is original in description without straining his
similes and analogies...."

124 _____. "Round About Parnassus," (title of column). Saturday Review of LIterature, 8 (January 16, 1932), 461.
Comments on Descent to the Dead, saying "the language is
beautiful, and robust even though the mood induced has been
a dwelling on death, in the midst of cairns and dolmens and
circles of great stones.... There are also passages so intensely imbued with his own individuality that one could not
mistake them for the work of anyone else." Concludes by
saying that "we have to judge him by higher standards than
we apply to other poets. The range of his pondering and
the power of his language necessitate that. This handful of
present poems is but an aside compared with the main body
of his work. Whatever may be the truth he is one of the
most striking poets of our period."

125 _____. "Review of Solstice and Other Poems." Saturday Review of Literature, 13 (November 2, 1935), 20.
Begins by observing that "Jeffers will never get away from
the rock and the hawk and the cruel trap of life and the un-
caring face of nature. His themes have become rather redun-
dant." On the other hand Benét says, "but he is wielding
some of the grandest language of our time. He seems to have
little flexibility in his temperament, but his stoicism is impressive."

126 _____, and Norman Holmes Pearson, eds. Oxford Anthology
of American Literature, 2 vols. New York: Oxford University Press, 1938. Robinson Jeffers, Vol. 2, pp. 1354-1383.
Prints in its entirety "The Tower Beyond Tragedy," the
short poems, "Noon" and "Night," "Ante Mortem," "Tor
House," and a selection from Tamar: "Invocation." Also an
excerpt from Cawdor: "The Death of the Eagle," and finally
"Love the Wild Swan," and "Self-Criticism in February."
Any student of Jeffers would applaud the generous inclusion
of the poet in this anthology. In the "Commentaries" section
it is said: "Jeffers is the Nay-Sayer, and the expression of
his dark philosophy, thought nihilistic, is extraordinarily

powerful. The man himself is like a force of nature. The
long, powerful rhythms that he has made his own, like the
welter and assault of waves on his own Carmel coast, the
evocative strength of description, the right metaphor, the
illuminating epithet, will be found throughout his work.

127   BENNETT, Melba Berry. Robinson Jeffers and the Sea. San
      Francisco: Gelber Lilienthal, 1936. Includes poetry by
      Jeffers pertaining to the sea. Reprinted Folcroft, Penn.:
      Library Editions, 1973. 173 pages.
            In the Introduction, Miss Bennett says: "This book, then,
      is not an explanation of the influence of the sea on Jeffers
      and his work, but rather is a questioning study of this in-
      teresting and significant phase of his talent, and a compila-
      tion of all materials pertaining to the sea contained in his
      poetry. It is also an attempt to arrive at, and to help other
      students arrive at, an understanding of the man's poetry,
      and by analysis and quotation, to isolate and thus focus
      attention on his preoccupation with the sea.
            The work is contained within 14 chapters, preceded by a
      Foreword by Una Jeffers, the fragment of an original Jeffers
      poem, the Introduction, and a quotation "Ocean" from Caw-
      dor. The chapters, filled with quotations, are basically a
      chronological review of Jeffers' life and works.
            Although lacking any value as an interpretative work, the
      volume is beautifully arranged and an asset to the student
      of Jeffers who is seeking to assess the impact of the sea,
      perhaps the single most important factor, on the poetry of
      Robinson Jeffers.

128   _____, first ed. and founder. Robinson Jeffers Newsletter,
      November 19, 1962.
      "In order to keep members of the Committee and National
      Council informed of developments, this is the first of a pro-
      posed series of newsletters to be issued on an occasional
      basis." Editorship continued through Number 22, August,
      1968. Mrs. Bennett died in the fall of 1968, and the editor-
      ship passed to Dr. Robert J. Brophy, Department of English,
      California State College at Long Beach.

129   _____. The Stone Mason of Tor House: The Life and Work
      of Robinson Jeffers. Los Angeles: Ward Ritchie, 1966.
      Foreword by Lawrence Clark Powell.
            Reviewed by E. L. Mayo, Poetry 111 (February, 1968),
      335-336. This work is largely the outgrowth of the author's
      close relationship with Una Jeffers, who died in 1950. Theirs
      was a stormy beginning, but gradually Una accepted Bennett
      and made no stipulation except that nothing be published un-
      til after Jeffers' death. The work is in 22 chapters, followed
      by a bibliographical listing of primary sources, and a very
      good index.

The chapters follow the course of Jeffers' life and work, from "The Young Robin," through "Sunset." In his Foreword to this biography, Lawrence Powell, another Jeffers scholar, regards the volume as invaluable for the future. It is the first biography of Jeffers, and although undoubtedly better works will follow, it is nonetheless a repository for many materials which in the future would be irretrievably lost, or never called into existence.

130 BENTON, Johnny. "An Interpretative Analysis of Robinson Jeffers' The Women at Point Sur." Ph.D. diss., University of Oklahoma (Norman), 1967. DA, 28 (1967), 1548A.
      This study assumes that Jeffers is an interesting figure, that he wrote with a power that is embodied in the term singularity, which includes particularity and puzzling strangeness. An attempt is made to reveal facets of the singularity through an analysis of one work. The "voice" of the work (point of view) is one of its strongest characteristics, and this dissertation seeks to show how to make that voice heard for an audience.

131 BJORKMAN, Edwin. "An American Poet." Asheville Times, July 31, 1927.
      Review of works by Jeffers and also comment on works about Jeffers by George Sterling.

132 BLACK, MacKnight. "Robinson Jeffers, for First Time, Treats Theme of Sacrificial Love." Philadelphia Record, Dec. 21, 1929.
      Review of Dear Judas, etc.

133 BLAIR, Walter, Theodore Hornberger, et al. American Literature: A Brief History. Glenview, Ill.: Scott, Foresman & Co., 1974, revised edition. Jeffers, pp. 221-222, 314.
      Jeffers started his career as a conventional versifier, but his later poetry--that most admired by critics--follows a metrical scheme which, as he said, is a "compromise" avoiding both "arbitrary form and capricious lack of disruption of form." Because he had a better knowledge of ancient poetry and a greater liking for it than most modern American poets have, Jeffers achieved metrical effects which are new, individual, and arresting. As the most blackly pessimistic of contemporary American poets, Jeffers has often been compared with Eugene O'Neill, and it is true that they shared a temperamental melancholy which is sometimes called Celtic, as well as Greek.

134 BLAND, H.M. "The Poetry of Today." Overland Monthly, 85 (December, 1927), 373-375.

135 BLANKENSHIP, Russell. American LIterature as an Expression of the National Mind. New York: Henry Holt, 1931. Robinson Jeffers, pp. 627-632.

Has been called the greatest American poet since Whitman,
but so sweeping a verdict may be premature. Jeffers is a
primitive. No poet of our time has drawn so little of his
material from the outward facets of contemporary life. His
active dislike of people makes him flee from society to the
solitude of the natural world. He hates the volatile passions
of the crowd.... People and their changing moods are dis-
pleasing to him; he seeks the unchanging aspects of rocks,
mountain ledges, and the open sea.

136   BLUESTONE, Stephen. "Robinson Jeffers and the Prophets:
      On the Book of Jeremiah and 'The Inhumanist.'" Notes on
      Contemporary Literature, 5 (September, 1975), 2-3.
            In "The Inhumanist" Jeffers comes closest to an explicit
      identification with the role of the prophet. The poem is, to
      a very great extent, organized along the lines of a biblical
      prophetic "book." Jeffers' choice of 52 "chapters" is ex-
      tremely suggestive: the Book of Jeremiah also has the same
      number of chapters. Also, as in prophetic literature, the in-
      ternal structure of the poem is discontinuous: the meter is
      varied according to no consistent pattern from chapter to
      chapter, narrative and lyrical passages alternate unpredictably,
      and the poet's manifest subject matter constantly changes.

137   BLY, Robert, ed. New of the Universe: An Anthology. San
      Francisco: Sierra Club Books, 1980.
            Prints three poems by Jeffers, without seeming to notice
      what they say: "Science," "Animals," and "Oh Lovely Rock."

138   BOGAN, Louise. Achievement in American Poetry: 1900-1950.
      Chicago: Henry Regnery, 1951. Reprinted in paperback,
      Gateway Edition, 1951. Jeffers, passim.
            No discussion of Jeffers; is referred to in chapter,
      "Poetry at the Half-Century."

139   _____. Selected Criticism: Prose and Poetry. New York:
      Noonday Press, 1955. "Landscape with Jeffers," pp. 67-69;
      and "Modern Syndrome," pp. 302-304.
            In the first comment Such Counsels You Gave to Me is the
      subject. This is a story of mother-son incest and a father's
      murder. The characters arouse little sympathy in the reader:
      "mother and son seem not so much puzzled and depraved as
      simple-minded." The son talks as if he were capable of any-
      thing, but in fact he is capable of nothing. The mother,
      like other Jeffers women, is capable of anything but winds
      up in a weak moral struggle, allowing her son to assume the
      blame for murder. Review first in Nation, 145 (October 23,
      1937), 442.
            Other comment on Medea, Jeffers' rendition of the Euripides
      play. "By a process of cutting and expansion and abrupt
      shifts in emphasis, Jeffers creates a creature so obsessed

by jealousy, pride, and a paranoid fear of ridicule that she passes from the normal world into the regions of insanity. Jeffers pitches his tone so high that it becomes a shriek of hysteria." Review first in New Yorks, 22 (May 11, 1946), 94.

140 BOYERS, Robert. "A Sovereign Voice: The Poetry of Robinson Jeffers." Sewanee Review, 77 (July-September, 1969), 487-507. Reprinted in Mazzaro (1970), pp. 183-203.
More than any other poet of the modernist or post-modernist periods, Jeffers has served as a whipping boy to a variety of well-placed poets and critics who have found it stimulating to deal with him exclusively on their terms, though never on his.... Throughout his career Jeffers tried to resolve the ambiguities of his vision that would take him further from concern with his fellows. However, he never advocated violence among men and tried to achieve a perspective wherein the violence that men did commit could be made tolerable. It is a tragic vision, and a vision at least worthy of our attention, and capable of giving pleasure. The felicities of Jeffers' poetry ought no longer to be denied, but received with gratitude. If not among our supreme poets, there have been few who were his equal.

141 BOYNTON, Percy H. Literature and American Life. Boston: Ginn & Co., 1936. Jeffers, pp. 860-863.
In Robinson Jeffers the mood of defiance and despair reached the most abysmal depths. Jeffers regards man with such disdain that one speculates on why he troubles to consider what he describes as "the animals Christ was rumored to have died for." He denies his subjects all nobility, he refuses them any sympathy, and he expends splendid powers in his frugal treatment of lust, hate, and despair.

142 BRAITHWAITE, W. S., ed. Anthology of Magazine Verse for 1916 and Yearbook of American Poetry. New York: L. J. Gomme, 1916. Jeffers, p. 238.

143 _____. Ibid. for 1924. Boston: B. J. Brimmer, 1924. Jeffers, p. 124.

144 _____. Ibid. for 1925. Boston: B. J. Brimmer, 1925. Jeffers, pp. 146 and 161.
Reviews of Tamar and Other Poems.

145 _____. Ibid. for 1926. Boston: B. J. Brimmer, 1926. Jeffers, pp. 91-93 et passim.

146 _____. Ibid. for 1927. Boston: B. J. Brimmer, 1927. Jeffers, pp. 110-112 et passim.

147   . Ibid. for 1928. New York: H. Vinal, Ltd., 1928.
          Jeffers, p. 524 et passim.

148   . Ibid. for 1929. New York: G. Sully, 1929.
          Robinson Jeffers, passim.

149 BREEN, Robert S. "Symbolic Action in Oral Interpretation of
          Robinson Jeffers' Roan Stallion." Ph.D. diss., Northwestern
          State University, 1950.

150 BREWER, W. A. "Review of Roan Stallion, Tamar and Other
          Poems." San Francisco Chronicle, March 14, 1926.

151   . "Review of The Women at Point Sur." San Francisco
          Chronicle, December 4, 1927.

152 BRICKELL, Herschel. "Some Good Poetry." North American
          Review, 233 (June, 1932), 576.
              Review of Thurso's Landing. The title poem in the Jeffers
          volume is a long narrative in blank verse, which again evi-
          dences the dark genius of Jeffers, a poet whose range is not
          wide, but a poet who has gazed into the abyss that surrounds
          the world and discerned things in its blackness....

153 BROOKS, Van Wyck. Opinions of Oliver Allston. New York:
          E. P. Dutton, 1941. Jeffers, p. 196.
              For this poet the human heart was vile and humanity the
          "mould to break away from" For others also, of this period,
          life was ugly and there was next to nothing to be done about
          it. In fact, they turned literature into a sort of wailing wall
          from which nothing rose but the sound of lamentations and
          curses.

154 BROPHY, Robert J. "Structure, Symbol, and Myth in Selected
          Narratives of Robinson Jeffers." Ph.D. diss., University of
          North Carolina, 1966. DA, 27 (1967), 2524A-2525A.
              The purpose of this study is to enlarge the appreciation
          of the artistry and scope of Jeffers' poetry by examining in
          some detail five narratives and one lyric poem: "Tamar,"
          "Cawdor," "Roan Stallion," "At the Birth of an Age," and
          "The Tower Beyond Tragedy." In the concluding chapter
          the study is brought to a focus in an analysis of "Apology
          for Bad Dreams," functioning as Jeffers' ars poetica, explain-
          ing why his themes are violent and almost inevitably apoca-
          lyptic.
              This dissertation was published in 1973.

155   . "A Textual Note on Robinson Jeffers' 'The Beginning
          and the End.'" Papers of the Bibliographical Society of
          America, 60 (July-September, 1966), 344-348.
              Remarks directed to the text that was published in the

spring of 1963 after Jeffers died in January of 1962. This
book was scarcely noted by the reviewers in only a handful
of journals. Thus the volume has suffered the fate sadly
the lot of the poet himself--of being passed over by a public
still unattuned to his impressive prophetic verse. In an effort to preserve his verse as it was written, certain corrigenda should be noted in the first printing. To point up the
authenticity of the text as originally edited it seems equally
important to preface this note with some remarks concerning
the manuscript, method of editing, and the problems and
solutions involved in the final version.

156 _____. "The Tor House Library: Jeffers' Books." Robinson
Jeffers Newsletter, 23 (April, 1969), 4-11.
Article is based on the author's experience, in November
1967, of visiting the Jeffers home to catalog the books in
Jeffers' personal library. There are some 2000 of these books,
with an arrangement that is "mostly miscellaneous." It has
astonishing breadth, yet it does not represent the extent of
the poet's reading, nor does it entirely reflect his tastes.
On the other hand, there are many books in the library which
do not at all reflect his reading or his tastes and interests.
The volumes belong to the whole family, early and late....
In conclusion: the Jeffers library, at least as it now stands,
affords no startling discoveries: neither key handbooks of
symbolism or mythology, nor annotated texts.

157 _____. "Two Reviews." Robinson Jeffers Newsletter, 23
(April, 1969), 3-4.
The two books are The Selected Letters of Robinson
Jeffers, edited by Ann N. Ridgeway (1968), and Fragments
of An Old Fury by Brother Antoninus (1968). Both volumes,
of course, are valuable contributions to a growing interest in
the poet.

158 _____. "Jeffers Research: Dissertations, a Summary and
Reflection." Robinson Jeffers Newsletter, 24 (September,
1969), 4-9.
An excellent presentation, listed alphabetically, of thirteen
doctoral dissertations done between 1932 and 1967 on the
poetry of Robinson Jeffers. The article is based on an annotated bibliography of the theses on Jeffers at Occidental
College Library, in Dissertation Abstracts, and a "cursory
examination" of microfilms. Almost all of the originals can be
found catalogued and available for reading in the Occidental
College Library. Many of them are also available through
University Microfilms (Ann Arbor, Michigan), both as microfilms and Xerography copies.
Note: These thirteen dissertations are listed within the
body of this Bibliography.

159 _____. "Jeffers Research: Masters' Theses, Occidental College
Library." Robinson Jeffers Newsletter, 25 (February, 1970),
4-8.

A listing of twenty-three theses on Jeffers' poetry, completed between 1930 and 1966. Arrangement is chronological to show developments in critical assessment. The texts are catalogued and available at Occidental College.

160 _____. "'Tamar,' 'The Cenci,' and Incest." American Literature, 42 (May, 1970), 241-244.

In his Foreword to Selected Poetry, Jeffers acknowledges debt to Shelley's "The Cenci" in relation to his own verse narrative "Tamar." So casually does he mention it that it is easy to discount any significance; however, a comparison of structure, symbol function, and poetic vision reveals a remarkable similarity between the two dramas--especially in a way that elucidates the disquieting use of incest which is both a dramatic event and a multi-relevant symbol central to each work.... Both "The Cenci" and "Tamar" have essentially two-part structures, the first part centering on the incest, the second dramatizing the transcendence which is its product. The notable difference is that Shelley's play gives Count Cenci prominence in the first part, his daughter Beatrice the central role in the second; whereas, Jeffers' work centers on Tamar throughout.

161 _____. "Landscape as Genesis and Analogue in Jeffers' Narratives." Robinson Jeffers Newsletter, 29 (August, 1971), 11-16.

Begins by quoting in their entirety three letters "presumably" written by Jeffers to a Mr. Munson who intended a study of Thurso's Landing. Nothing is known of Mr. Munson or his study. The authenticity of the letters cannot be absolutely guaranteed, since they exist only in carbon copies. The letters reflect a number of personal characteristics of Jeffers, but perhaps more important they reveal the central role of landscape in the poet's consciousness and the inspiration it affords. Landscape is not merely background. "The scene impressed me first and the narrative poem grew out of it," Jeffers said. First came the impact of the landscape, then the falcons, and finally the dramatic implications for human endurance. The relationship between man, animal, and landscape is developed in practically all Jeffers' narratives.

162 _____. "The Summer Jeffers Festival." Robinson Jeffers Newsletter, 30 (January, 1972), 1-5.

A program guide to the third annual Jeffers Poetry Festival which was held at Monterey Peninsula College, July 30-31, 1971. Three sessions were held, Friday P.M., Saturday A.M., and Saturday P.M., during which there were papers, talks, readings by poets, scholars, friends, and enthusiasts for

Jeffers from all parts of the United States. In addition to a
listing of all the activities, the editor of Newsletter undertakes
to summarize most of the presentations.

163 _____. "Topography and the Narrative Scene." Robinson
Jeffers Newsletter, 30 (January, 1972), 13-14.
    Notes serve as Preface to a new map which undertakes to
index and locate the major narrative poem sites by way of
coordinates. In the course of this mapping the discovery
was made that most of Jeffers' later narratives do not seem
to specify particular sites. Does this lack of specification
mark a shift in the poet's artistry, or was his subject matter
more topical yet in a way more disengaged from the coast's
ritual reality?

164 _____. "'Crumbs or the Loaf': An Interpretation." Robinson
Jeffers Newsletter, 31 (May, 1972), 8-9.
    Sees the poem, which is quoted in its entirety, as a
statement by Jeffers on the use of his lyric and narrative
forms of poetry. He alludes to Jesus who also concluded
that the truth he would preach is too difficult for the slow,
biased, reactionary ears of his hearers. They must be
reached in stages, so hence the parable. Jeffers in effect
is saying: "My Narratives or My Lyrics." For him the narratives are for those who cannot comprehend the lyrics,
"straight on."

165 _____. "The Apocalyptic Dimension of Jeffers' Narratives."
Robinson Jeffers Newsletter, 32 (July, 1972), 4-7.
    In many if not all of Jeffers' stories there comes a moment,
often startling and disconcerting, and almost inevitably un-
explained, when the dramatic action is interrupted by a
glimpse of larger processes that seem to be running parallel
to or underneath the action at hand and subsuming it. Cites
examples in Tamar, "The Loving Shepherdess," Thurso's
Landing.... The pattern is a persistent one, recurring
regularly and without explanation or visible outcome. Unless
we find Jeffers an inept artist, his thus provoking the reader
must be intentional and his lack of explanation must be part
of his technique. Indeed, it would seem that the point he is
intent on making cannot be communicated in any other way
but by a kind of subliminal "tease," an impression left to
rankle, a place which does not easily fit the puzzle as we
put the scenes together.

166 _____. "Jeffers' 'Cawdor' and the Hippolytus Story." Western American Literature, 7 (Fall, 1972), 171-178.
    His poems are written, Jeffers says, to work out a personal
"salvation." In each of the narratives, Jeffers exposes a
different facet of this salvation. In "Cawdor" Jeffers seeks
to purify the notion of security by reviewing the pit-falls of

settling for anything less than the harsh reality of things.
He does this in a cosmic context of the Life-Force in which
we, both the human race in general and as individuals,
must find the "common sense of our predicament as passionate bits of earth and water...." The plot of "Cawdor" adapts
the Hippolytus-Phaedra story. Theseus here is Cawdor, a
prosperous farmer and rancher; Hippolytus is his son Hood,
who has turned nomad-hunter in preference to crop tending;
Phaedra is Fera (which means "wild beast"), a girl whom a
forest fire has orphaned and made homeless.

167   _____. "Jeffers' 'Medea': A Dionysian Retribution." Robinson Jeffers Newsletter, 33 (September, 1972), 4-6.
        Relates the Medea character to other characters in Jeffers,
and concludes that this adaptation of Euripides was by no
means the first encounter which Jeffers had had with the
story. Medea is the pre-rational answer which primitive
forces make to civilized presumptions. She is raw power
responding to genteel cruelty and cultured rationalization.
Civilization has cornered and robbed her, then cast her
aside. Her responses are instinctive, the remorseless sudden
ascendency of Dionysus over Apollo.

168   _____. "Jeffers Scholarly Resources: A Proposed Series."
Robinson Jeffers Newsletter, 33 (September, 1972), 11-14.
        Initiates a series of short summaries of the major manu-
scripts and other holdings at libraries throughout the United
States of Jeffers materials. So much of the material is un-
catalogued in libraries that the task seems formidable. In
this issue is mentioned the Jeffers collection at the University
of Alabama and the Sara Bard Field collection at the University of California (Berkeley).

169   _____. "Jeffers Scholarly Materials: The Mabel Dodge
Luhan Correspondence." Robinson Jeffers Newsletter, 34
(February, 1973), 7-9.
        Article is a listing of letters by Mrs. Luhan to a countless
number of people to whom she was hostess at her fashionable
salon on Taos, New Mexico. These letters, of which there are
321 in Mrs. Luhan's hand to Una Jeffers, are in the Library
of the University of California (Berkeley), along with other
materials relating to the subject. She also knew D. H. Lawrence, and some of the material relates to him and his wife
Frieda.

170   _____. "The Ritual Ending of 'Roan Stallion.'" Robinson
Jeffers Newsletter, 34 (February, 1973), 11-15.
        Gives a brief background to the poem, saying it has always
been something of a stumbling block to the understanding and
popular acceptance of Jeffers. It is the ending which readers
and critics find objectionable, the violent and bloody killing

of the stallion. This reading of the poem sees the conclusion
as parallel to the ancient ritual of tragedy, in which the god-
hero was slain in order to be resurrected in the cycle of
birth-death-rebirth, endlessly.

171 _____. "'Salmon-Fishing': The Ritual Gesture at the Heart
of Things." Robinson Jeffers Newsletter, 35 (May, 1973), 6.
Gives the background and season for the event of salmon
fishing, seeing it in highly symbolic and mythic terms. The
season is winter, and the fishermen are seen as related to
the "ancient sun-worshippers at Stonehenge. At solstice the
sun-hero dies or is killed in ritual combat, so that his young
successor may lead the bound world into rejuvenescence."
The fishermen are for Jeffers another link with the cosmic
mono-life process of the god he loves. Men are not central,
but they are inexorably agents of the god in the great ritual
which assures continued life in all things.

172 _____. "Una Jeffers-Blanche Matthias Correspondence."
Robinson Jeffers Newsletter, 35 (May, 1973), 7-9.
The correspondence discussed here is in the Beinecke
Library, Yale, and was acquired in the Fall of 1972. There
are 164 letters and upwards of a hundred notes and postcards,
all signed by Una Jeffers. The Matthias letters to Una have
not survived. "Yet there is much revelation here--especially
of Una's eager spirit, responsiveness, and effervescence, that
makes the series stand unusually well on its own." Una speaks
mostly for herself, her own interests, her own political opinions,
her own literary tastes. What we learn from the letters is
not so much new insights into Jeffers, the man and the artist,
but rather the lively and warm context which surrounded his
interior hermitage.

173 _____. "Biographical & Psychoanalytic Criticism: A Response."
Robinson Jeffers Newsletter, 37 (December, 1973), 4-5.
Comment is directed largely at the Shields' dissertation,
"The Divided Mind of Robinson Jeffers," which concludes that
much of Jeffers can be explained--or explained away--by means
of Freudian analysis. Brophy feels that perhaps this is not
the best way to understand Jeffers: for the most part confusion and misunderstanding in Jeffers can be overcome if the
reader is familiar with Greek and other mythologies. His problems were essentially more far-reaching than those Freud en-
compasses--the need for immortality, immunity from pain, personal importance, and the illusion of effectiveness.

174 _____. "'Night': A Prayerful Reconciliation." Robinson
Jeffers Newsletter, 37 (December, 1973), 6-7.
Jeffers frequently wrote with therapeutic intent, for both
his own and the reader's sake. There are human biases
which are exorcised only with vigilance and perseverance,

and there are aspects of being which are ever slighted because of their threatening aspect--mutability, death, and annihilation. Jeffers' lyric "Night" is such a poem, written in the form of a reverent prayer to the Divine Matrix. The theme is inner reconciliation to the terrors of human finitude and personal obliteration, the impending advent of nothingness, its closeness in the midst of life.

175   _____. "Jeffers Scholarly Materials: Una Jeffers-De Casseres Correspondence." Robinson Jeffers Newsletter, 37 (December, 1973), 11-12.
The material described here is in the Brooklyn Public Library. It contains 21 letters from Jeffers to Benjamin De Casseres, New York writer and critic. There are also seven letters by Una to Mrs. De Casseres, to "Ben," or to both. In addition there is a two-part manuscript of the poem "Night," with about 18 deletions, additions, and corrections on the first sheet, about 17 on the second, the last two lines being crossed off entirely and rewritten sideways on the page. Finally the collection also yields eight photographs of the Jeffers twins, Tor House, Hawk Tower, etc.

176   _____. Robinson Jeffers: Myth, Ritual, and Symbol in His Narrative Poems. Cleveland: Case Western Reserve University Press, 1973. Foreword by William Everson.
Consists of 320 pages with Bibliographical Notes and Index. Is arranged in five basic chapters, with Introduction, Conclusion, Epilogue, and Appendix. The five narratives studied are "Tamar," "Roan Stallion," "The Tower Beyond Tragedy," "Cawdor," and "At the Birth of an Age." In the Introduction the author clearly outlines the scope of his study: to examine in some detail five narratives and one lyric poem to illustrate Jeffers' use of myth and ritual patterns. The method chosen is contextual rather than topical: that is, each poem is analyzed structurally, textually, and thematically in its own context. Each chapter begins with an introduction to the poem and a short analysis of its structure. This is followed by a close reading of the poem, emphasizing myth patterns, ritual undercurrents, and their meanings. The five narratives selected represent Jeffers at his best and most typical, and they cover a spread of mythical materials-- Hebrew-Christian, Roman, Greek, and Teutonic--representing both ancient plots and settings, and the adaptation of these to modern times and characters.

177   _____. "T. S. Eliot and Robinson Jeffers: A Note." Robinson Jeffers Newsletter, 38 (April, 1974), 4-5.
Although they were roughly contemporaries and faced the same disintegrating world, there are very few links between the careers of these two poets. Only two references to Eliot are made by Jeffers in Selected Letters, and hardly more than that by Eliot about Jeffers. It is interesting to note, however

that Eliot expressed more concern and awareness of Jeffers
than did Jeffers for Eliot. When Jeffers died in 1962, Eliot
expressed the opinion that Jeffers was underevaluated--Jef-
fers and Conrad Aiken have never been "adequately appreciated."

178 _____. "Distancing in Jeffers' Lyrics." Robinson Jeffers
      Newsletter, 38 (April, 1974), 5-6.
      Notes that Jeffers is often badly represented in anthologies
      and the result is one of total misunderstanding. Poems are
      thrown against one another without regard to the "distance"
      which Jeffers assumed in his poetry. There are three dis-
      tinct stages, or three distances, which Jeffers takes from his
      subject matter: close-up, harsh, direct; a middle ground,
      using the poem to work out an answer; far-distanced emotion-
      ally from his material. These three categories do not neces-
      sarily correspond to any periods in Jeffers' life and may in-
      deed be only three moments in the same problem.

179 _____. "Jeffers Manuscripts: University of North Carolina
      Library." Robinson Jeffers Newsletter, 38 (April, 1974), 17.
      This material consists of two manuscripts, four pages each,
      of first and second drafts of the poem "An Artist." They
      provide an interesting study of Jeffers' method of composition
      and revision. The first draft, in pencil, is unusually criss-
      crossed, corrected, and disjointed. The second draft (typed)
      has only slight alterations. The title is changed from "The
      Artist" to "An Artist." There are 22 changes in word choice
      or phrase, five in punctuation. The differences between this
      second draft and the text found in Selected Poetry are minimal.

180 _____ (unsigned). "Kirwan on Jeffers." Robinson Jeffers
      Newsletter, 39 (July, 1974), 6-8.
      Article is about James Martin Kirwan, "a gifted young
      artist who has burst upon the Jeffers scene." More specifi-
      cally it is an atempt to describe three posters which this artist
      has done based on Jeffers' works. He has what he calls "The
      Journey" trilogy and another one called "Cassandra." The
      first is based on Be Angry at the Sun, the second "Shine,
      Perishing Republic," and the third "Ourselves to Know."
      The "Cassandra," of course, is based on Jeffers' poem
      "Cassandra."

181 _____ "Biblical Resonances in Jeffers' 'Signpost.'" Robinson
      Jeffers Newsletter, 39 (July, 1974), 10-12.
      Begins with a brief statement as to Jeffers' background in
      biblical knowledge, pointing out that even after he abandoned
      institutional Christianity in preference for a personal pantheism,
      he did not abandon the biblical symbolism so frequently used
      in his poetry. For instance, although he did not believe that
      Jesus was the event of cosmic history, he still found in him the

imagination and language of a mystic whose words are emi-
nently adaptable to his own fervent religious vision.   The
sonnet "Signpost" is a case in point.   Jeffers says: "I point
the way," certainly a parallel to Jesus's dictum "I am the
way."

182 _____.   "Jeffers Scholarly Materials: California State University at Long Beach."   Robinson Jeffers Newsletter, 39 (July,
1974), 21-26.
       Article is a listing of the Jeffers' materials which this
college acquired in 1973, "a major Jeffers Collection."   Lists
ten categories of the collection:

1.   First editions, many signed copies
2.   Limited signed editions
3.   All dust-wrappers
4.   Many presentation copies
5.   20 unpublished poems typed by the poet
6.   9 autograph letters signed
7.   Periodical appearances, including Jeffers' first paid
     appearance in print
8.   All key anthological appearances
9.   Every important biographical, bibliographical, and
     critical work
10. A wealth of miscellaneous material: holographs,
     foreign editions, theses, newsletters, signed photos,
     family snapshots, recordings, etc.

183 _____.   "Jeffers' 'Second-Best':   A Vocational Crises."
Robinson Jeffers Newsletter, 40 (November, 1974), 7-9.
       Both "Apology for Bad Dreams" and "Second-Best" are
personal compositions, the first answering the question of
why he writes tragedy, and the other one answering why he
writes at all.   It is a question that nearly all American writers
have asked themselves.   For Jeffers it was a particularly
urgent question, and "Second-Best" emerges as a merciless
self-examination--followed quickly by a firm vocational affirmation.... His vocation always seems best described in religious
terms, and the roles that reach deepest are those of prophet,
apocalyptist, ritualist, and mystic.   He contemplates, is God's
sense organ, his "intelligencer."   With these high expectations,
he is not second-best.

184 _____.   Robinson Jeffers.   Boise: Boise State University
Press, 1975.   50 pages, Western Writers Series, # 19.

185 _____ (as editor of Newsletter).   "Eulogy on the Death of
Rev. William Hamilton Jeffers," by Dr. Kelso.   Robinson
Jeffers Newsletter, 43 (December, 1975), 6-11.
       This material has been reprinted from the Minutes of the
Board of Directors of Western Theological Seminary, November

16, 1915. Dr. Jeffers died at Pasadena, California, on December 20, 1914. The Eulogy covers his career as teacher and preacher, with emphasis on his high standing and reputation in both fields.

See also Karman, James, for further material on the subject of Jeffers' father.

186 _____. "Jeffers Scholarly Materials: Gleeson Library, University of San Francisco." Robinson Jeffers Newsletter, 43 (December, 1975), 18.

The card catalog lists 46 works by Jeffers, including translations into German, Czech, and Italian and some rare special printings; 22 works on Jeffers, including theses and monographs; 9 letters and manuscripts. Most of this material has not been published. Among these materials are telegrams and notes to Judith Anderson, letters by Una to various correspondents, Judith Anderson's script for "The Tower Beyond Tragedy," 22 photos of Jeffers, family, and Tor House, etc.

187 _____. "Jeffers Theses and Dissertations: A Summary Listing." Robinson Jeffers Newsletter, 45 (June, 1976), 8-10.

Lists 33 Masters Theses, alphabetical by author, with title, reference to Newsletter in which abstract appears, and institution where thesis was completed.

Lists 27 Dissertations, alphabetical by author, with title, reference to Newsletter in which abstract appears, institution where work was completed, and a reference to Dissertation Abstracts where work is listed and discussed.

188 _____. "The Prose of Robinson Jeffers: An Annotated Checklist." Robinson Jeffers Newsletter, 46 (September, 1976), 14-36.

Lists over 120 items from around 1905 to 1976, with length (in words) of composition and place of publication. Each entry is also accompanied with a brief annotation as to content, thematic intention, etc. Excellent contribution to Jeffers scholarship which had not been attempted previously.

189 _____. "A Note on Jeffers' Prose." Robinson Jeffers Newsletter, 47 (December, 1976), 5-6.

Is a continuation of above article with an appeal for several troublesome items not included in the first checklist.

190 _____. "Jeffers Scholarly Materials: Albert Bender Collection at Mills College (Oakland, Calif.)." Robinson Jeffers Newsletter, 47 (December, 1976), 29-32.

Article is a listing of the materials in three divisions: Manuscript holdings, Letters, and Other Materials. Under manuscripts are listed "Original" (mostly in pencil), and "Typescripts." There are several extended quotations copied as Book Inscriptions. Under letters are listed those from

Jeffers, from Una Jeffers (201 of which are addressed to
Bender), a couple of notes from Donnan and Garth Jeffers,
and some carbon copies of Bender's letters to the Jeffers
family. Under other materials are listed photographs, clippings, a map of Jeffers Country, and a typed checklist of
the Jeffers-Bender collection at Occidental College.

191 _____. "The Berg Collection: New York Public Library."
Robinson Jeffers Newsletter, 48 (March, 1977), 24-25.
    Calls this "an interim report," which means it was not
made by someone "on-the-spot," and may be superseded later.
This one is based on a card catalong photocopy. It is listed
by "Letters of Robinson Jeffers," "Letters of Una Jeffers,"
"Letters of Others," and "Other Manuscripts." Also several
photographs, including one of Edna St. Vincent Millay and
Robinson Jeffers, are listed. In the manuscripts are four
holograph poems.

192 _____. "Jeffers Scholarly Materials: University of California,
Santa Barbara." Robinson Jeffers Newsletter, 54 (October,
1979), 29-31.
    Lists 12 letters in the "Corle Collection," along with some
clippings and four photos. The other listing is the enormous
Judith Anderson Papers, 44 file boxes in 45 categories with
separate box of photos, clippings, etc.

193 _____. "The Poet as Essential to the Nation's Life: Robinson
Jeffers." Robinson Jeffers Newsletter, 55 (December, 1979),
43-45.
    An abstract of a Phi Beta Kappa lecture delivered at Cali-
fornia State University, Long Beach, April 2, 1979. Jeffers
embraced an almost lifelong commitment to pay his "Birth" to
the human race, to tell mankind, especially his own country,
what it did not want to hear but needed to hear for its own
sake. Hermit, recluse, isolate, he was in his way the nation's
most public figure. Whether his readers believe in what he
said or not, they cannot but be affected by his vision.

194 _____. "Jeffers Scholarly Resources, University of Maryland."
Robinson Jeffers Newsletter, 58 (May, 1981), 35.
    Brief account is based upon the librarian's response. The
materials consist of five letters from Jeffers to persons at
Boni & Liveright, 1928, concerning Cawdor--from the time of
submission to receipt of author's copies. They also mention
Dear Judas, a work in progress. Two postcards also refer
to the limited edition of Dear Judas.

195 _____. (unsigned). "Jeffers Scholarly Materials: Melba
Bennett Collection, Palm Springs." Robinson Jeffers Newsletter, 61 (July, 1982), 38-40.

Ms. Bennett left her extensive Jeffers holdings to two
libraries, Occidental College receiving the bulk of materials,
suited to a primary research library; and to the Public Library in Palm Springs, perhaps fifty volumes by and about
Jeffers. First editions are signed by Jeffers.

196 _____. "An Index to the Poems of Robinson Jeffers." Robinson Jeffers Newsletter, 63 (June, 1983), 31-44.
   Begins with a listing of sources and an abbreviation by
which each one is identified. The poems are listed in alphabetical order, with work in which it appeared, and the page,
or pages. Is offered "as a convenience to help identify titles
and locate texts," and is not a final version.

197 _____, ed. Robinson Jeffers Newsletter, Number 23, April,
1969 to Present, Fall 1985.

198 _____, ed. with Afterword. Dear Judas and Other Poems.
New York: Horace J. Liveright, 1929. Reprinted New
York: Liveright, 1977.

199 BROWN, E. K. "The Coast Opposite Humanity." Canadian
Forum, 18 (January, 1939), 309-310.

200 BROWN, John Mason. Seeing More Things. New York: McGraw-
Hill, 1948. "In the Grand Manner," pp. 231-237. About Medea,
   Miss Anderson approaches antique tragedy unafraid. Playing Medea and playing her to the last drop of cruelty,
frenzy, and revenge that is in her, she cannot raise "Tragedy to the skies," but instead at the dictation of the text,
she burrows with it into the heat of hades, flinching from
none of the horrors to be found there.... Jeffers has not
attempted the impossible task of prettifying the Medea story.
He has employed the poet's skill to streamline the text, to
bring it closer to the contemporary stage, to rid its speeches
of those stylistic villainies. Jeffers' language, though not
always satisfactory, has a driving quality about it. What it
loses as poetry, it gains as theatre.

201 _____. Dramatis Personae. New York: Viking Press, 1963.
"Judith Anderson's Medea," pp. 208-213.
   A review of Jeffers' adaptation of the Greek play, which
opened at the National Theatre, October 20, 1947. Praises
Miss Anderson in the most superlative terms: "So right is
she for Medea, so right is Medea for her, that it almost seems
as if Euripides, not Mr. Jeffers, must have had Miss Anderson
in mind." Reviews the actress's career and concludes that she
has never been afraid to portray a character "to the last drop
of cruelty, frenzy, and revenge." Most actresses simply
cannot accomplish this. In the end, however, this reviewer
leaves the theatre somewhat "cold" and thinks it was because

of Jeffers' particular slant on the character of Medea, the
utter lack of tragic grandeur, the presentation of a woman who
"merely wades deeper and deeper into a sea of horrors."

202 BROWN, Leonard. "Our Contemporary Poetry." Sewanee Re-
     view, 41 (January-March, 1933), 43-63. Jeffers, passim.
        A review of The New Poetry: An Anthology of Twentieth
     Century Verse in English, edition by Harriet Monroe and
     Alice Corbin Henderson (1932). Of Jeffers, the reviewer
     says: "...one of the more lately arrived luminaries in the
     contemporary heavens, has been likened to the Greeks; his
     work does have a kind of classical overtone at times, but it
     is in the manner rather than in the meaning of his poetry
     that we find this flavor. But even the classic qualities of
     this style are so overladen with a dark melodrama that we
     come finally to suspect even his so-called Greek temper....
     If we go beyond the selections given from Jeffers by Miss
     Monroe in this anthology to the longer poems, we come upon
     material which is not remotely classical."

203 _____, et al., eds. Literature for Our Time. New York:
     Henry Holt, 1947. "Foreword to The Selected Poetry of
     Robinson Jeffers," pp. 348-349, and 4 poems.
        Prints a selection from "Roan Stallion," under Machine
     Against Man; "Shine Perishing Republic," "The Purse-Seine,"
     and "The Answer," under The Individual in a World Society.
     Each division of the anthology is prefaced with a short intro-
     duction, but the authors are not commented upon significantly.

204 BROWN, M. Webster. "Robinson Jeffers: A Poet Who Studied
     Medicine." Medical Journal and Record, 130 (November 6,
     1929), 535-539.
        Reviews briefly the history of medical men who have won
     something of fame as poets. It is, however, rare that we
     find a poet who has studied medicine with no idea of becoming
     a physician, but simply for the purpose of adding to his gen-
     eral knowledge. This is true of Jeffers, and his acquaintance
     with physiology, medicine and abnormal psychology intensifies
     and enriches the poetic message. Continues by quoting numer-
     ous excerpts from Jeffers to illustrate the poet's knowledge of
     medicine, but at the end feels that such quoting does not do
     justice to this poet, "the one poet America has produced with
     a real title to greatness since the world was startled by the
     'barbaric yawp' of Walt Whitman."

205 BUKOWSKI, Charles. Mockingbird Wish Me Luck: A Book of
     Poems. Los Angeles: Black Sparrow Press, 1973. "He
     Wrote in Lonely Blood," a poem written to Jeffers and the
     book Be Angry at the Sun. Reprinted in Robinson Jeffers
     Newsletter, 46 (September, 1976), 40.

206 BURGESS, R. L. "One Hundred and Three Californians." Poetry,
     27 (January, 1926), 217-221.
         Review of Continent's End, an Anthology of Contemporary
     California Poets, edited by George Sterling, Genevieve Tag-
     gard, and James Horty. Comments briefly on various poets
     and says of Jeffers: "our big new man, whom we are so
     proud of New York's having discovered in romantically belated
     fashion, is awarded the honor of conferring the title upon the
     collection from one of his own poems...." In general, does
     not regard the anthology too favorably, calling it too regional,
     too much concerned with the local and regional.

207 _____. "A Very Great Californian," editorial. San Jose
     Evening News, February 1, 1926.

208 _____. "The Seaward Print of Unreturning Feet; a Tribute
     to George Sterling." Overland Monthly, 84 (December, 1926),
     Jeffers, 379 et passim.

209 BURNS, Aubrey. "Will Against Will Clashes in Epic by Mount
     Carmel Poet." Dallas Morning News, May 8, 1932.
         Review of Thurso's Landing and Other Poems.

210 BUSCH, Niven. "Duel on a Headland: A Portrait of Robinson
     Jeffers." Saturday Review of Literature, 11 (March 9, 1935),
     533. Reprinted in New Directions: The Student in a Chang-
     ing World. ed. Warren Bowers. Philadelphia: Lippincott, 1937.
     Pp. 443-448.
         Biographical sketch of Jeffers, his family--Una and the
     two sons--their house at Carmel, and the surrounding envi-
     ronment of which the Jefferses are so much a part. It is
     referred to as a "weird household," but Jeffers "and his wife
     run a successful corporation. She has the knack, so neces-
     sary to the business half of literary partnerships, of giving
     shrewd advice without taking credit for it." Jeffers said,
     "My life is happier than most lives--quite ridiculously con-
     tented. I should like to go on like this for several centuries."

211 BUSH, Douglas. Mythology and the Romantic Tradition in Eng-
     lish Poetry. Cambridge: Harvard University Press, 1937.
     Reprinted New York: Pageant Book Company, 1957. Chapter
     XV, "American Poets," pp. 481-525. Jeffers passim.
         In Jeffers we have the most undisciplined soul and mind
     that we have yet encountered, the most striking of many
     proofs that Latin and Greek cannot make a classical artist
     out of a romantic, in this case a decadent romantic.... Al-
     though the classics have not wrought order out of Jeffers
     stormy broodings on the plight of humanity, they have led
     him to ancient myth. Poems which have mythological back-
     grounds are "The Tower Beyond Tragedy," "Solstice," and

numerous shorter works. On the whole, Jeffers' many volumes have not shown much evidence of growth. It is not
surprising that many American reviewers should have has-
tened to deify the apostle of a new religion. Most Greeks
would have considered him an unbalanced barbarian.

212 BUSHBY, D. M. "Poets of Our Southern Frontier." Overland
     Monthly, 89 (February, 1931), 41-42.
        Comparison of Robinson Jeffers and E. A. Robinson.

213 CALVERTON, V. F. and S. D. Schmalhausen, eds. Sex in
     Civilization. New York: Macaulay Co., 1929. "A Note on
     the Poetry of Sex," by Arthur D. Ficke, pp. 666-667.

214 _____. "Pathology in Contemporary Literature." Thinker,
     4 (December, 1931), 7-16. Reprinted in Our Neurotic Age,
     ed. by S. D. Schmalhausen.

215 _____. American Literature at the Crossroads. Seattle:
     University of Washington Book Store, 1931.

216 _____. The Liberation of American Literature. New York:
     Charles Scribner's, 1932. Jeffers, pp. 473-474 et passim.
        In Robinson Jeffers, another aspect of literary pathology
     emerges into the foreground. Jeffers envisions the world as
     a monstrous miscarriage of fate. Believing that we are much
     closer to the animals than to the angels, he is much more
     fascinated by instinctive man than by intellectual man....
     Jeffers is more than il-logical; he is a-logical in his whole
     approach to life. Only God remains for him, with whom by
     subduing ourselves we may finally become one--if we have
     the courage to face our doom. Never has such desperately
     dooming poetry been written in this century, never such mad,
     chaotic, crucifying verse which overwhelms by a power that
     is more thunderous than tragic.

217 CAMBON, Glauco. The Inclusive Flame: Studies in American
     Poetry. Bloomington: Indiana University Press, 1963.
     Jeffers, passim.
        Jeffers not discussed; referred to several times.

218 CANBY, Henry Seidel. "North of Hollywood." Saturday Review
     of Literature, 10 (October 7, 1933), 162. Reprinted in
     Seven Years' Harvest. New York: Holt, Rinehart, and
     Winston, 1936. Reprinted Port Washington: Kennikat, 1964.
     Pp. 146-150.
        Review of Give Your Heart to the Hawks and Other Poems.
     Canby says, "In spite of its morbidity, and perhaps because
     of it, here is a poem that troubles the water as if there
     passed by some angel of judgment." Jeffers has been known

as a poet of cruelty and horror, who has celebrated in dramatic narrative, sensational to the point of melodrama, the
harsh incoherences between men's expectancy and his fate.
The inhumanity of his monotonously beautiful coast seemed
to weigh upon him until, ignoring its cities and bungalows,
he peopled the empty canyons of its wilderness with figures
in which perverted passions broke through suppressions into
blood and fire. His rather loose verse took on aspects of
grandeur as it lifted the mountains and the sea to a plane
of wild imagination, then too often broke into sensationalism
as the passions and despairs of his homely people were un-
loosed, like hopeless souls of sinners in some old illuminated
manuscript, writhing toward the eternal pit.

219 CANTWELL, Robert. "Robinson Jeffers Better Novelist Than
     Poet." New York World Telegram, March 29, 1932.

220 CARGILL, Oscar. Intellectual America: Ideas on the March.
     New York: Macmillan, 1941. Fourth printing, 1959. Jeffers,
     pp. 741-761.
         "...for Robinson Jeffers the fate of man has a majesty
     that needs 'nor God nor goal.' Indeed though Death will
     reap at last all the heritage of Man, Death cannot alter the
     character of man.... We may deplore his lack of sympathy
     with our problems, yet at his best Jeffers enriches our
     thought by demonstrating the glory and beauty of an imperi-
     ous will, our sword and shield, possibly, in other circum-
     stances than he has imagined. At his worst, Jeffers is still
     symptomatic of the moral confusion of his time, its mirror
     and mouthpiece. If the future chooses to judge us by Jef-
     fers' most abortive work the future will not go far wrong."

221 CARMELITE: Robinson Jeffers Supplement, edited by Ella Winter.
     December 12, 1928. Carmel-By-The-Sea, California. 16 pages.
         Contents:

         "Portrait of Robinson Jeffers," by J. Hagemeyer, pp.
             1-3.
         "Jeffers, the Neighbor," by Lincoln Steffens, p. 3.
         "Portrait of Una Jeffers and Note," by D. H., pp. 3-5.
         "The Judgment of His Peers," comment by Edgar Lee
             Masters, S. B. Field, J. DeAngelo, W. Bynner,
             C. E. S. Wood, C. Sandburg, and J. Rorty, p. 5.
         "Two Portraits of Robinson Jeffers, at 18 and today
             (1928)," pp. 6-7.
         "Robinson Jeffers, Stone-Mason," by Ella Winter, with
             two photographs of Tor House, pp. 7-10.
         "Birds of the Jeffers Country," by L. Williams, with
             a photograph, p. 10.
         "Flora of the Jeffers Country," by L. Rowntree, pp.
             10-11.

"Biography," from Author's Who's Who, p. 11.

"The Butcher Looks at Jeffers," excerpts from poems,
    p. 11.

"Joy," a poem addressed "To my friend Robinson
    Jeffers," by A. D. Ficke, p. 11.

"Onorio's Vision of Our Lady," woodcut by R. Boynton,
    p. 12.

"The Eagle Flight in <u>Cawdor</u>," by D. Hagemeyer, p.
    13--Review of <u>Cawdor and Other Poems</u>.

"Time and Western Man," by James Rorty, pp. 13-14.

"Jeffers as Prose Writer," p. 14.

"Two Portraits of Robinson Jeffers with His Children,"
    p. 14.

"A Bibliography of the Books by Robinson Jeffers,"
    p. 15.

"Anecdotes of the Jefferses," p. 16.

"Linoleum Cut," by S. Wood, p. 16.

222   CARPENTER, Frederic I. "The Values of Robinson Jeffers."
      <u>American Literautre</u>, 11 (January, 1940), 353-366.
         Jeffers has often been called the poet of denial, the de-
      stroyer of morality and of human values. It is the purpose
      of this essay to inquire how far this is true. A poet may
      deny the authority of existing values, may be unable or un-
      willing to describe a new order, and yet may imply and even
      occasionally define the outlines of such an order.... The
      problem of values is fundamental to the understanding of
      Jeffers' poetry, but many of his statements on this subject
      are contradictory. Although he believes that human values
      are real and necessary his poems also exclaim frequently that
      humanity itself is "a spectral episode," and "needless." But
      granting the contradictions, his poetry as a whole does re-
      peatedly emphasize certain values. Some of these may be
      classed as "human," others as "natural."

223   . "Death Comes for Robinson Jeffers." <u>University Re-</u>
      <u>view</u>, 7 (December, 1940), 97-105. Reprinted in Carpenter,
      <u>American Literature and the Dream</u>. New York: Philosophical
      Library, 1955. Pp. 144-154.
         Article is based upon the premise that to the mind of
      Western man, life has always seemed the greatest good and
      death the greatest evil. But now, the modern poet believes
      men's minds may have changed. Upon this reversal of values,
      Robinson Jeffers has sought to build a new philosophy, in
      which life shall no longer be the only good, nor death the
      ultimate evil. Many of his finest poems have celebrated
      death and night and have questioned the goodness of life.
      This questioning of life, and this celebration of death, have
      been important in causing the rejection of his poetry by many
      readers and critics.

224 _____. Robinson Jeffers. New York: Twayne, 1962. Also
published in paperback.
Consists of 159 pages, with Notes to chapters, a Selected
Bibliography, and Index. In six chapters:

1. The Life and Times of Robinson Jeffers
2. The Poetry of Myth: The Long Poems
3. The Short Poems
4. Philosophy and Religion
5. "The Atom to Be Split"
6. Conclusion

Does not aim at solving any of the problems surrounding
Jeffers' career, but rather surveys his initial reception in
the 1920's to his almost total obscurity in the end. Over
the years Jeffers' reputation--both critical and popular--has
fluctuated more than that of any contemporary author. Never
an easy author to read, all Jeffers' poetry leads toward the
philosophic attitude of "Inhumanism" and most readers and
critics are repelled by the utter nihilism apparent in this
philosophy.

225 _____. "Robinson Jeffers and the Torches of Violence," in
Poetry and Fiction in the American Twenties, edited by R. E.
Langford and W. E. Taylor. DeLand, Fla.: Everett Edwards
Press, 1966. Pp. 14-17.
Begins with brief commentary on the violence which has
been increasing in literature in general since the 1920's and
thinks that the average reader or critic may see in Jeffers
the very epitome of this tendency. In the early 1920's be
began writing the poetic narratives of physical and emotional
violence which made him famous. This trend culminated in
The Women at Point Sur, after which he had to stop and
reconsider the direction in which he was going. Jeffers
created a rationale of his reasons for having so much violence,
chiefly because he felt that it was necessary for tragedy, but
ironically his work was never truly tragic. If Jeffers' imagination and literary rationalization of the problem was sometimes
confused, it is not surprising. After his death we are only
beginning to recognize the illumination which "the torches of
violence" may produce.

226 _____. "Robinson Jeffers and 'Humanity'--Some Anecdotes."
Robinson Jeffers Newsletter, 10 (April, 1965), 2. Reprinted
in Newsletter, 15 (September, 1966), 1-2.
Recalls some of the incidents in his relationship with Robinson Jeffers--an uncommon friendship since the two had apparently nothing in common. Author visits Jeffers in 1935 and
finds that Jeffers the poet and Jeffers the man were almost
two different people. He had created the literary "persona"
who scorned "humanity" and hated intrusion upon his solitude.

But he welcomed, often almost longed for communication with individuals interested in poetry and in ideas. Or he scorned humanity in the abstract, rather than humanity as individuals. And although he truly valued solitude, he also valued individual friendships and suffered from the deprivation of such friendly meetings as that with the Irish poet who did not dare to call on him.

227   _____. "Review of Robinson Jeffers: Poet of Inhumanism," by Arthur Coffin. American Literature, 43 (November, 1971), 477.

This new study is interesting for several reasons. As the latest of a series of books published since Jeffers' death in 1962, it bears witness to the extraordinary vitality of his poetry, which was sometimes pronounced dead before its author.... Coffin's book both suffers and gains from its philosophical approach. Three of his chapters discuss the relationship of Jeffers and Nietzsche, while the other chapters consider Jeffers in relation to Schopenhauer, to Lucretius, and to others. The author avoids the old sterile analysis of influences but emphasizes what Sainte-Beuve called "Families of minds."

228   _____. "Robinson Jeffers Today: Beyond Good and Beneath Evil." American Literature, 49 (January, 1977), 86-96.

Reviews Jeffers' poetic activities from 1941 to January 20, 1962, at the time of his death. The objective of this article is to follow the events which have caused a renaissance in Jeffers' reputation and to suggest some of the reasons for it. The reasons which are given consist of books--biography and criticism--which have been published, editions of Jeffers which are being brought out, the founding of a Jeffers Newsletter, a Jeffers Festival, etc. In conclusion it is suggested that Jeffers continues to interest because he is much in line with current criticism which explores mythic themes and deep psychological problems.

229   _____. "'Post Mortem': 'The Poet Is Dead.'" Western American Literature, 12 (1977), 3-10.

Article is essentially an address which was delivered on the weekend of November 21-23, 1975, at the first "Robinson Jeffers Festival" to be held outside of California. This Festival was celebrated at Southern Oregon State College, Ashland, Oregon. On the program William Everson, an avowed disciple of Jeffers, read from Jeffers' poetry and from his own elegy, "The Poet is Dead."

The address is a comparison-discussion of Jeffers' poem "Post Mortem" published in 1927, and Everson's elegy, which makes use of some of Jeffers' imagery and poetic phrases, spoken as it were, with the tongue of the dead poet, in

order to realize his presence in the world which he has just
left. These two poems complement each other--the first
looking forward to the time when the poet should have died;
the second remembering the dead poet and naturalizing him
in our living world.

230 _____. "The Inhumanism of Robinson Jeffers." Western
American Literature, 16 (Spring, 1981), 19-25.
   When Jeffers described Inhumanism in the Preface to
The Double Axe, he emphasized only a "philosophical shifting
of emphasis and significance from man to not-man," asserting
that the idea "has objective truth and human value. It offers a reasonable detachment as a rule of conduct." Article
reviews some recent comments on Jeffers' use of this word
and then traces the course of development of the concept
of "humanism" from its appearance in the Renaissance to the
twentieth century. In conclusion it is said that "the positive
meanings of Inhumanism are difficult if not impossible to de-
fine. They are related to the nature of science--especially
the pure science of astronomy. The phrase 'cosmic naturalism' comes close."

231 CERWIN, Herbert. "Notes on Robinson Jeffers." Robinson
Jeffers Newsletter, 33 (September, 1972), 3-4.
   A personal article in which the author says: "I was sev-
enteen and a young newspaper reporter when I met Robinson
Jeffers in Carmel in the 1920's. What impressed me most was
his sculptured face, as if it had been carved out of stone.
His eyes were narrow slits. There was nothing of a recluse
about him.... The poet said I was the first newspaperman
to interview him, and he asked how I had heard about him.
I told him that Lincoln Steffens had suggested him and I had
gone to the library and obtained a copy of 'Roan Stallion.'"

232 CESTRE, Charles. "Robinson Jeffers." Revue Anglo-Américaine.
4 (August, 1927), 489-502.

233 CHATFIELD, Hale. "Robinson Jeffers: His Philosophy and His
Major Themes." Laurel Review, 6 (1966), 56-71.
   Begins with a fairly comprehensive review of what some
critics have said about Jeffers, and hopes to bring about an
end to some of the "innumerable prejudices and falsehood that
have somehow managed to marry themselves to Jeffers' poetry."
Article deals mainly with two questions, the preponderance of
violence and evil in his poems. Believes that the poet would
like the human being to face up to the unpleasant realities
of nature. Nature is exceptionally clever in devising means
but she has no ends which the human mind is able to discover
or comprehend. The other problem is that of death, with
which Jeffers seems to be obsessed. He does not worship
death, nor does he love war. He knows that death is a fact

that must be either ignored or endured, and he chooses endurance. He knows as far as war is concerned that it is
man's "grim folly," and says in one of his poems "I would
burn my hand in a slow fire ... to change the future."

234 CHERRY, William Grimes III. "An Analysis of the Major Char-
     acters of Selected Long Poems by Robinson Jeffers as Reflec-
     tions of the Author's Philosophy and Poetic Theory." Ph.D.
     diss., University of South Carolina, 1973. DA, 34 (1974),
     5371A.
        This study focuses upon the principal figures of ten major
     works while tracing Jeffers' developing philosophy of Inhu-
     manism from its tentative statement in Tamar (1924), to its
     fullest expression in The Double Axe (1948). This analysis
     attributes the singular power and flavor of Jeffers' verse to
     his conscious decision to create through these purposely un-
     realistic characters, symbolically, the aura of timelessness.
     Jeffers attempted a literature of permanence by intensifying
     in his figures those characteristics that he considered perma-
     nently recognizable, and he punished them in moralistic
     fashion for possessing these same traits.

235 CHILDS, Myrtokleia. "Thurso's Landing: Jeffers in Familiar
     Setting." Carmelite, 5 (March 31, 1932), 8.

236 CHURCH, Samuel H. "A Pittsburgh Poet Discovered." Carnegie
     Magazine, 2 (November, 1928), 180-182.

237 CLARK, Walter Van Tilburg. "A Study in Robinson Jeffers."
     Masters Thesis, University of Vermont, 1934.

238 CLURMAN, Harold. Lies Like Truth: Theatre Reviews and
     Essays. New York: Macmillan, 1958. "Judith Anderson,"
     pp. 88-90.
        Comments on the 1947 production of Medea as written by
     Robinson Jeffers and acted by Judith Anderson. Does not
     share the general enthusiasm for Miss Anderson's Medea.
     Says he has "three major objections to her performance."
     First, she works too hard, and at the end we experience
     only fatigue; second, her approach is chiefly physical; and
     finally, this Medea is neither a person nor a concept. Noth-
     ing is communicated.
        Continues with comment on the 1951 production (by the
     American National Theatre and Academy) of Jeffers' "The
     Tower Beyond Tragedy." Thinks this production belongs
     somewhere in the "limbo of the theatre's well-intentioned but
     unsightly efforts." Not even Miss Anderson can give its
     pain and violence any meaning. Jeffers' poem was not written
     for the stage and makes a brazenly joyless sound without echo,
     as if all feeling were buried deep in stone.

239 COFFIN, Arthur Bonneau. "Ideological Patterns in the Work of
     Robinson Jeffers." Ph.D. diss., University of Wisconsin,
     1965. DA, 26 (1965), 3329.
        In six chapters, this dissertation undertakes to identify
     the chief ideas and to explain how they are embodied in the
     poems. The first chapter is an introduction to the relevant
     scholarship and to the method used in this study. Jeffers'
     theories about poetry and the function of the poet are brought
     together and organized in order to facilitate subsequent dis-
     cussion of the ideas; and on the basis of the poet's use of
     the ideas involved, the poet's work is divided into three
     periods--the Twenties, the Thirties, and the work from Be
     Angry at the Sun onward to the posthumous collection.
        The following published work is derived principally from
     the dissertation.

240 _____. Robinson Jeffers: Poet of Inhumanism. Madison:
     University of Wisconsin Press, 1971.
        Consists of 300 pages, in eight chapters, with Introduction,
     Notes, Bibliography, and Index. The chapter titles are based
     on the elements of influence for that period in Jeffers' life:

        1. The Poet and the Poetry
        2. Jeffers and Schopenhauer
        3. Jeffers and Nietzsche, the Beginning
        4. Jeffers and Nietzsche, the Middle Period
        5. Jeffers and Nietzsche, the Final Period
        6. The Idea of Culture Ages
        7. The Greek Tragedians
        8. The Order of Nature

        Jeffers' poetry, which often appears to be a monotonous
     litany of doom, reveals upon close study a dynamic quest for
     satisfactory answers, and regarded in the light of Nineteenth-
     Century philosophical inquiry and contemporary Twentieth-
     Century literary reaction to that thought, it assumes fresh
     significance and stature.
        Review by Robert Brophy, Robinson Jeffers Newsletter,
     29 (August, 1971), 4-5.

241 _____. "Robinson Jeffers: Inhumanism and the Apocalypse."
     Robinson Jeffers Newsletter, 30 (January, 1972), 6.
        Abstract of paper read at the Summer of 1971 Jeffers
     Festival. This paper examines the theological implications of
     the ideological structure which Jeffers assembled during the
     course of his poetic career and identified as Inhumanism--a
     shifting of emphasis from man to not-man. The former Apoc-
     alyptic tradition assures judgment, punishment, and new
     beginnings: the latter, a fictive construct, provides a struc-
     ture with which man, occupying the Now, can impose a sense
     of order on the future, the Sartrean Not-Yet.

242 COMMAGER, Henry Steele. <u>The American Mind</u>. New Haven:
     Yale University Press, 1950. "Cult of the Irrational,"
     pp. 120-140.

    The most uncompromisingly scientific of the literary spoke-
men of determinism, Jeffers is, at the same time, the most
romantic. Living, by choice, close to nature, and acknowledg-
ing no obligation but to nature, his affluent poetry is a scientific as well as philosophical commentary on the life of man.
With Jeffers, the philosophical reaction to the world of science
opened up first by Darwin, came full circle. Man, the last
born of nature's long travail, was seen not as her chiefest
glory but as her most cruel blunder, because having endowed
man with the critical faculty, she enabled him to realize the
futility and horror of his existence.

243 CONNER, Frederick William. <u>Cosmic Optimism: A Study of the
     Interpretation of Evolution by American Poets from Emerson to
     Robinson</u>. Gainesville: University of Florida Press, 1949.
     Jeffers, pp. 332-339.

    Jeffers not only recognized the indifference, the insensi-
bility of the cosmos, but made of this indifference a kind of
Nirvana. Cosmic optimism was essentially a projection of
human values into a theory of the universe, but what Jeffers
prizes in nature is precisely that it is not human. What he
despises in man is that he falls short of both this thoughtless
violence and the rock-like impassibility which Jeffers admires
equally. Man's salvation is not to be achieved by the fulfillment of his humanity, but by abandoning it, by imitating the
granite imperturbability of inorganic nature.

244 COOPER, Monte. "Pain Matched by Courage." <u>Memphis Com-
     mercial Appeal</u>, June 12, 1932.
    Review of <u>Thurso's Landing</u>.

245 COUCHMAN, Robert. "Review of <u>Thurso's Landing and Other
     Poems</u>." <u>San Jose Morning Herald</u>, May 10, 1932.

246 COX, Mary Margaret. "The Role of Women in the Narrative
     Poetry of Robinson Jeffers." Masters Thesis, University of
     North Carolina, 1964.

247 CRAWFORD, N. A. "Robinson Jeffers, Poet in the Somber Cloth
     of Tragedy." <u>Baltimore Evening Sun</u>, September 17, 1927.
    Review of <u>The Women at Point Sur and Other Poems</u>.

248 CRONON, William. "Robinson Jeffers Collections: Stanford
     University." <u>Robinson Jeffers Newsletter</u>, 42 (August, 1975),
     15-16.

    At first glance one is led to believe that Stanford is one
of the largest holders of Jeffers materials in the country.
There are four collections: Albert Bender, George Sterling,

Margery Bailey, and American Authors Collections. But there
is little of major biographical or bibliographical interest here.
There are copies of Jeffers' and Una's letters to George
Sterling, and a Jeffers' letter to Margaret Cobb, the only
original in the collection. All others are by Una, in one of
which is a manuscript draft of the poem "Suicide's Stone."
We learn little of Una's personal life from these letters and
even less of Jeffers. Mostly they show Una in the role of
handling business, manuscript sales, autographing of special
editions, refusing personal appearances Jeffers did not care
to make. Some of the letters are accompanied with little
personal notes, but they indicate that she was busy and in
a hurry.

249 CUSHING, M. A. "Criticism of 'Tower Beyond Tragedy' Produc-
     tion." The Peninsulan (Burlinghame, Calif.), 1 (November
     10, 1932), 4.

250 CUNNINGHAM, Cornelius Carmen. "The Rhythm of Robinson
     Jeffers' Poetry as Revealed by Oral Reading." Quarterly
     Journal of Speech, 32 (October, 1946), 351-357.
          Begins with a background on the importance of oral reading
     to a total understanding of the poetry under consideration.
     It is the purpose of this article to show the results obtained
     by adapting oral reading to the end of solving problems with
     respect to the prosody of poets. The poet chosen is Robinson
     Jeffers, who probably presents the most challenging problem
     in prosodic analysis of all the poets writing in English
     today.... Presents several poems in scansion and tabulates
     the results, identifying the patterns of rhythm. In conclu-
     sion, the article advises that the counterpart of Jeffers'
     rhythm can be found in the flight of the birds--eagles, gulls,
     hawks--especially the hawks: the way they soar and swoop.
     In reading Jeffers' poetry aloud, don't forget that soar and
     swoop.

251 DALY, James. "Roots Under the Rocks." Poetry, 26 (August
     25, 1925), 278-285.
          Review of Tamar, etc. When Jeffers' first volume appeared
     in 1916, its most appreciative critics were somewhat dismayed
     by the contrast between his philosophy, which was modern,
     and his technique, which belonged to a period thirty years
     past. They greeted him as an authentic poet, a fine fruition
     of the land he celebrated; but they pointed out that he did
     not hesitate to make awkward inversions for the sake of rhyme,
     and that he seemed over-fond of thee and thou. The strength
     that came shouldering through the highly conventional meters
     of poem after poem showed that here was a poet whose develop-
     ment called chiefly for a resolute avoidance of the established,
     the ready-made, in verse.

252 DAVIDSON, Gustav. "A Mount Carmel Saga." The Forum, 78
     (December, 1927), 596-597.

253 DAVIS, H. L. "Jeffers Denies Us Twice." Poetry, 31 (Febru-
     ary, 1928), 274-279.
         Review of The Women at Point Sur. This reviewer begins
     on a highly optimistic note: "The most splendid poetry of
     my time. Nothing written by this generation can begin to
     come up with it. Every page is a triumph. I cannot praise
     it more than it deserves. And yet--the poem itself is dead,
     as lifeless as a page of Euclid." Article continues with telling
     the story, which really does an injustice to the total compo-
     sition, and the critic concludes by saying: "Make no mistake
     about the poetry; these years have never seen better than
     this, with its depth and beauty and barbaric splendor. There
     are no prose passages, there is no flagging, no marking time.
     Every page is a triumph. It appears to me, in looking back,
     that Jeffers has given his account of human terror and jeal-
     ousy and selfishness, vice and foulness and weakness, as
     having wished to divorce his mind from these and all things
     human, and see them only as incidents in the long procession
     of planets, no more to be ignored than they, and no more to
     be pitied. But they are more to be pitied. The poet is not
     as the planets are, but human; and to forget that is to be a
     renegade."

254 DE CASSERES, Benjamin. "Robinson Jeffers: Tragic Terror."
     Bookman, 66 (November, 1927), 262-266. Reprinted Austin,
     Tex.: J. S. Mayfield, 1928. Pamphlet.
         It is as difficult to conceive Robinson Jeffers in any other
     place than Carmel, California, as it would be to think of
     William Blake in Pittsburgh. If ever a man and a Spirit of
     Place had conspired for a mystical union it is here. That
     portion of California--its hills, sea, blue lupin, golden pop-
     pies, sea-gulls, dirt roads, pines, firs, hawks, herons and
     lighthouses ... belongs as absolutely to Robinson Jeffers, as
     Wessex belongs to Thomas Hardy.

255 _____. The Superman in America. Seattle: University of
     Washington Book Store, 1929. Jeffers, pp. 22-25 et passim.
         Reviews the cult of Superman in America "which began
     long before Nietzsche first gave poetic and philosophic vitality
     to a biological and psychological law as old as the race: the
     superior man is a law unto himself." Names and discusses
     several writers whom he considers supermen, among them
     Emerson, Thoreau, and Whitman. In the discussion of later
     writers he says of Jeffers: "he is the poet of Crazy Beauty.
     He is in the stream of the Dreadful Beauty--that thin stream
     on the borderland of our consciousness on the hither side of
     which we remain men, on the yon side of which there walk
     the tall and Beauty-ravished gods and the sublime madmen.

Jeffers is a man obsessed with the dream of a race that will wrench itself free of all hitherto accepted standards. He begins where Nietzsche left off. He is the most portentous figure, either artistically or personally, of the post-Nietzschean literary world."

256 _____. "Robinson Jeffers." University North Carolina Daily Tar Heel, 40 (January 24, 1932), 1.

257 DELL, Floyd. "Shell Shock and the Poetry of Robinson Jeffers." Modern Quarterly, 3 (September-December, 1926), 268-273.
    The acclaiming of a poet as "great" should at least give us new information concerning the psychology of the critical climate at that moment in history. The appearance of the poet Robinson Jeffers upon the literary horizon and the enthusiastic acclaim which his work has received from many of the advanced leaders of the American intelligentsia offer us this present opportunity for such an inquiry.... While this inquiry will not undertake any esthetic criticism of Jeffers' work, it may be said at the outset that it is certainly work of unusual and remarkable quality, and that its dramatic and narrative powers would naturally attract attention to it. However, the attribution of "greatness" to a writer implies something more than a recognition of his possession of such powers: It implies a profound approval of his content--not necessarily his subject matter, but his treatment of it, in short his attitude toward life.

258 DE MOTT, Robert J. "Robinson Jeffers' 'Tamar,'" in The Twenties, edited by Warren French. Deland, Fla.: Everett Edwards, 1975. Pp. 405-425.
    In "Tamar" Jeffers' lyricism joins with descriptive power to create a sensitive and poetic rendering of reality. In his narrative poem, description is essential for setting the scene, as well as for describing human actions. The effect of his verse, five beats to the line, quickened and sometimes doubled in others, creates a long and intensive line which manifests a basic harmony, wholeness and comprehensiveness Jeffers perceives in the natural world.... In "Tamar" Jeffers sustained the total movement of the poem by injecting his lines with the weight of both physical and psychological reality. The result was a combination of penetrative vision, surging elemental power and heightened dramatic tension characterized by what Jeffers termed a "detached and inclusive view-point." After eight years absence from publishing, Jeffers emerged in this poem "to rip the veil from reality only to realize that the vision he created was potentially demonic and self-defeating."

259 DEUTSCH, Babette. "Brains and Lyrics: Review of Tamar and Other Poems." New Republic, 43 (May 27, 1925), 23-24.

Calls the opening poem, "Tamar," a powerful dramatic narrative on the stern Greek model, given a native setting and written in a free verse that has in it the long roll and swing of the elder seas. Jeffers has his own style, which is worthy of his high moods and gnarled thinking. It is possible not to share the Oriental philosophy expressed in certain of his poems, but it is impossible to have strong poetry without the force of some equal conviction beating like a heart in its body.

260 _____. "Bitterness and Beauty." New Republic, 45 (February 10, 1926), 338-339.

Review of Roan Stallion, Tamar, etc. Article comments on three volumes besides Jeffers. This second volume by Jeffers which includes the contents of the first, together with almost as many new pieces, confirms the reader in the belief that Jeffers ranks with the foremost American poets, not only of his generation but of all the generations that preceded him.... This new volume shows clearly the stern Greek strain the Californian possesses. Jeffers' poetry is Greek in that it shows the large serenity of Greek thought at its highest, and it deals bravely in contemporary terms with the old terrible importunate Greek themes.

261 _____. "Or What's a Heaven For?" New Republic, 51 (August 17, 1927), 341.

Review of The Women at Point Sur. The poem leaves one with the feeling of having witnessed a Pyrrhic victory. Its meanings are too often obscure, and its drama too often sordid without relevance. There are too many characters, too many events that seem to have no organic relation to the whole. It is not up to some of his earlier work.

262 _____. "Brooding Eagle." New Republic, 57 (January 16, 1929), 253.

Review of Cawdor and Other Poems. Does not see any evidence that Jeffers has lost any of his immense power, but he has failed to use it "as terribly" as he can in this work. Yet such greatness as the poem possesses is not inherent either in its background or its fable, but rather in Jeffers' personal vision. Action and atmosphere are not caught as inextricably in the same net here as was the case in the other narrative poems. The black fate of the hero-victim is perhaps too special to be impressive. The most notable passages in the poem, though linked up with the narrative, could be deleted without hurting it vitally, and could, indeed, stand alone as separate lyrics. They center about the motif of a caged, maimed eagle, and the lines that take their drive from the image of the dying bird are particularly fine.

263 _____. "The Future of Poetry." New Republic, 60 (August 21, 1929), 12-15.

Article is concerned with several poets other than Jeffers.
As to this poet, the critic says: "In the work of Robinson
Jeffers, a poet who is not drawn into the tangle of theosoph-
ical thought, one finds even more distinctly a vision of the
universe large enough to inform a long philosophical poem.
It is, in the case of Jeffers, a terrifying vision, but, stead-
fastly confronted, it has the reconciling gift of all truth."

264 _____. "Sweet Hemlock: Review of Dear Judas, etc." New
York Herald Tribune Books, January 12, 1930.
Says "those who care for truth and poetry will make this
book their own. Those who do not will scarcely have troubled
to read this inadequate praise of it."

265 _____. "Comfort in Hell: Review of Descent to the Dead,
etc." New York Herald Tribune Books, January 31, 1932.
Remarks that neither the form nor the content will offer
surprises to those who have followed this poet's progress.
Here is simply a confirmation of his strength. He is one who
has looked on life as on death and feared neither one. The
mood is sustained throughout, with just enough variation to
avoid monotony.

266 _____. "The Hunger of Pain: Review of Thurso's Landing,
etc." New York Herald Tribune Books, March 27, 1932.
Does not believe that Jeffers has reached the peaks of
lyricism as in "Tamar" and "Cawdor," but technically this
work shows no change in the poet's ability. He continues to
employ his long, deep-breathed, billowing line. Here he is
more than usually devoid of ornament. The quality of poetry--
music and high imagination--remains.

267 _____. This Modern Poetry. New York: W. W. Norton,
1935. Chapter 7, "The Burden of the Mystery," pp. 187-
209. Jeffers, pp. 193-199.
Jeffers balances a religious and classical education with
the scientific equipment of a medical student and the special
knowledge of a forester. He spent much of his youth travel-
ing and studying in Western Europe and is restrained by his
greater learning from "brash pronunciamentos." He is a
poet who writes novels (in verse) which objectify his feeling
about man and the universe. HIs poetry also symbolizes a
serious inner conflict not uncommon in our time. His finest
passages achieve a harmony which is acceptable because it is
no facile cheerfulness but has as its fulcrum a tragic intensity.

268 _____. "In Love with the Universe: Review of Solstice,
etc." New York Herald Tribune Books, October 27, 1935.
The poem which opens Jeffers' latest volume restates his
familiar themes with no loss of power, and with the additional
interest of a greater technical variety. This is not the kind

of poetry that inflames the heart against the brutalities of
the strong, the greedy, and the stupid. It is poetry that,
fixing its eye upon the stars, is less troubled by the human
drama.

269 _____. "Review of Such Counsels You Gave to Me and Other
     Poems." New York Herald Tribune Books, October 31, 1937.
         Points out that the title poem is written in the long surg-
     ing line with the abrupt half for moments of tension that is
     peculiarly Jeffers' own, and, like his other narratives, draws
     some of its strength from the poet's knowledge of medicine
     and astronomy. It has the suspense that a story needs, and
     is not without power and beauty. However, it does not rise
     to the height of his previous performances.

270 _____. "Review of Be Angry at the Sun." New Republic,
     106 (March 23, 1942), 402.
         In the main, Jeffers sticks to his old themes and his fa-
     miliar style. The title poem, which brings the book to a
     close, reiterates the poet's aloofness from man's recurrent
     follies and crimes, and his dedication to the cold lonely
     passion for truth, however bleak. In his Preface to this
     volume Jeffers apologizes for the unusual number of "timely
     pieces" and hopes that the few timeless lyrics will outlive the
     current evils.

271 _____. Poetry in Our Time. New York: Holt, Rinehart, &
     Winston, 1952. "A Look at the Worst," pp. 1-27. Jeffers,
     passim.
         Makes a number of remarks in comparing Jeffers with
     Thomas Hardy. She says, however, that "Jeffers' motifs
     vary little from poem to poem, although the tragedy has
     different nodes. His recurrent themes are the danger of an
     all-too-human love, the self-delusion of man's self-importance,
     and over against these, the peace whose source lies in con-
     templation of the impersonal universe, acceptance of its inhu-
     man harmony...."

272 DE VOTO, Bernard A. "Rats, Lice, and Poetry." Saturday Re-
     view of Literature, 17 (October 23, 1937), 8.
         Refers once to Such Counsels You Gave to Me and Other
     Poems, but the essay is not a review of the book. Is rather
     an overall and generalized discussion of Jeffers, and not a
     favorable one at that. Scorns Jeffers' preference for rocks
     and animals over the human species, pointing up at the end
     that man is the only being who tries to solve his dilemmas
     and will go on trying to do so, independently of the scorn
     or approval of literary persons. Ironically, the reviewer
     says, "Oh, and about lice and rats, they can't read."

273 _____. Minority Report. Boston: Little, Brown, 1940. 257-
     264.

Title, "Lycanthropy," means the magical ability to assume the characteristics and form of a wolf. Is used here in a viciously ironic sense.

274 DE WITT, John. "Mrs. Nash of Hermosa Beach." Robinson Jeffers Newsletter, 52 (December, 1978), 27-29.

Biographers have given little information about Mrs. Nash, seamstress for Mrs. De Witt during the 1910-1915 period. She was asked to chaperone Jeffers and Una on a trip, the year before their marriage. She refused, but was deeply depressed over the matter. Years later it was learned that she had died in her bathtub, having been asphyxiated by the fumes from a gas heater.

275 DICKEY, James. "First and Last Things." Poetry, 103 (February, 1964), 316-324.

Article is a review of eleven books of poetry, including The Beginning and the End by Robinson Jeffers. Now that Jeffers is dead, his last poems have been issued, culled from handwritten manuscripts by his sons and his secretary. Though some of the pieces were obviously left unfinished-- there are several different ones which have the same passages in them--it is worth noting that they are actually no more or less "finished" than the poems Jeffers published in book after book while he lived. Now, in some fashion we must come to terms with Jeffers, for he somehow cannot be dismissed as lesser men--and no doubt better poets--can. As obviously flawed as he is, Jeffers is cast in a large mold; he fills a position in this country that simply would have been an empty gap without him: that of the poet as prophet, as large-scale philosopher, as doctrine-giver.

276 DICKINSON, Hugh. "Robinson Jeffers: The Twilight of Man," in Myth on the Modern Stage. Urbana: University of Illinois Press, 1969. Pp. 113-145. Review by David Dougherty, Robinson Jeffers Newsletter, 29 (August, 1971), 3-4.

Jeffers' inhumanism is considered only as a concept that provides background to the dramatic form under discussion. Dickinson's thesis is that Jeffers learned the craft of the dramatist as he became more objective in the plays. Thus, "The Tower Beyond Tragedy" suffers from an excess of in-humanist (therefore undramatic) philosophy, whereas "The Cretan Woman" relies on the dramatic effect rather than the thought content. The study provides an excellent look at this too frequently ignored aspect of Jeffers' art. The main body of the study consists of an examination of the alterations Jeffers made on his models.... The essay considers only four of the plays which have models in Greek drama.

277 DIGGORY, Terence. Yeats and American Poetry: The Tradition of the Self. Princeton: Princeton University Press, 1983.

"The Inhuman Self: Robinson Jeffers," pp. 118-133.
Jeffers becomes the source of a tradition. But what of
that other direction of tradition, the past, that we often
consider the only direction? If Jeffers has descendents,
does he also have ancestors? In the Hungerfield volume he
refers to himself as "The Old Stonemason" who thirty years
before had pulled himself and the stones he used to build
his tower "out of the tide-wash." The obvious intention is
to claim the sea, the great mother from which all life sprang,
as ultimate, and inhuman ancestor. But he also speaks here
not only of a biological but of an imaginative origin. The
man Jeffers already existed, but he had not conceived of
himself until the time he describes, and he, not the ocean,
did the conceiving. He owes the ocean only the blocks
from which he builds both his tower and himself. Jeffers
thus completes the tradition of the self by making himself
his own ancestor, extending himself into the past as well as
the future.

278 DOLAN, Kathleen T. "Robinson Jeffers, Virile Poet of a Philos-
     ophy of Decay." Masters Thesis, Columbia University, 1948.

279 DOUGHERTY, David. "The Annihilative Vision: Craftsmanship
     and Dramatic Action in the Narratives of Robinson Jeffers."
     Ph.D. diss., Miami University, 1970. DA, 32 (1971), 425A.
     Most critical assessments of Jeffers' poetry have emphasized
     the philosophical content of his verse instead of the artistic
     merit of his poems. The study of the narratives has been
     largely confined to isolating thematic content, with consequent
     inattention to form and technique. Such approaches have
     tended to obscure the fact that Jeffers is primarily a poet
     who expresses himself in lyric, narrative, and dramatic gen-
     res, not primarily a philosopher who chooses poetry as a
     vehicle for ideas.

280 _____. "Tragedy, Inhumanism, and Robinson Jeffers."
     Robinson Jeffers Newsletter, 30 (January, 1972), 6-7.
     Article is abstract of paper read at the Jeffers Festival,
     Summer of 1971. This study examines the middle period,
     about 1928 to 1941, during which Jeffers emphasized the
     tragic vision. Especially in "Give Your Heart to the Hawks"
     man achieves a certain human dignity; though man is in no
     way the center of the universe, or particularly noble or sig-
     nificant in himself, he reclaims a portion of that dignity nec-
     essary to the tragic vision through his response to pain and
     suffering. The hero's suffering burns away the inessential
     and reveals the particular man's spark of nobility, without
     affirming the nobility of the species.

281 _____. "Themes in Jeffers and James Wright." Robinson
     Jeffers Newsletter, 33 (September, 1972), 7-11.

Not a poet who attracted disciples, repudiated the main-
stream of modern poetry, the growth of the Eliot-Pound
aesthetic, and found his own path to the organism of form.
Jeffers discovered his own use for the more traditional sonnet, meditative lyric and narrative forms. His reclaiming
and alteration of traditional forms certainly set Jeffers at odds
with the formulators of the modern aesthetic and with their
followers. Later, however, a clear rebellion against the
school of Eliot was taking place, exciting new poets--James
Wright, Gary Snyder, W. S. Merwin, etc.--were discovering
the poetic freedoms claimed by Jeffers.... Article continues
with illustrations of similarities between Jeffers and Wright,
perhaps the most nearly imitative of the younger group.

282 DREW, Fraser B. "The Gentleness of Robinson Jeffers." Western Humanities Review, 12 (August, 1958), 379-381.
Reviews terms of violence and brutality with which Jeffers
is typically associated. There is, however, another side to
this poet who treats of man's cruelty to man and beast and
of man's lust, filth, and degradation. There is a gentleness
and a tenderness which can lighten the burden and linger
after the nightmare as nightmare is forgotten. This gentleness is quickly apparent to the people who know Jeffers personally. And the reader who cannot know the poet in person
may readily find these same qualities in his poetry. Article
cites numerous passages in which this gentleness is apparent,
most of them related to the poet's wife Una or their two sons.

283 _____. "The Loving Shepherdess of Jeffers and Scott."
Trace, 31 (April-May, 1959), 12-16.
Sees this poem and the character of Clare Walker as an
anomaly among Jeffers' works: Here is the poet of violence
and terror, telling one of the tenderest stories in modern
literature without sentimentality and achieving as fine a
tragedy as he had ever re-created from Greek or Celtic or
California legend. Article discusses briefly the question of
where he had found Clare and how he had changed the girl
who suggested the tale of the gentle shepherdess. Thinks
the answer is in Scott's novel The Heart of Midlothian.

284 _____. "Carmel and Cushendun: The Irish Influence on
Robinson Jeffers." Eire-Ireland, 3 (Summer, 1968), 72-82.
Finds in Jeffers' Irish poems, especially Descent to the
Dead, an achievement which should not be overlooked. The
Northern landscape forms at least a third of the inspiration
for the poet and his themes. Good deal of article traces Jeffers' first-hand knowledge of Ireland, his and Una's visits
there, and the relationship of these experiences to certain
specific poems: 16 from Descent, two from Thurso's Landing,
another from Solstice--each evoking the primitive cleanness
and elemental violence of the Irish landscape in its history,
much of which remained with him long after his return home.

285 _____. "Una and Robinson Jeffers at Lough Carra." Eire-
    Ireland: A Journal of Irish Studies, 11 (Autumn, 1976),
    118-125.
        Article is a kind of extended footnote to article listed
    above. This study deals with the long interest Una had in
    George Moore and his work and comes primarily from the un-
    published travel journals of the several visits the Jeffers
    made to Ireland.

286 DRINKWATER, John, H. S. Canby, W. R. Benét, eds. Twenti-
    eth Century Poetry. Boston: Houghton Mifflin, 1929.
    Jeffers, p. 379.

287 DUBOISE, Novella E. "A Study of Some Parallel Ideas Found
    in the Literary Works of E. A. Poe and Robinson Jeffers in
    Light of Scientific Progress." Masters Thesis, University
    of Kentucky, 1942.

288 DUDLEY, Dorothy. Forgotten Frontiers: Dreiser and the Land
    of the Free. New York: Harrison Smith & Robert Hass,
    1932. Robinson Jeffers, p. 315 et passim.

289 DUNCAN, J. E. The Revival of Metaphysical Poetry: The His-
    tory of a Style, 1800 to the Present. Minneapolis: Univer-
    sity of Minnesota Press, 1959. Jeffers, passim.
        Does not discuss Jeffers; is useful for a general back-
    ground discussion and for good insight into Jeffers' great
    contemporary, T. S. Eliot.

290 DUPEE, F. W. "Review of Dear Judas and Other Poems." Mis-
    cellany, 1 (March, 1930), 34-36.

291 EBERHART, Richard. "A Tribute and Appreciation." Robinson
    Jeffers Newsletter, 27 (November, 1970), 6-7.
        Jeffers was sensitive to the human predicament and showed
    in his long poems the struggles and follies of mankind, the
    enormity of his passions, scope, and futility. The clarity
    and disposition of his mind made him severe and in his short
    poems, by which he is best remembered, he expressed the un-
    human beauty of things, the eternal forbidding and beautiful
    world of rocks, stones, tides, the vast impersonal forces of
    nature. In the perspective of his imagination he saw the
    rise and fall of nations, the coming and going of dictators,
    the endless procession of man's wars as moving realities against
    the impersonal nature and grandeur of time and fate. Harsh-
    ness, strength, the impersonality of things, fate, struggle,
    pain and death are his measures.

292 EISELEY, Loren C. "Music of the Mountain." Voices, December-
    January, 1932-1933. Pp. 42-47.

The secret of the poet's strength is something simple and
elemental. It is that very rare phenomenon which happened
once at Walden and a few other places: the complete identification of the individual with his environment, or, rather,
the extension of the environment into the individual to such
a degree that the latter seems almost a lens through which is
projected a portion of the diversified and terrific forces of nature.

292a   . "The Bird and the Machine," in The Immense Jour-
ney. New York: Random House, 1955.
    Has been described as a prose counterpart of Jeffers'
"Hurt Hawks" in its description of the freeing of captive
hawks. On one occasion Eiseley said: "Sometimes of late
years I find myself thinking the most beautiful sight over
New York might be the birds after the last man has run away
to the hills."

293 EISENBERG, Emanuel. "A Not So Celestial Choir: A Review of
The Women at Point Sur." Bookman, 66 (September, 1927),
102-103. Also printed in Parkersburg [W. Virginia] News,
September 11, 1927.
    Calls the work an "electrifying poem, and an unforgettable
story, surging with vigor and heat and pain; but it is only
for an eclectic minority of persons."

294   . "The Lean Season." Bookman, 66 (October, 1927),
222-223.
    Review of A Miscellany of American Poetry: 1927. Refers
briefly to Jeffers in a discussion of recent poetry. Thinks
Jeffers will attain greater heights than any other poet in this
country, but the United States will never accept him as offer-
ing a genuine expression of American values.

295   . "Jeffers Lends Rich Violence to Christ Legend."
New York Evening Poet, January 4, 1930.
    Review of Dear Judas and Other Poems. The ambition of
the poem is defeated and turns into a graphic illustration of
Jeffers' defects and virtues. But the title poem is a moving
and beautiful work, with the importance attached to all of the
poet's long compositions. Some of the shorter poems in the
volume are impressive in their own right.

296 ELDRIDGE, Paul. "Review of Roan Stallion, Tamar, etc."
American Monthly, 17 (February, 1926), 373.

296a ERISMAN, Fred, and Richard Etulain, eds. Fifty Western
Writers. Westport, Conn.: Greenwood Press, 1982. Chapter on Jeffers, pp. 215-227, by Robert Brophy.

297 EVERSON, William (Brother Antoninus). "Earth Poetry." Sierra
Club Bulletin, 55 (July, 1970), 13-15.
    Comments on the ecology scene, using Jeffers' poetry.

298 _____ . "Continent's End (The Collected Poems of Robinson
        Jeffers): A Proposal." Robinson Jeffers Newsletter, 31
        (May, 1972), 10-15.
            A review of Jeffers' published volumes, with comment and
        criticism as to how they should be arranged in a Collected
        Edition of Jeffers. He also anticipates the problems which
        such an undertaking would involve; the establishment of the
        text; the securing of permissions, and the finding of a pub-
        lisher. In conclusion he says: "Here is a labor to daunt
        the most ambitious editor. But what a challenge! The work
        calls. The time approaches. Procrastination can only con-
        found the difficulties. Let the man stand forth. And let
        him be supported by all who recognize the obvious: that the
        greatest need in the cause of Jeffers today is the publication
        of the Collected Poems."

299 _____ . "Archetype West," in Regional Perspectives: An Ex-
        amination of America's Literary Heritage, edited by John
        Gordon Burke. Chicago: American Library Asso., 1973.
        Jeffers, pp. 207-305.
            Includes a great deal other than Jeffers. As for Jeffers
        he says: "The direction Jeffers took could not have been
        predicted either from the persons of Joaquin Miller or the
        naturalistic dream of Frank Norris or the social benignity of
        Edwin Markham. All the expensive energy of affirmation of
        these western visionaries seems negated in Jeffers, and yet
        actually his deceptive stretegy has been to press negation
        to its conclusion in order to reach its other side and touch
        the core of affirmation which the archetype keeps specify-
        ing...."

300 _____ . "Astrological Note: Jeffers as Pisces Ascendant."
        Robinson Jeffers Newsletter, 36 (October, 1973), 7-8.
            Article is based on a loose sheet of information, in Una
        Jeffers' hand, which the author found while he was doing
        research in the Jeffers collection at the University of Texas
        at Austin. This information indicates that Jeffers was born
        at 1:00 a.m., January 10, 1887, thus giving a Libra ascend-
        ant to the poet. The recollection of his mother, however,
        says that he was born at 10:00 a.m., January 10, 1887,
        making him a Pisces ascendant: "A chart much more con-
        vincing for what we know of Jeffers' character."

300a _____ , ed. with Introduction. Robinson Jeffers' Cawdor and
        Medea. New York: New Directions, 1970. Pp. vii-xxx.
            This book places in the hands of a new generation of
        readers two of the long, somber, and God-tormented poems
        of Robinson Jeffers. In Cawdor his aim was to write a simple
        narrative, classically sound, in which his doctrine of "Inhu-
        manism" is implicit not obtrusive.... The case of Medea is
        more complex and more difficult to discuss, bringing as it

does into sharper focus than Cawdor the whole matter of
Jeffers' relation to the tragic tradition in literature. In the
matter of form the two poems share a common feature. One
is narrative and the other dramatic, one is modern and the
other is classical, yet both were tailored to exterior require-
ments. (Cover photograph [rugged seascape] is by Thomas
Merton, design by Carla Packer.)

300b   , ed. with Introduction. Robinson Jeffers' Californians.
Aromas, Calif.: Cayucos Press, 1971. Reprint of 1916 edition,
Macmillan Co. Pp. vii-xxvi.
        The justification for reissuing any immature work by a
major artist lies chiefly in one thing: what it can tell us of
the greater achievement to come.... To sum up, what
emerges as the principal impression of Californians is an
emptying of the agonized Jeffersian landscape, a kind of in-
sular unrealization that leaves it merely pastoral and inert.
There is as much emphasis on actual place-names as would
later occur, but they are approached from a different segment of the psychic hemisphere. The torment is quite lacking,
and we hardly seem to be in the same world. What the event
was that changed the pastoral landscape of Californians into
the tortured landscape of Tamar doubtless will never be certainly known. But unquestionably between the two works
something radical and conclusive did occur.

300c   , ed. with Preface, Introduction, Afterword, and Notes
on the Poems. The Alpine Christ and Other Poems. Aromas,
Calif.: Cayucos Press, 1973.
        Hitherto thought to be destroyed, this work is the first
of two volumes bridging the gap between Californians (1916),
and Tamar (1924). The volume includes two long poems, "The
Alpine Christ," and "A Woman Down the Coast," plus seven
short poems written in 1916-1917. The discovery of most of
the original typescript on the obverse of later Jeffers' manuscripts at the University of Texas was made by William Everson, who deals in depth with the meanings of the work. The
poems are organized in a sequential way to show the poet's
creative development.

300d   , ed. with Afterword. Tragedy Has Obligation. Santa
Cruz: Lime Kiln Press, 1973.
        Written in 1943, but previously unpublished, the poem was
unearthed from the Jeffers collection at the University of
Texas. Addressed to Hitler, it is a stern admonition and
appeal never to surrender. It is, of course, sardonic irony,
and might have been misunderstood. The poem shows no
admiration, considerable disdain, some pity. It makes a plea
for the war-loser to transcend fate, to step out of the closing
trap and, by an act of tragic awareness, burn pure. Everson also discusses Jeffers' attitude toward Roosevelt and the

anguished anticipation of the future involvements of America
coming out of the war.

300e   , ed. with Preface, Introduction, and Afterword.
        Brides of the South Wind. Aromas, Calif.: Cayucos Press,
        1974.
             Includes 15 unpublished sonnets and ten other previously
        unpublished poems, to present all poems known or believed
        to have been written between 1917 and 1922. This period is
        crucial to an understanding of Jeffers. Poems are arranged
        into a meaningful chronological progression showing the evo-
        lution of Jeffers' poetry through this important period.

300f   , Foreword. The Double Axe and Other Poems, Includ-
        ing Eleven Suppressed Poems, ed. with Afterword by Bill
        Hotchkiss. New York: Random House, 1948. Reprinted
        New York: Liveright, 1977.
             In The Double Axe Jeffers proves himself to be an excel-
        lent political poet, adept at the rougher aspects of political
        infighting. No other contemporary verse comes to mind that
        is quite so brusque, savage, and intransigent. But his des-
        cent into the political arena was an unmitigated disaster.
        The Double Axe was universally consigned to oblivion, effec-
        tively ending Jeffers' role as a creditable poetic voice during
        his lifetime. Jeffers believed American participation in World
        War II was a tragic mistake, wasting American lives and re-
        sources to fish in what he considered the witches brew of
        Europe. These issues are still with us today, and the repub-
        lication of this work will doubtless provoke a corresponding
        reaction, though hardly to the same degree.

300g   . On Writing the Waterbirds and Other Presentations:
        Collected Forewords and Afterwords, 1935-1981, edited by
        Lee Bartlett. Metuchen, N.J.: Scarecrow Press, 1983.
        Jeffers, pp. 157-269; items listed above. Index p. 276.

301 FAIRBANKS, Jonathan. "The Impact of the Wild on Henry
        David Thoreau, Jack London, and Robinson Jeffers." Ph.D.
        diss., University of Otago (New Zealand), 1966.

302 FARRAR, John. "A Furious Poet from Pittsburgh." Bookman,
        62 (January, 1926), 604.
             Review of Roan Stallion, etc. There is no question that
        Jeffers has amazing powers of expression. There are pages
        and lines of great strength and beauty. "Roan Stallion" is
        an unforgettable and thoroughly unpleasant performance. It
        is only fair to warn many readers that they will be horrified
        by its magnificent but perverse imagining. Jeffers has given
        to what might have been a disgusting and ugly performance a

sort of deep rooting in the soil that imparts the quality of a
Greek myth.

303 _____. "This Stream of Poets." Bookman, 65 (March, 1927),
80-81.
Article is a brief commentary on several books of poetry
by a variety of authors. Critic is not much impressed with
any of them, although he says that Robinson Jeffers by
George Sterling is a "fine piece of criticism." As for Jeffers
he says "I must take him on faith. I am willing to believe
all that my friends say about him, and I have enjoyed some
of his magnificent lines, yet he still puzzles me...."

304 FARRELL, James T. "The Faulkner Mixture." New York Sun,
October 7, 1932.

305 FEIDELSON, Charles, Jr. Symbolism and American Literature.
Chicago: University of Chicago Press, 1953. Jeffers, passim.
Jeffers not discussed; referred to several times.

306 FICKE, Arthur D. "A Note on the Poetry of Robinson Jeffers."
Carmelite, 1 (December 19, 1928), 17.

307 _____. "A Note on the Poetry of Sex," in Calverton and
Schmalhausen, eds., Sex in Civilization (1929), pp. 666-667.

308 FIELD, S. B. "Memories of George Sterling." Overland Monthly,
85 (November, 1927), 340-341.

309 FIRKINS, Oscar W. "Review of Californians." Nation, 105
(October 11, 1917), 400-401.
Comments on the vitality of the verse. Thinks Jeffers
has many failings and names five or six of them. If Jeffers
has the patience, he probably will become a great poet.

310 FITCH, W. T. "Is There Literary and Artistic Culture in California?" Overland Monthly, 84 (December, 1926), 379 et
passim.

311 FITTS, Dudley. "A Review of Selected Poetry." Saturday Review of Literature, 19 (April 22, 1939), 19.
Jeffers' great virtues are the ability to tell a story and to
sustain tremendous rhythms for long periods. His curious
verse-form, a development of Whitman's, is perfectly suited
to narrative. In his description of scenery he is always
effective. What he lacks in restraint, and, above all things,
humor. By humor one does not mean a sense of fun, but a
sense of balance, of design, of proportion.

312 _____. "Hellenism of Robinson Jeffers." Kenyon Review, 8
(Autumn, 1946), 678-685. Reprinted in The Kenyon Critics:

Studies in Modern Literature from The Kenyon Review, edited
by John Crowe Ransom. Chicago: World Publishing, 1951.
Reprinted Port Washington: Kennikat Press, 1967. Pp. 307-
312.

    A Review of Medea. Thinks the Jason-Medea myth is
suited to Jeffers. The element of incest is missing but is
replaced by an element of violence. Jeffers makes several
changes in the ancient play, among which is making Jason
more appealing and Medea less appealing. In this poem he
is incapable of tragic force. He lacks insight and control.
His characters to him are speaking puppets, not fleshly men
and women with whom he can sympathize.

313   . "A Review of The Double Axe and Other Poems."
New York Times, August 22, 1948.

    This new book of poems is largely a failure. Everything
he writes began to look alike several years ago, and this
does not improve upon his situation. His recent adaptation
of Medea was at best almost comic in its vulgar ranting that
made up most of it.

314   . "A Review of Hungerfield and Other Poems." New
York Times, January 10, 1954.

    As is so often true of Jeffers' work, the best poems in
the present collection are not the long, tortured narratives
but the short and quasi-lyrical pieces. The successful moments in the long poems are relatively few and always pre-
carious.

315 FLANNER, Hildegarde. "Two Poets: Jeffers and Millay." New
Republic, 89 (January 27, 1937), 379-382. Reprinted in
After the Genteel Tradition, edited by Malcolm Cowley. New
York: W. W. Norton, 1936. Pp. 155-167, 124-133.

    More than any of their contemporaries, Jeffers and Millay
have been known to the wider public that does not read much
poetry. Each has expressed a spirit peculiar to the age.
Each has rebelled against the standards of puritanical respect-
ability that prevailed when they began writing, but revolt
with Jeffers never took the form of fulfillment or pleasure
that it took with Miss Millay. His attitude is supremely negative, his verse has been set down in tragic and distorted
images. Jeffers has reduced human behavior to a criticism
of human motives. Millay's poetry was also a criticism of
society, but it was largely limited to a reaction against gen-
tility. To the Western poet there fell a task more definite
and more susceptible to failure--a long look forward and back-
ward into history to pass judgment on man.

316 FLETCHER, John Gould. "The Dilemma of Robinson Jeffers."
Poetry, 43 (March, 1934), 338-342.

    A review-essay based on Jeffers' volume Give Your Heart

to the Hawks, but including a good deal of general information on the poet. He arrived on the scene just when all the talk and discussion of the "New Poetry" was dying down and a new group of postwar radicals was arriving to revive Ezra Pound and proclaim T. S. Eliot. These poets produced an intensely intellectual, critical, metaphysical type of poetry that left no room for anyone of different temperaments. Against this current Jeffers has stood aloof.... But his poems tend to get less and less interesting as he repeats in every poem the characters with strong streaks of neurotic obsession. Unless he can find a new set of characters, a new background, and a new outlook, his poetry may slip into oblivion. This is Robinson Jeffers' dilemma.

316a FLEWELLING, R. T. "Tragic Drama--Modern Style." Persona-
      list, 20 (July, 1939), 229-241.
          Article is devoted largely to a discussion of Jeffers' "The
      Tower Beyond Tragedy." In Part I, the critic reviews the
      basic "Nature of Tragedy," in Part II, "The Ancient Treat-
      ment of Tragedy," and, in Part III, "Modern Tragedy," which
      is represented in the Orestes-Electra story told in "The Tower
      Beyond Tragedy." In a brief Conclusion some comparisons
      are drawn: Ancient drama drew its power from belief in the
      essential nobility of man; Jeffers does not escape the modern
      concept that man is a mere pawn in the movement of natural
      events. In Jeffers' handling of the myth, Orestes refuses
      the kingship of Mycenae and offers his kingdom for a ship
      that will take him to the ends of the earth. For Orestes,
      victory is in the conquest of his own spirit.

317 FLINT, Frank Stewart. "Recent Verse." The Criterion (Lon-
     don), 8 (December, 1928), 342-346.
         Review of Roan Stallion, etc. Calls Jeffers a tragic poet,
     his poems memorable, their movement, their pathos giving
     intense pleasure.

318 _____. "Verse Chronicle." Criterion, 11 (January, 1932),
     276-281.
         Review of Dear Judas. Says Jeffers is a lonely figure,
     chanting ancient heroic virtues and pities in sweeping meas-
     ures.

319 FOLK, B. N. "Robinson Jeffers Taken to Task." Catholic
     World, 179 (July, 1954), 270-273.

320 FONZA, David. "The Inhumanist and Poet of Violence." Levia-
     than, May 19, 1977. Pp. 5-6.
         This generally favorable article was occasioned by the re-
     issue of the three Liveright-Norton volumes of Jeffers. It
     speculates on Jeffers' place in the modern consciousness and
     especially in the current milieu of poets. Finding Jeffers an

isolate, immoderately caught up in violence through a career
which spanned two wars, he still gives the poet credit for
an immense integrity and openness. Critic lauds Jeffers'
attempt to reconcile man to the world and God and he values
the poet's disdain for the introverted spirals in which many
other modern poets are caught. He sees Jeffers as mediating
toward a more realistic and moderate poetics.

321 FORD, Lilian C. "New Major Poet Emerges." Los Angeles Times,
April 11, 1926.
Review of Roan Stallion, etc.

322 FOX, C. J. "Full Circle: The Zeitgeist and Robinson Jeffers."
Antigonish Review, 43 (1980), 91-104.
Rarely have relations between the "fickle current of opinion" and a prominent poet come full circle so specifically as
in the case of Robinson Jeffers. In the twenties he was
opposed to America's self-proclaimed role as "world policeman."
In the thirties he refused to follow other leading writers into
left-wing campaigns, and in the forties he was denounced as
an isolationist and professional hater of America's hero, Frank-
lin Roosevelt. This opposition had the effect of ending Jeffers' role as a creditable poetic voice during his lifetime. He
died in 1962 and in a few years he was critically acclaimed as
being "more or less perfectly into tune with the anti-interven-
tionist ideas of the new Left in the era of Vietnam."
Article continues with good documentation of thesis, with
many quotations and references to Jeffers' works.

323 FRANCIS, Sowmu. "Inhumanism in the Poetry of Robinson Jeffers and Wallace Stevens." Robinson Jeffers Newsletter, 63
(June, 1983), 8.
Written in Madras, India, June 1980, in which he says:
"Reality in the early decades of the Twentieth Century presented a bleak aspect. Man seemed insignificant in the cartog-
raphy of the universe. Among the artists who attempted to
reconcile such a bleak vision of life with the demands of
existence, Jeffers and Stevens are significant in the similarity
of their emphasis. Stevens condensed the scientific view of
reality in the adjective 'inhuman.' He used the term in the
poetic context along with 'superhuman,' to effect a process of
semantic elevation--from a neutral descriptive level to that of
a non-denominational denotation for the divine.

324 FRANKENBERG, Lloyd. "Review of Be Angry at the Sun."
New York Herald Tribune Books, November 30, 1941.
Despite the violence of his action, Jeffers is not essentially a
dramatic poet. His scenes are not designed for the development
of character or incident but rather to expose subconscious and
primitive layers. The characters are motivated by his own desire to break the crust of the senses. The climaxes, more often
than peaks, are pits. The critical faculties are in abeyance. The

volcanic process is not selective in its activity: the ludicrous
is disgorged quite as easily as the monstrous. His stories
are carried along at break-neck speed, preventing the immediate application of an analysis that might threaten his effects.

325 _____. Pleasure Dome: On Reading Modern Poetry. Boston:
Houghton Mifflin, 1949. Jeffers, passim.
Does not discuss Jeffers; is referred to in passing. Book
may offer valuable insight on the methods of modern poetry
and also revealing commentary on many of Jeffers' contemporaries.

326 FRENZ, Horst, ed. American Playwrights on Drama. New York:
Hill and Wang, 1965. "The Tower Beyond Tragedy," by
Robinson Jeffers, pp. 94-97.
The essay appeared first in The New York Times on November 26, 1950. Discusses the composition in terms of the
reasons he wrote it: "In making poems of contemporary life,
I had found my mood cramped by the conventions and proba-
bilities of the time; particularly by our convention of under-
statement. It is our custom to avoid lyrical speech, and to
express any great passion in whispers, or perhaps not at all.
The human voice is a terrible organ, we must not extend it.
To express a violent motion violently, or a beautiful one beautifully, would be shocking in daily life; but it is normal in
Greek tragedy." He did not want to take two or three Greek
tragedies, change them considerably, and make them into a
poem, and so was glad to add something of his own at the
end: "This was the pantheistic mysticism of Orestes which
comes to him like a religious conversion after he has commit-
ted his criminal act of justice.... Orestes at last escapes the
curse; he turns away from human lust and ambition to the
cold glory of the universe." He escapes to the "tower beyond
tragedy."

327 FRIAR, Kimon. "On Translation." Comparative Literature Studies, 8 (September, 1971), 197-213.
Does not discuss Jeffers, but is an excellent study of the
problems of translations in general. Jeffers' Medea is given
as an example of the "free adaptation or paraphrase" of the
Euripides play. In this form of translation the poet uses
the original work of another simply as a springboard, as a
source of inspiration, and adapts it with extremely deviant
degrees of "faithfulness" as he sees fit, limiting himself only
by the creative powers of his own free-flying imagination.

328 FRY, Amelia, interviewer. "Recollections and Reminiscences by
Benjamin Lehman." Robinson Jeffers Newsletter, 63 (June,
1983), 12-18.
Excerpted from "Recollections and Reminiscences of Life in
the Bay Area from 1920 Onward." Interview with Benjamin
Lehman.

329 GARDINER, Harold C., ed. American Classics Reconsidered:
      A Christian Appraisal. New York: Scribner's, 1958. Jef-
      fers, passim.
         Jeffers not discussed; referred to briefly in chapter on
      Whitman.

330 GARLAND, Gary. "Mann and Jeffers: Myth Definition and Sub-
      sequent Technique." Robinson Jeffers Newsletter, 37 (Decem-
      ber, 1973), 7-11.
         Although both authors utilize myth in their creative works,
      they define myth differently and the definitions become a
      prime determiner of literary technique. Continues with dis-
      cussion of Mann's Joseph and His Brothers and Jeffers' "At
      the Birth of an Age." Myth for Mann is essentially the eter-
      nal "Now," which transcends time. Myth also clarifies man's
      position in relation to the universe and allows a vision in
      terms of past and future. Through myth, man is able to
      fathom the depths of his nature and achieve a better under-
      standing of himself. Myth is never clearly defined in Jef-
      fers. He was familiar with Greek, Mideastern, Egyptian,
      Norse and other mythologies. For Jeffers it seems that the
      story was never important--since all the stories are basically
      the same--but rather the process which moves the universe
      and is God. The process itself is by its nature motion, and
      the motion is cyclic, from the smallest measurement of night
      and day to the astronomical phenomenon of the expanding and
      contracting universe. The process is the universe in all of
      its aspects and man's place is unimportant.

331 GATES, G. G. "The Bread That Every Man Must Eat Alone."
      College English, 4 (December, 1942), 170-174.
         Frequently the poetry of Robinson Jeffers is dismissed
      as the work of a nihilist, a Fascist, a romantic. Quite fre-
      quently, too, his poetry is taken literally as a complete de-
      nouncement of all men. There is also a tendency on the part
      of some to describe his poetry as an either/or. By some,
      though, Jeffers is considered too powerful as a writer to be
      accepted as either one thing or another or completely ignored.
      His point of view, regardless of any question of its validity,
      is now being voiced by a number of individuals who sense
      deep worldly wrongs. This article, without making any value
      judgment, attempts to give an understanding of Jeffers'
      point of view. Stated briefly the poet's thesis is the neces-
      sity of the individual to find a proper balance of universal
      power found in the external world and the elementals of human
      life as found in primitive types of human beings.

332 GEORGOUDAKI, Catherine. "Jeffers' Medea: A Debt to Eurip-
      ides." Revue des Langues Vivantes (Brussels), 42 (1976),
      620-623.

333 GESSLER, Clifford. "Robinson Jeffers: A Giant Husky and
     Brawling." Honolulu Star-Bulletin, October 15, 1927.
     Review of The Women at Point Sur.

334 _____. "Forthcoming Poetry." Honolulu Star-Bulletin,
     August 24, 1929.
     Review of Dear Judas, etc.

335 GHISELIN, Brewster. "Paeonic Measures in English Verse."
     Modern Language Notes, 57 (May, 1942), 336-341.
         In Robinson Jeffers' "The Songs of the Dead Men to the
     Three Dancers" about every ninth foot is a paeon. The first
     of the three parts of this poem is mainly anapestic. Its
     movement is varied with a few dissyllabic feet, numerous pae-
     ons, and at least one sequence of four unaccented syllables--
     a natural and not unique development, with obvious implica-
     tions. This is accentual verse--not in its ancient forms, but
     as it has been written during the past fifty or seventy-five
     years.

336 GHORMLEY, Wilbur Hamilton. "Lineal Data of Joseph Jeffers and
     Barbara Moore." Robinson Jeffers Newsletter, 54 (October,
     1979), 3-5.
         Joseph and Barbara Jeffers were the parents of William
     Hamilton Jeffers (Robinson Jeffers' father), the 7th of nine
     children. Article contains a good many facts of the ancestry
     of the Jeffers' family, including some references to Robinson
     and his career as "the poet."

337 GIBSON, W. H., and Philip Horton. "Robinson Jeffers: Pro
     and Con." Nassau Literature (Princeton), 91 (November,
     1932), 11-23.
         Begins with a general review of Robinson Jeffers' life
     and character as he lives at Tor House on the Pacific Coast,
     Then he discusses Jeffers' poetry: "so far-reaching in its
     implications, at times so obscure, so immense in its outlook
     over time and space, so rawly and at times so delicately emo-
     tional, so often self-contradictory, and finally, so unmistaka-
     bly poetry, that no critic so far has been able to pigeon-hole
     it or to analyze it clearly and completely...."
         In the other half of the article, the critic says he judges
     literature on its form and content, and in both respects he
     finds Jeffers "execrable." There is no form, no evidence of
     discipline necessary to the true artist. Quotes several pas-
     sages to illustrate the bad taste of Jeffers' metaphors. As
     to content, Jeffers is sensational, extreme, sometimes senti-
     mental, and generally repulsive.

338 GIERASCH, Walter. "Robinson Jeffers." English Journal (col-
     lege edition), 28 (April, 1939), 284-295.

Article is a somewhat generalized account of Robinson Jeffers and his poetry, with some emphasis on the influence of the California geography on the poet. Central to this, however, is Jeffers' belief in the merit of permanence. He finds this not in human things, not even in living things, although hawks come near to symbolizing animately the impersonal quality Jeffers respects. However, permanence truly resides in fire, in darkness, in the stars, and in the rhythm of universal motion.... Jeffers has created a world that most readers cannot like or believe in, but which they find it hard to resist. The power of his imagination and the sweep of his long lines are more effective than those of any other half-dozen contemporary poets.

339 GILBERT, Rudolph. <u>Shine, Perishing Republic: Robinson Jeffers and the Tragic Sense in Modern Poetry</u>. Boston: Bruce Humphries, 1936. 197 pp. Reprinted New York: Haskell, 1965.

Consists of five separate essays:

1. The Poet of Our Time
2. His Philosophy
3. Mysticism and Symbolism
4. Tragedy: An Approach to the Not Self
5. Attitude Toward Poetry, Civilization, and Nature.

Has selective bibliography, but no index.

340 _____. "Robinson Jeffers: the Philosophic Tragedist," in <u>Four Living Poets</u>. Santa Barbara, Calif.: Unicorn Press, 1944. Pp. 23-41.

Robinson Jeffers has chosen, or has been chosen by destiny, to use as his poetic vehicle events of the past to express ageless truths. "We know of no living English or American poet who may be compared with Jeffers, either in creative power, philosophic, psychological insight or lyric utterance. We sense in him a unity of thought with some of the greatest poets of the past; he seems the prophetic voice at once of a passing era and of one in its birth pangs." Jeffers stands as the poet of his own age and day. Nowhere else in modern poetry can we find so nearly complete a view of the complex emotional colors of life which underlie all the contemporary experiences of humanity en masse.... No other modern poet has measured humanity in its greatness as well as in its brutalities with so passionate and lusty a measure as Jeffers.

341 GILDER, Rosamond. "Review of Jeffers' <u>Medea</u>," in <u>Theatre Arts Anthology: A Record and a Prophecy</u>, edited by Rosamond Gilder, et al. New York: Theatre Arts Books, 1950. Pp. 669-672. First published in December, 1947.

Jeffers has created a terrifying image of evil. It is the
apotheosis of the religion of hate--the ultimate fiery end of
the doctrine of an eye for an eye. Medea calls for justice
but actually she seeks vengeance. She seeks "annihilation."
Judith Anderson's Medea is pure evil, dark, dangerous, cruel,
raging, ruthless. Every detail of voice and body contributes
to a masterly performance, although Jeffers' handling of the
Greek theme evokes more terror than pity. John Gielgud
plays Jason, a role not at all commensurate with the great
actor's talent. At the end he quietly touches the death of
tragic despair when he sees his children murdered.

342   GILL, Nancy Elizabeth. "Robinson Jeffers: The Greatest
      Beauty." Ph.D. diss., Pennsylvania State University, 1979.
      DA, 40 (1979), 2061A-2062A.
          This dissertation is an exploration of some of the "conflicts
      and excesses" that seem to be responsible for Jeffers' poetry.
      It treats his life and poetry as personal history, as a history
      of emotional conflict, of fragmentation of soul, brought about
      by a lack of introspection, a refusal to acknowledge the cen-
      tral experiences of his life, to explore his feelings, motives,
      choices, and behavior, and to claim primary responsibility for
      them. The study is presented in three chapters, with the
      third devoted largely to analysis of Jeffers' works, and a
      conclusion that his refusal to see, accept, and understand
      himself made it impossible for him to tell the truth in his
      poems.

343   GILLIAM, Harold. "The Abiding Genius of Jeffers." Robinson
      Jeffers Newsletter, 46 (September, 1976), 37-39. Reprinted
      from San Francisco Sunday Examiner & Chronicle, June 20,
      1976. "This World" column, p. 24.
          An admiring tribute to Jeffers, "who lived 43 years on the
      coast near Carmel and wrote some of the most eloquent poetry
      ever written about the American land." Article reviews Jef-
      fers and his wife Una's coming in 1914, the building of Tor
      House, which now stands "like a remnant of another age."
      The surprising facts are, however, no one seems interested
      in preserving the house, in exempting it from the astronomi-
      cal taxes which have been levied against property in that
      area, and in general keeping Jeffers' house--as we have kept
      the houses of other American writers--for future generations.
      The poet once expressed his hope that the house would stand
      until worn away by the elements.

344   GINGERICH, Owen. "The Galileo Affair." Scientific American,
      297 (August, 1982), 143 et passim.
          It is an irony of history that Galileo's own methods of
      scientific argument were instrumental in showing that what
      passes for truth in science is only the likely or the probable;
      truth can never be final or absolute. What makes science so

fascinating is the task of pushing ever closer to the unattain-
able goal of complete knowledge. It is this process that the
poet Robinson Jeffers had in mind when he wrote: "The
mathematicians and the physics men have their mythology;
they work alongside the truth, never touching it; their equa-
tions are false but the things work."

345 GLICKSBERG, Charles I. "The Poetry of Doom and Despair."
     Humanist, 7 (August, 1947), 69-76.
          Article is a discussion of several poets of the modern era,
     including Jeffers who is called "the most talented poet of
     modern pessimism." Jeffers' vision of the universe extends
     beyond the individual; it involves the whole race in a common
     doom. What Jeffers looks forward to with unphilosophical im-
     patience is the dreamless, peace-clothed death when the body
     is again fused in primal unity with matter.... Passionately
     brooding on the mystery of existence, Jeffers praises the
     great silence, the goal of death toward which all sentient
     things, man included, tend. The tide that spilled life on
     earth draws seaward again; in the midst of the fever of living
     the soul remembers the primal silence, the womb of Night.
     Nothing endures. The ages pass away as relentlessly as the
     seconds. The life of mankind, Jeffers, concludes, is essen-
     tially like the life of man; a pilgrimage from birth to death,
     a journey from darkness to darkness.

346 GORDON, Don. "The Poet in the Stone House." Robinson Jef-
     fers Newsletter, 17 (April, 1967), 3-4. Originally published
     in Statement by Don Gordon (1943).
          Poem dedicated to Jeffers, who liked the poem.

347 GORHAM, Herbert. "Jeffers, Metaphysician." Saturday Review
     of Literature, 4 (September 17, 1927), 115-116.
          Review of The Women at Point Sur.
          This "bright shell of rolling lines and sonorous utterances
     and philosophical innuendos so starred with astonishing images
     that smash out at the reader with the force of a gigantic blow
     suggests a colossus in California," Gorman says. He continues
     by saying that he cannot give Jeffers the praise that some
     critics offer but will admit that the narratives "are not all
     sound and fury." There is a core of intensive and exalted
     poetry but it is semi-smothered by a number of wilful urges,
     sexual obsessions, fogginesses of utterance, undisciplined
     ardors, prophetic predilections. The lion roars a little too
     loudly at times.

348 GRAHAM, Bessie. The Bookman's Manual. New York: Bowker,
     1928. Robinson Jeffers, p. 186.

349 GREENAN, Edith. Of Una Jeffers. San Francisco: Ward Ritchie
     Press, 1939.

Consists of 67 pages with only 250 copies of the book printed. A note by Robinson Jeffers says: "The characters are two unusual women. This little book has made me realize more fully many lovely memories; and especially the undeserved good fortune that has followed me like a hound, ever since I knew the woman whom Edith Greenan, too, seems to use for the pole star."

The work contains five illustrations, including a handsome portrait of Jeffers, and was written by the girl to whom Edward Kuster (Una's first husband) was engaged. Miss Greenan somehow felt that marriage would not be a success unless she knew Una. It was a unique relationship. The book closes with a letter from Una to Edith in 1939. Una had read the manuscript and was pleased. It prints for the first time three poems and a fragment by Robinson Jeffers.

350 GREENBERG, Clement. "Review of Be Angry at the Sun." Nation, 154 (March 7, 1942), 289.

Thenewnarrative poem is as bad as ever, if not worse--probably worse. How Jeffers won his reputation on the basis of his narratives is beyond seeing. They contain some of the worse poetry in English and couch a humanity too narrow ever to be taken very seriously in poetry or out of it. Elsewhere, in the verse play included in this book and in the short poems, this narrowness does not harm, lacking the space in which to make itself felt.

351 GREGORY, Horace. "Jeffers Writes His Testament in New Poem." New York Evening Post, Deember 31, 1931.

Review of Descent to the Dead and Other Poems.

352 _____. "Jeffers Again Hurls Indictment at Civilization." New York Evening Post, March 31, 1932.

353 _____. "Suicide in the Jungle." New Masses. 25 (February 13, 1934), 18-19.

Compares O'Neill and Jeffers and finds Jeffers the better poet, but he erred in associating with a corrupt society. He was a great nature poet, but more important he was able to show the underside of the great American dream at a time when this dream had become largely a nightmare. Bias is in favor of Marxist interpretation.

354 _____, and Marya Zaturenska. A History of American Poetry, 1900-1940. New York: Harcourt, Brace, 1946. "Jeffers and the Birth of Tragedy," pp. 398-412.

Argues that Nietzsche's essay "The Birth of Tragedy" is essential to understanding Jeffers. It was a Nietzschean "reality" that Jeffers perceived. Also sees the story of King Midas as essential to understanding Jeffers, in the despair, the verdict that Man would have chosen best had he chosen

not to be, not to be born. That being impossible, it is best
"quickly to die."

Jeffers' poetry, whatever its flaws may be, needs no defense, and he has phrased his own answer to those who have
taken the trouble to dispute his general views; in "Self-
Crticism in February" he wrote: "What is most disliked in
those verses/Remains most true...." His last answer is always a return to Nietzsche. But it is probable that his
"philosophy" will have less endurance than those gifts which
enabled him to create parables of human blindness and suffering, to see, as if for the first and last time, the austerities
of a Pacific or Irish coast line, and to make his reader aware
of the physical beauty that inhabits the California landscape
and the sky above it.

355   _____. "Review of Hungerfield and Other Poems." New York
Herald Tribune Book Reviews, January 24, 1954.
Something that is not resignation, yet has the serenity
of self-knowledge, enters the fourteen short poems of this
book. In taking the road beyond middle age, few American
poets have stepped so far with a more deeply expressed
humility and courage. With this book and those that may
follow it, Jeffers' contribution to the poetry of our day is
of mature inspiration and accomplishment. His position is
secure and singular.

356   _____. "Poets Without Critics: A Note on Robinson Jeffers,"
in New World Writing, 7th Mentor Selection, 1955. Pp. 40-52.
Frequently reprinted as in the following: The Dying Gladi-
ator and Other Essays, New York: Grove Press, 1961, pp.
3-20; Spirit of Time and Space, pp. 267-279; American Critical Essays: Twentieth Century, edited by H. L. Beaver,
excerpt, pp. 70-88.
Robinson Jeffers' accomplishments and the modesty of his
private life, now saddened by the death of his wife, should
serve as an example to the present as well as the next generation of writers. Within the last thirty years he has made no
compromise with the changing fashions of the day. Some
readers object to his aloofness, but Jeffers has reestablished
the position of the poet as one of singular dignity and courage. He is neither voiceless nor without his readers; and he
is not without wisdom in seeming to await the verdict of pos-
terity.

357 GRIFFITH, B. W. "Robinson Jeffers' 'The Bloody Sire' and
Stephen Crane's 'War Is Kind.'" Notes on Contemporary Lit-
erature, 3 (January, 1973), 14-15.
Points up passages in which the phrasing seems similar.
In philosophies, however, the two poets are quite different.
Crane is purely ironic; Jeffers avoids irony, preferring to
say outright what he intends. Both are in a single accord,

however, in expressing the belief that war is a manifestation of man's childish and animal tendencies to fight.

358 GRIFFITH, R. H. Robinson Jeffers, An Artist. Austin, Tex.: privately printed by J. S. Mayfield, 1928. Pamphlet.

359 GROSS, Harvey. Sound and Form in Modern Poetry: A Study in Prosody from Thomas Hardy to Robert Lowell. Ann Arbor, Mich.: University of Michigan Press, 1964. Jeffers, pp. 88 et passim.

Refers to Jeffers in a discussion of Whitman, and uses Jeffers as an example of one "who commands rhetoric and is persuaded into believing that he also commands prosody." He quotes a passage from Jeffers and says: "Meaning fights through the morass of the rhythms; syllable, stress, and syntax do not move but writhe, heave, grunt, and lie down again, gasping with the effort. The heavy stresses, impaled by alliteration, die on the page."

360 GUSTAFSON, Richard. "The Other Side of Robinson Jeffers." Iowa English Institute Yearbook, 9 (Fall, 1964), 75-80.

After the publication of The Double Axe, Jeffers has been dismissed as a "carping pessimist, a steel-eyed fascist, and a crazy old ranter." His reputation is now at its lowest point, though he still appears in anthologies. HIs indignation is no stronger than that of Ginsberg or Ferlinghetti, yet they titillate with their nastiness whereas we simply turn away in discomfort from Jeffers. We forget that Jeffers is the most successful writer of long narrative poems in our century. We forget that he founded his own style, a loose but idiomatic and fluent, five-stress line. He developed native settings and formulated a consistent philosophy of their actions. Although modern taste disregards all verse narratives, a shifting fashion will probably resuscitate those of Jeffers, and we will see him in his true light.

361 HACKMAN, Martha. "Whitman, Jeffers, and Freedom." Prairie Schooner, 20 (Fall, 1946), 182-184.

In recent years Whitman has enjoyed a renewed popularity, while the opposite has been true of Jeffers, whose style, if not his thought, is strangely reminiscent of Whitman's and owes much to the older poet. After a brief popularity in the twenties and thirties Jeffers has been neglected, and since 1941 he has virtually ceased to publish. He has been considered alternately a fascist, a misanthrope, and a negativist. These charges are only half true. Certainly he is not a fascist, since one of his profound respects is for freedom. He lacks Whitman's undiscriminating and all-embracing love for his fellows, but he respects the essential qualities

of human nature, stripped of its artificialities and conventions.
He strives to achieve a view of the universe so broad that all
things, living and dead, appear in their proper perspective.

362 HAGEMEYER, Dora. "How Jeffers and Lawrence 'Do' the Atmos-
     phere." Carmel Cymbal, 1 (May 18, 1926), 6, 11.

363 _____. "Poet's Garden and a Visitor." Carmel Cymbal, 2
     (September 29, 1926), 9.

364 HALE, W. H. "Jeffers Refines His Fury." Yale Daily News
     Literary Supplement, 4 (November 21, 1929), 1.

365 _____. "Robinson Jeffers: A Lone Titen." Yale Literary
     Magazine, 95 (December, 1929), 31-35.

366 HAMBURGER, Kate. From Sophocles to Sartre: Figures from
     Greek Tragedy, Classical and Modern. Translated from the
     German by Helen Sebba. New York: Frederick Unger, 1969.
     "Phaedra," pp. 117-122.
          Jeffers very subtly reveals a homosexual tendency in his
     character of Hippolytus in The Cretan Woman. In Jeffers he
     is the real hero--a delicately organized character in whom
     even the homosexual tendency is aesthetically sublimated. He
     loves his friends and shuns the realm of sexual love and pro-
     creation. Thus Aphrodite, who appears in Jeffers' play, is
     exalted to the cosmic principle of love, and anyone who sins
     against this great principle must be punished and destroyed.
     Phaedra represents something of this primal cosmic principle
     which is beyond good and evil.

367 HANSEN, Harry. "The Dark Jeffers." New York World, July
     19, 1927.
          Review of The Women at Point Sur. Also printed in
     Greensboro News, July 24, 1927.

368 _____. "Long Poem by Phenomenon of Nature." Kansas City
     Journal Post, August 7, 1927.
          Review of The Women at Point Sur.

368a HARMSEN, Tyrus G. "Jeffers Collection--Occidental College."
     Quarterly News Literature, 27 (Winter, 1961), 3-9.
          See 1976 article listed below; largely duplicates with ex-
     ception of being brought up to date.

369 _____. "Jeffers Scholarly Materials at Occidental College."
     Robinson Jeffers Newsletter, 44 (March, 1976), 21-23.
          Traces the growth of the Jeffers Collection from 1903 to
     1905 when Jeffers was a student at Occidental College and
     contributed verses to the College literary magazines, The
     Aurora and The Occidental. Perhaps the second milestone
     was Dr. Powell's dissertation and subsequent book in 1932

and 1934. This study undoubtedly stimulated an interest in Jeffers as a prominent alumnus of the College. From that point on the collection has grown over the past forty years. A checklist of the Jeffers collection was presented in 1955. This article attempts an overview, without going into every detail of the holdings. The following are typical categories:

Printed materials
Issues of periodicals and newspapers which contain first
    printings of Jeffers' poems
Autograph manuscripts and first drafts
Prose works by Jeffers
About 75 letters by Jeffers
Copies of theses and dissertations about Jeffers
Photographs of Jeffers, the family, and Tor House
Una Jeffers materials: about 230 letters and cards
Manuscripts of E. Greenan's Of Una Jeffers and Melba
    Bennett's The Stone Mason of Tor House

370   _____. "Three Unpublished Letters of Robinson Jeffers."
Robinson Jeffers Newsletter, 47 (December, 1976), 10-12.
    Letters given to Occidental College by Dan S. Hammack, Jr. His father, Daniel Stewart, and Jeffers were classmates at Occidental (Class of 1905). The first two letters are in Jeffers' handwriting; the third is typewritten, and the closing portion has been cut away; hence the abrupt ending and lack of signature. The dates on the first two letters are 1914, and the third is December 1917.

371   _____. "John Robinson Jeffers, Student at Occidental College." Robinson Jeffers Newsletter, 50 (March, 1978), 21-24.
    In 1903, for reasons of health, Dr. Jeffers decided to move to a warmer climate and so brought his family first to Long Beach and later to Highland Park, where they built a home. At that time Occidental College was located in Highland Park, and it was chosen for Jeffers' continued education; he had previously attended Western Penn (now the University of Pittsburgh). During his two years at Occidental, Jeffers took a classical course of study, including the following subjects: The Bible, Economics, English, Rhetoric, Natural Science, History, Latin, Philosophy, Mathematics, Astronomy, and Greek. Jeffers' grade in each course is listed, and in many instances the name of his teacher. Following the article are three pages of pictures of buildings at Occidental.

372   _____. "Occidental College Library: Recent Jeffers Acquisitions." Robinson Jeffers Newsletter, 62 (January, 1983), 35-36.
    Materials include the Sydney Alberts' archives relating to his research on the Bibliography (1933); 9 letters from Una to Hazel Pinkham and one letter from Jeffers to Hazel; four copies of the Lawrence Clark Powell thesis.

373 _____, and Melba B. Bennett, compilers. "Bibliography of
Jeffers' Works in Translation." Robinson Jeffers Newsletter,
19 (November, 1967), 2-3.
   Lists some 25 items, covering 1953 to 1967, with place of
publication, title of Jeffers' work in the foreign language,
and the translator.

374 HARRIS, J. Robert. "Robinson Jeffers' Poetic Definitions of
God." Masters Thesis, University of Saskatchewan, 1971.

375 HART, James D. "Review of The Selected Letters of Robinson
Jeffers, 1897-1962." American Literature, 41 (May, 1969),
302-303.
   Out of these letters comes insight into Jeffers' poetry; more
than that, out of them comes greater understanding of the
poet. They are edited simply and sparingly. The reader
may wish for more annotation, but in general the integrity of
the editor's handling of the materials is satisfactory. The
student of Jeffers is appreciative of the fact that they have
been made available.

376 HART, William D. "Robinson Jeffers: A Study of 'The Tower
Beyond Tragedy.'" Masters Thesis, Columbia University,
1951.

377 HARTSHORNE, Charles, and William Reese. "Jeffers: Tragic
Pantheism." Robinson Jeffers Newsletter, 39 (July, 1974),
9-10.
   This article is a reproduction of the Jeffers section in
Hartshorne and Reese's book Philosophers Speak of God
(University of Chicago Press, 1969), pp. 208-210. The commentary is perceptive but not especially original: "Here we
see a typical result of combining the all-inclusiveness of
deity with a one-sided or mono-polar conception of the nature
of deity thanks to which the full reality of the world is ren-
dered homeless, since it can neither qualify God nor have its
being outside him."

378 HARTSOCK, Earnest. "Review of The Women at Point Sur."
Atlanta Journal, July 24, 1927.

379 _____. "Review of The Women at Point Sur." Bozart (Atlanta),
1 (September-October, 1927), 14.

380 HASLAM, Gerald. "Predators in Literature." Western American
Literature, 12 (1977), 123-131.
   Begins with an informative review of the love-hate relationship humans share with predatory animals and birds in ancient
and modern literature. Limits his article to birds of prey and
to two authors, Robinson Jeffers and Walter Van Tilburg Clark.
Of Jeffers he writes: "Jeffers was an original: a passionate,

powerful poet who tapped archetypal, primordial depths in
his examination of humans and nature. Jeffers intimates in
some of his poetry that within each human being dwells a
caged eagle, a suppressed wildness that breaks free only in
moments of violence, in times when survival is at stake, or
when sensual lust overwhelms the mere mechanics of pleasure.
At that point one perceives God as energy, the beast becomes
a Christ-like life force within, and life itself is cyclical, pain
becomes an affirmation of life."

381 HATCHER, Harlan. "The Torches of Violence." English Journal,
         23 (February, 1934), 91-99.
         Covers a good many authors and selections other than Jef-
     fers. Cites a dozen examples or more of ghastly and brutal
     murder, incest, rape, suicide, insanity, execution and death
     in general. Our writers have become preoccupied with death:
     a cruel and inhuman withholding of it in Jeffers' Cawdor, for
     instance. Jeffers has seen life gasping in "a net of cruelty,
     inextricably involved." This vision has been so intense that
     all margins are burned away. At his best he creates beauty
     out of this ugliness, and his horrors are legitimate represen-
     rations of his understanding of life.... But as his work has
     progressed, it has led one reluctantly to suspect that the au-
     thor has searched more diligently for new aspects of terror
     than for more acute meanings, and that the very attempt to
     extend and to intensify the violence has succeeded only in
     enervating it....

382 HAURY, Beth B. "The Influence of Robinson Jeffers' 'Tamar' on
         Absalom, Absalom!" Mississippi Quarterly, 25 (1972), 356-358.
         The connection between Faulkner's novel and the story of
     King David is manifest in the title. The biblical account is
     not, however, Faulkner's sole source of inspiration concerning
     the tragic story of incest. Affinities between "Tamar" and
     Faulkner's novel indicate that Faulkner knew Jeffers' poem
     and drew upon it in writing his own modern version of the
     old myth. The remainder of the brief article is based on four
     points: Faulkner's characterization approximates that in
     "Tamar"; both works make use of certain linguistic repetitive
     devices; the works also share a common use of sun imagery;
     and, lastly, similarities exist between both authors' use of
     fire imagery.

383 HAYDEN, A. E. "Robinson Jeffers: Poet-Philosopher." Uni-
         versity Review, 5 (Summer, 1939), 235-238.

384 HAZLITT, Henry. "Our Greatest Authors: How Great Are
         They?" Forum, 88 (October, 1932), 245-250.

385 HERZBERG, M. J. "Jeffers Tells an Unpleasant Narrative of
         Crime." Newark Evening News, September 3, 1927.

386 HICKS, Granville. "The Past and Future of William Faulkner."
     Bookman, 74 (September, 1931), 17-24.
         How does Faulkner fare if we compare him with the contem-
     porary he most resembles in choice of subject, with Robinson
     Jeffers, in whose poems is paralleled every offence against
     human law that Faulkner's novels chronicle? Jeffers has a
     vision, which expresses itself in symbols of lustful deeds
     and bloody crimes. Jeffers writes the poetry of annihilation,
     Faulkner the record of thwarted lives and savage deaths.
     That calm detachment betrays a secret, for if he is not a
     man possessed, as Jeffers unquestionably is, what is he?

387 _____. "A Transient Sickness." Nation, 134 (April 13, 1932),
     433-434.
         Review of Thurso's Landing, etc. Thurso's Landing is
     perhaps the most human poem he has written, in the sense
     that its characters act from comprehensible motives.... It
     moves swiftly, in lines terser and firmer than those the poet
     has hitherto composed, sweeping forward on the wings of an
     imagery even nobler than that we have known. There is a
     kind of vitality in this and all of Jeffers' poems, but the
     vitality is there not because his vision is inevitably true but
     because it is a possible truth. He sees only the way of
     death....

388 _____. The Great Tradition: An Interpretation of American
     Literature Since the Civil War. New York: Macmillan, 1933.
     Jeffers, pp. 262-267.
         Jeffers has been expressing his rage at the indifference
     of the universe by portraying it as a malicious demon.
     Though he knows that man is at worst only an animal, the
     bitter recognition that he is not a god makes him hate the
     race as if it were a race of fiends. Nothing in man's experi-
     ence seems to him so significant as suffering, and no quality
     of man's nature seems to him admirable except the capacity
     to endure suffering. Jeffers chooses his events not because
     they are representative in any statistical sense but because
     they do symbolize what seem to him the significant and re-
     vealing moments of human life.

389 HIGHET, Gilbert. People, Places and Books. New York: Ox-
     ford University Press, 1953. "An American Poet," pp. 22-28.
     Later reprinted as "Jeffers the Pessimist," in Powers of Poetry.
     New York: Oxford University Press, 1960. Pp. 129-134.
         Highet says: "It is sad that the word Romantic has been
     so misused and vulgarized. If it had not been, we could call
     this American poet a romantic figure. Most of the many mean-
     ings implied in the word would fit him; unorthodox, strongly
     individual, imaginative and emotional, daring, careless of rou-
     tine success, a lover only of the material things which can be
     loved without desire (not money and machines, but mountains,

waters, birds, animals); lonely too, lonely. Yes, he is a
romantic figure."

390 HILLYER, Robert. "Nine Books of Verse." New Adelphi (London), 2 (March-May, 1929), 232-236.
Review of Roan Stallion, etc.

391 _____. "Five American Poets." New Adelphi, 2 (March-May,
1929), 280-282.
Review of Cawdor, etc.

392 HOLDEN, W. S. "The Bloody Stones of Mycenae." Argonaut,
111 (November 11, 1932), 5-6.
Critique of production of "The Tower Beyond Tragedy."

393 HOLMES, John. "Review of Solstice and Other Poems." Boston
Transcript, October 19, 1935.
If possible, the rage and violence, the unreasoning and
unhuman hatred are pitched a few notes higher than they
ever have been pitched before. In the long poems called "At
the Birth of an Age" Jeffers seems to reach bedrock at last
(an awe-inspiring thought) as he returns to the days of
Attila for a story that fits his mood and style more closely
than any other long poem he has written. This is the chief
poem of the book, the one exciting item he gives us.

394 _____. "Review of Be Angry at the Sun." New York Times,
February 22, 1942.
The chief difference between this and previous volumes is
that history has finally caught up with Jeffers. This is
nearer to utter catastrophe, and some of this poet's violence
pales beside today's fact. He speaks more frequently and
more openly than before of living men and women and places.
He speaks of Hitler often. There are few hawks in this book,
fewer invented people, more living figures, more doom, and,
in varying degrees of poetic power, the same themes announced
years ago.

395 HOPKINS, Virgil Elizabeth. "A Comparison of the Poetry of
Whitman and Jeffers." Masters Thesis, University of Washington, 1940.

396 HOTCHKISS, Bill. "The Sivaistic Vision: Art and Theme in
Robinson Jeffers." Ph.D. diss., University of Oregon, 1974.
DA, 35 (1975), 5408A.
Jeffers has wide literary precedent in both theme and art
and is keenly aware of such precedents--these having with-
stood the test of the "thousand years" he himself proposes.
This dissertation is an attempt to apply a precedential frame-
work of values to the work of Jeffers. Long and short poems
are examined, with special emphasis on "Tamar," a poem which

is "representative of Jeffers' narrative style and a good deal
better than is generally recognized." This study concludes
that Jeffers may be compared favorably with such tragic
writers as Euripides, Aeschylus, and Marlowe--and is, in
fact, one of our master writers.

397 _____. "Critical Afterword." The Women at Point Sur.
Drawings by Nancy Olson. Auburn, Calif.: Blue Oak Press,
1975. Pp. 176-189.
Poem has been out of print 30 years. Numerous research
libraries do not have the book, and hence it remains perhaps
the least known and least understood of the narratives of
Robinson Jeffers, a writer held by a growing number of
scholars to be the greatest poet of the present century. This
longest of Jeffers' works aroused violent storms of controversy
upon its publication. Fervent cries of damnation were coun-
terpointed by chants of enthusiastic praise. A troubled Van
Doren questioned whether this were not the culmination of Jeffers' philosophical vision--where could he go from here?

398 _____. Jeffers: The Sivaistic Vision. Auburn, Calif.: Blue
Oak Press, 1975.
Publication of dissertation listed above.

399 _____. "For Robinson Jeffers." Robinson Jeffers Newsletter,
48 (March, 1977), 5-6. Reprinted from Climb to the High
Country. New York: W. W. Norton, 1978.
Thirty-five-line poem, in which the poet says "You were
the master spirit: you saw through the terrible agony of
God's self-immolation...."

400 _____, ed. with Afterword. The Double Axe and Other Poems,
Including Eleven Suppressed Poems. Foreword by William
Everson. New York: Random House, 1948. Reprinted New
York: Liveright, 1977.

401 HOWARD, Leon. Literature and the American Tradition. New
York: Doubleday, 1960. Jeffers, pp. 271-274.
Among the host of singers in the chaotic twenties there
arose only one new voice strong enough, for a while, to
rival Eliot's; and that was the voice of the California poet
Robinson Jeffers. As well educated as Eliot, though interested in the sciences as well as in the classics, Jeffers had
studied abroad and published one volume of rather conventional verse before marrying and settling upon the California
coast near Monterey, where he built the stone tower in which
he was to live the rest of his life in retirement. He was completely untouched by the "new" poetry of Pound and Eliot,
but his own was new enough in its own right, and his images
had the strength of his own wild surroundings.

402 HRUBESKY, Donald William. "Robinson Jeffers--An Inverted
     Whitman." Ph.D. diss., Kansas State University, 1971. DA,
     32 (1972), 3253A.
         This study examines in detail the major philsophical judg-
     ments contained in the poetry of Walt Whitman and Robinson
     Jeffers and investigates the implications these judgments have
     in relation to man, America, and the world. Both poets, on
     a superficial level, reveal similar poetic forms and concern
     themselves with certain areas, particularly human sexuality,
     which likenesses have prompted comparisons and suggested
     a possible Whitman influence on Jeffers. In addition, the two
     poets reflect what has been called a cosmic consciousness, an
     awareness of the complex interaction of the physical universe
     and a religious perception of its essential unity that both
     poets visualize as the manifestations of the divine spirit.
     There is a common starting point in the poets, but from that
     point they look in different directions, and what they observe,
     the objects they value, and the predictions they make mark
     them as virtual opposites.

403 HUGHES, John W. "Humanism and the Orphic Voice." Saturday
     Review, 47 (May 22, 1971), 31-33. Review of Arthur Coffin's
     book Robinson Jeffers: Poet of Inhumanism (1971).

404 HUGHES, Langston. I Wonder as I Wander: Autobiography.
     New York: Hill & Wang, 1956. Robinson Jeffers, pp. 282-
     285. Reprinted in Robinson Jeffers Newsletter, 55 (Decem-
     ber, 1979), 28-31.
         Recalls the time he spent as guest in the cottage belonging
     to Noel Sullivan at Carmel-by-the-Sea. Had gladly accepted
     the offer since he wanted an opportunity "to be quiet and
     write." Was amazed at the number of interesting people in
     the area, including the Jefferses, whom he met when he
     walked along the ocean with Greta, the dog. Of the Jefferses
     he says: "Tor House had no electricity or gas, and its
     rough exterior belied the cozy fireplace comfort of the tiny
     rooms within. Una Jeffers, in contrast to the grave and taci-
     turn Robin, was a dynamic, talkative and beautiful little wom-
     an, gracious to friends, but protecting her poet husband
     from strange intruders with a sharp tone--and a rifle if need
     be...."

405 HUGHES, Richard. "But This Is Poetry." Forum, 83 (January,
     1930), 6, 8.
         Review of Dear Judas, etc.

406 HUGHES, Robert N. "Poetic Technique in the Verse of Edna
     St. Vincent Millay, Robinson Jeffers, and Edwin Arlington
     Robinson." Masters Thesis, Ohio State University, 1932.

407 HUMPHRIES, Rolfe. "Hail Cal-i-forn-i-aye." New York Herald

Tribune Books, February 7, 1926.
Review of Continent's End.

408 _____. "Poet or Prophet?" New Republic, 61 (January 15,
1930), 228-229.
    Jeffers' latest book is undoubtedly the most spectacular
event of the poetic year. The strength of Jeffers hits you
between the eyes. No one can deny his tremendous power,
his unique manners, the compulsive force of his narratives,
his accurate, sensuous, poetic vision of the lonely acres
about his home. His weaknesses come from the same source
as his strength, and they are almost equally formidable--a
laxity of language; a proclivity for talking symbol, not sense;
a scant artistic ruthlessness, particularly in knowing what to
leave out ... an inability to project character, or too loose
an ability to project himself.

409 _____. "More About Robinson Jeffers." New Republic, 62
(April 9, 1930), 222.
    Letter about Dear Judas; is a postscript to the article
"Poet or Prophet?" At the time of that writing Humphries
had not read George Moore's novel The Brook Kerith (1905).
Thinks that the explanations by which Jeffers accounts for
the behavior of Judas and Jesus are closely paralleled in
Moore's book. Also Jeffers' poem "The Loving Shepherdress,"
in the same volume seems clearly related to Moore's post-
crucifixion Jesus. Does not insist on Jeffers' imitation but
offers it as an interesting reference.

410 _____. "Two Books by Jeffers." Poetry, 40 (June, 1932),
154-158.
    Review of Descent to the Dead and Thurso's Landing.
These newest books confirm rather than alter the impression
made by the former work of Robinson Jeffers. He either
knocks you, or leaves you cold. Begins with the premise
that Jeffers' longer narrative poems are meant to be descrip-
tions of scenery and stage directions on whose writing the
dramatist has lavishly expended his finest art. For the
rest, they are dramas depending on the author's personal
intensity, expressed in a rhythm that induces an almost hypnotic response; and, finally, on the shocking character of
the stories he has to tell. All of these measures contribute
to dramatic effectiveness, and all of them are perfectly legiti-
mate, time-honored techniques.

411 _____. "Robinson Jeffers." Modern Monthly, 8 (January and
February, 1935), 680-689, 748-753.

412 HUNT, Tim. "The Interactive Voice of Jeffers' Hungerfield."
Robinson Jeffers Newsletter, 43 (December, 1975), 12-17.

Jeffers' last long poem, Hungerfield, has been described
as a narrative framed by a lyric. The long, middle part
tells the story of Hawl Hungerfield who battles an incarna-
tion of Death for the life of his mother and suffers disaster
for his presumption. The lyric that opens and closes the
poem is an elegy for Una who had died less than a year
before the poem was begun. The link between story and
elegy is obvious. Less obvious is Jeffers' attempt to inter-
fuse the lyric and narrative into a larger thematic and struc-
tural pattern, that of his own struggle to confront his sense
of grief and feelings of impotence before the omnipotence of
death. Whatever success the poem may have achieved, it
does offer the poet and the reader a series of confrontations
with issues raised by death.

413 _____, ed. with Afterword. The Women at Point Sur and
Other Poems. New York: Boni & Liveright, 1927. Reprinted
New York: Liveright, 1977.
Many have misunderstood Jeffers' insistence that we need
to break out of humanity as an invitation to repeat the all-too-
human depravities that his poems portray. This poem, for
example, shows what can happen when a rebellious seeker
after truth confuses that search with his self-pitying lust
for power. The Reverend Dr. Barclay of this poem goes beyond the bounds of sanity, coming to think of himself as
God. He thinks of himself as a savior, but his victims need
saving from him, a point which Jeffers obscured for many
readers by making his poem bewilderingly long and complicated.

414 HUTCHISON, Percy A. "An Elder Poet and a Young One Greet
the New Year." New York Times Book Review, January 3,
1926.
Review of Roan Stallion and Thomas Hardy's Human Shows.

415 _____. "Robinson Jeffers Attempts a New Beauty." New
York Times Book Review, September 11, 1927.
Review of The Women at Point Sur. Of this work Hutchin-
son says it has great intensity, but it is the revolting intensity of the bald and reeking confession of a psychopath. It
is not the intensity of Sophocles, for Sophocles never offended
against beauty.

416 _____. "Mr. Robinson Jeffers Brings Hamlet to California."
New York Times Book Review, December 16, 1928.
Review of Cawdor and Other Poems. Those who have
followed the work of Jeffers will still grant him his high
position. He is America's most dramatic worker in a form
other than prose. Cawdor is a scream on the affrighted air;
and when the sound and fury die away, one is inclined to
think that something of artificiality was used in the production of the noise.

417 _____ . "Robinson Jeffers Writes Two Passion Plays." New
      York Times Book Review, December 1, 1929.
          Review of Dear Judas and Other Poems. Jeffers in his
      own uncouth way moves to pity and horror as few poets have
      done since the Greeks. And "The Loving Shepherdess," in
      the strange and tragic beauty of its composition, is something
      even finer than what he has done hitherto. Hutchinson re-
      fers to this poem and the title poem "Dear Judas" as the two
      passion plays.

418 _____ . "Review of Descent to the Dead." New York Times
      Book Review, January 31, 1932.
          These poems are magical in tonal value and rhythm but
      can blind one to the fact that philosophically they are, at
      best, futile. But one does not wish to give them up. This
      is the dilemma into which the modern poet and reader are
      plunged, both unable to return to certain poetic traditions.

419 _____ . "Robinson Jeffers' Dramatic Poem of Spiritual Trag-
      edy." New York Times Book Review, April 3, 1932.

420 _____ . "Sound and Fury in Mr. Jeffers." New York Times
      Book Review, October 15, 1933.
          Review of Give Your Heart to the Hawks, etc. Jeffers
      has in him that love of cruelty so often present in modern
      literature that amounts almost to perversion. The amount of
      blood in this volume becomes appalling. Are the works by
      Jeffers nightmarish rather than real, despite their apparent
      reality? But no one can deny the effects produced at the
      moment. The poetry is unsure of survival, but his is the
      most striking personality in verse today.

421 JACK, P. M. "Bitter Dust." New York Sun, December 18,
      1931. Review of Descent to the Dead, etc.

422 _____ . "Cruelty and Power." New York Sun, April 8, 1932.
      Review of Thurso's Landing, etc.

423 _____ . "Review of Such Counsels You Gave To Me, etc."
      New York Times, October 17, 1937.
          It may be said that Jeffers brings a naive story to full
      maturity and mirrors the modern world in his incestuous and
      degenerate violences. But it is not well or truly written.
      It is not clear how much the characters are poetic symbols.
      What is clear, however, is that Jeffers can write, as displayed
      in his shorter poems, as well as any one when he tells us
      that the sea, the mountains, and the rocks will outlast any
      mortal person.

424 JARRELL, Randall. <u>Poetry and the Age</u>. New York: Knopf,
      1953. Reprinted paperback Vintage Books, 1959. Jeffers
      passim.
            Does not discuss Jeffers; referred to in chapter "A Verse
      Chronicle."

425 JEFFERS, Donnan (son). "Some Biographical Corrigenda."
      <u>Robinson Jeffers Newsletter</u>, 35 (May, 1973), 4-5.
            Comment is directed towards Melba Bennett's biography
      <u>The Stone Mason of Tor House</u>, which he says contained a
      number of minor inaccuracies. The errors could have been
      avoided had Mrs. Bennett allowed a member of the Jeffers
      family to read the manuscript. He did not want to publish
      these corrections during Melba Bennett's life time but now
      thinks the time has come to correct them. Donnan Jeffers
      quite accurately describes these errors as "mostly very
      trivial."

426 _____. "A Note on Tor House." <u>Robinson Jeffers Newsletter</u>
      42 (August, 1975), 6-9.
            Article affords an excellent tour of Jeffers' property, seen
      from within and also from the outside with the surrounding
      territory. The plot of land is surprisingly small, and the
      number of buildings on the property just about fill it up.
      The floor plans are described, rooms are described, furnish-
      ings named and described. The overall impression is one of
      unbelievable worth, not just because Jeffers built so much of
      the place and lived there for 43 years but also because of
      the rich store of antiques which Jeffers and Una collected.
      The present owners find it difficult to maintain the property
      but are reluctant to see it sold and scattered about the coun-
      try.

427 _____. "Portraits of Robinson Jeffers: A Preliminary List."
      <u>Robinson Jeffers Newsletter</u>, 45 (June, 1976), 7-8.
            Lists 11 works, by date, if known, artist, kind of compo-
      sition, and present whereabouts of the portrait, if known.

428 _____. "Some Notes on the Building of Tor Huse." <u>Robinson
      Jeffers Newsletter</u>, 53 (June, 1979), 8-25.
            Article first appeared in the Monterey <u>Peninsula Herald's</u>
      "Weekend Magazine," August 1978. The version printed here
      is expanded, with clarifying divisions as follows:

            1) A Prophetic Gift,
            2) The Jeffers at the Future Site of Tor House,
            3) The Building of the Original House,
            4) Life at Tor House in the Early Years,
            5) The Building of the Tower,
      6 & 7) The Building of the Dining Room and East Wing,
            8) The Conversion of the Old Garage into a Kitchen, and

9) The Building of the Connective Wing.

The article ends with a listing of Tor House Furnishings.

429   JEFFERS, Robinson.   Principal works listed chronologically:

Flagons and Apples. Los Angeles: Grafton Publishing, 1912.
Californians. New York: Macmillan, 1916.
Tamar and Other Poems. New York: Peter G. Boyle, 1924.
Roan Stallion, Tamar, and Other Poems. New York: Boni
    and Liveright, 1925.
The Women at Point Sur. New York: Boni and Liveright,
    1927.
Three Poems. Introduction by B. H. Lehman. San Francisco:
    Book Club of California, 1928.
An Artist. Privately printed: John S. Mayfield, c. 1928.
Cawdor and Other Poems. New York: Horace Liveright,
    1928.
Dear Judas and Other Poems. New York: Horace Liveright,
    1929.
Stars. San Francisco: Flame Press, 1930.
Apology for Bad Dreams. Paris: Harry Ward Ritchie, 1930.
Descent to the Dead: Poems Written in Ireland and Great
    Britain. New York: Random House, 1931.
Thurso's Landing and Other Poems. New York: Liveright,
    1932.
Give Your Heart to the Hawks and Other Poems. New York:
    Random House, 1933.
Solstice and Other Poems. New York: Random House, 1935.
Roan Stallion, Tamar, and Other Poems. New York: Random
    House, 1935. Modern Library edition. Contains a dozen
    or so poems not in the original publication, 1925.
Such Counsels You Gave to Me and Other Poems. New York:
    Random House, 1937.
Selected Poems of Robinson Jeffers. New York: Random
    House, 1938. Jeffers' own selections--615 pages arranged
    chronologically. Represents about half of published work.
    Selection is "more or less arbitrary." Seems to prefer
    shorter poems; very early poems not included, nor very
    long ones.
Be Angry at the Sun. New York: Random House, 1941.
Medea: A Modern Verse Rendering of the Euripides play.
    New York: Random House. Reprinted in Cawdor and
    Medea. New York: New Directions, 1970.
The Double-Axe and Other Poems, with Preface by Robinson
    Jeffers. New York: Random House, 1948.
Poetry, Gongorism, and a Thousand Years. Los Angeles:
    Ward Ritchie, 1949.
Hungerfield and Other Poems. New York: Random House,
    1954. Contains 115 pages, including "The Deer Lay Down
    Their Bones," and "The Cretan Woman."

The Cretan Woman. New York: Random House, 1954.
Themes in My Poems. San Francisco: Book Club of Califor-
nia, 1956.
The Beginning and the End, and Other Poems. New York:
Random House, 1963.
Selected Poems. Reprint of 1938 publication. 1965.
Selected Letters of Robinson Jeffers, edited by Ann Ridgeway.
Baltimore: Johns Hopkins University Press, 1968.

430 JEFFERS, Una. "A Correction." Nassau Literature (Princeton
University), 91 (January, 1933), 41.

431 _____. "Una Jeffers: Correspondent." Robinson Jeffers
Newsletter, 44 (March, 1976), 7-10.
Consists of two letters which Una wrote to their dear
friends Hans and Phoebe Barkan, in the early years of a
long friendship. The dates are March 1934 and May 27, 1934.
They reveal something of Jeffers' annoyance at visitors and
crowds which intruded on his isolation; more importantly,
however, they reveal much of Una, her love of music, her
reading habits, her love for the children, and her deep regard for the warmth of friends.

432 _____. "Una Jeffers: Correspondent." Robinson Jeffers
Newsletter, 45 (June, 1976), 10-13.
Consists of some excerpts from letters to Phoebe and Hans
Barkan, 1930-1932. These letters have no particular theme,
but are interesting for insights into the routine life of the
Jeffers' family. Una Jeffers was an easy letter writer and
may be described as chatty, familiar, and warm.

433 _____. "Una Jeffers: Correspondent." Robinson Jeffers
Newsletter, 46 (September, 1976), 8-13.
Consists of excerpts from letters to Phoebe and Hans
Barkan, 1933-1937, and one undated, unsigned, eight-page
set of travelling directions to Ireland. The date here is
probably 1938. Like the above, these letters relate ordinary
living and routine events--what they boys are doing, what
Jeffers is doing, what she is doing or reading.

434 _____. "Una Jeffers: Correspondent." Robinson Jeffers
Newsletter, 47 (December, 1976), 12-19.
Excerpts from letters to Phoebe and Hans Barkan, 1939-
1949. Is the concluding segment in this series, and takes
Una Jeffers up to the time almost of her death. Actually
her illness of cancer began to be apparent in 1948, and she
refers to it in one of her last letters. She refers also to
Katherine Mansfield's Letters and Journals, an author who
died young of tuberculosis, and knew she was dying.

435 _____. "Una Jeffers, Correspondent: Excerpt from Letters
to Blanche Matthias, 1927-1934." Robinson Jeffers Newsletter,

49 (June, 1977), 12-21.

Blanche and Russell Matthias were long-time friends of Una
and Robinson Jeffers. The Matthiases moved about a great
deal, also traveled widely, but the friendship was a lively
one, warm and close. A collection of over 200 letters and
cards from Una is now kept in Yale University's rare book
and manuscript library. The excerpts printed here were
copied from the letters deposited at Yale.

436   _____. "Excerpts from Letters to Blanche Matthias, 1935-
         1937." Robinson Jeffers Newsletter, 50 (March, 1978), 12-20.

Continues the series begun in Vol. 49 of Newsletter. In
September and October of 1937 the Jefferses were in Ireland,
Scotland, and later in London, and the letters printed here
comment at random on their trip. On their way home they
stop at Taos, New Mexico, and visit Mabel Dodge Luhan.
Finally arrive at Tor House, Carmel, just in time for Christ-
mas night dinner.

437   _____. "Matthias Letters, 1936-1941." Robinson Jeffers
         Newsletter, 51 (July, 1978), 23-51.

Begins with some undated fragments and letters, probably
around 1937. Una especially was not very careful about dat-
ing her letters, but they are included for the personal and
family life they reveal. In one letter Una talks about her
former husband's second and third wives. Some of the letters
remark on the war in Europe, but mostly the details are of
a lesser nature--what the Jefferses did, what the boys are
doing, the death of one dog, the acquisition of another, etc.

438   _____. "Matthias Letters, 1942-1944." Robinson Jeffers News-
         letter, 53 (June, 1979), 31-46.

Continues the series begun earlier. Adds further strength
to the record of the friendship. These letters, written during
the war, are filled with details of the war, but they are still
personal and fully recognizant of everyday life and those who
live it.

439   _____. "Matthias Letters, 1945-1950." Robinson Jeffers News-
         letter, 55 (December, 1979), 3-28.

Concludes the Matthias letters, the last one dated June 26,
1950, in which Una says she progresses about as fast "as a
sick snail." She died September 1, 1950. Some of these
letters are undated. In general they simply continue the line
of conversation begun in the much earlier letters.

440   _____. "Letters to Hazel Pinkham, 1912-1920." Robinson
         Jeffers Newsletter, 56 (June, 1980), 7-44. Continued in 57
         (November, 1980), 6-26, dates 1921-1925.

Begins the two-part publication. Una and Hazel were life
long friends although they seldom visited. These letters, 52

at the University of Texas and 12 at Occidental, shed light on Una's early life during which time she and Robin were beginning their lives together. They record many details of the birth of the Jeffers twins. In the first installment the letters are presented complete and almost entirely unabridged.

441   _____. "Una Jeffers Correspondent: Albert Bender Letters." Robinson Jeffers Newsletter, 60 (June, 1982), 5-16, Letters from 1927-1929; Part II, 61 (July, 1982), 18-38, Letters from 1926-1935; Part III, 62 (January, 1983), 15-34, Letters from 1936-1940.

442 JEROME, Judson. "Poetry: How and Why the Language of Robinson Jeffers." Revista de Letras (Oviedo), 1 (1969), 99-105.

443   _____. "Roan Stallion." Writers Digest (April, 1983), 52-55. Article includes a synposis of the poem with analysis of form, verse, folklore, and mythopoesis.

444 JOHNS, Orrick. "Review of Descent to the Dead, etc." Carmel Pine Cone, 18 (January 15, 1932), 5.
It is possible not to keep the attention always on the Jeffers ultimates, for the way is strewn with precious metal, visible life, wisdom that cuts the muddle with a sword. If his message seems sometimes a magnificent tree dying at the top, it is a tree that continually drops golden fruit.

445 JOHNSON, Merle. "(John) Robinson Jeffers, 1887--." Publishers' Weekly, 117 (April 19, 1930), 2143.

446   _____. American First Editions. New York: Bowker, 1932. Robinson Jeffers, p. 203.

447 JOHNSON, William Savage. "The 'Savior' in the Poetry of Robinson Jeffers." American Literature, 15 (May, 1943), 159-168.
Refers to "Meditation on Saviors," by Jeffers.
One of the concepts which appears most frequently in the poetry of Robinson Jeffers is that of the "Savior." In his poetry the Savior comes to represent a spirit of opposition to good, and yet the poet's attitude toward the savior type is ambiguous, for the conflict between his acquired intellectual system and his Christian inheritance has not been entirely resolved.... Jeffers' only extended discussion of the savior-concept is in the long poem "Meditation on Saviors." It is a confused and rather incoherent poem, but it is of interest as a personal confession of the dilemma in which the poet finds himself. Its chief purpose seems to be to establish in his own mind and person a right relation to the phenomenon contemplated.

448 JOLAS, Eugene. "Literature and the New Man." Transition (Paris), June 1930. Pp. 13, 19.

449 JONES, Howard Mumford. "Dull Naughtiness." Chicago Daily News, August 3, 1927. Also printed in Columbus (Ohio) State Journal, August 7, 1927.
     Review of The Women at Point Sur.

450 JORGENSEN, Virginia E. "Hearing the Night-Herons: A Lesson on Jeffers' 'Hurt Hawks.'" English Journal, 51 (September, 1962), 440-442.
     Brief article is directed toward teaching Jeffers' poem to a group of older high school students. Author considers such matters as underlying ideas, structure, the personal point of view of the poet, the metrics, the dramatic interest of the poem. In conclusion: "A short study should never try to encompass all a teacher knows (or thinks he knows) about a poem or poet. It should follow the interests and abilities of the class." Some of the grandeur of the wild country and wild creatures of a major American poet is evident in the personal feelings expressed here so deftly. But the real value of a study of this poem would seem to be in an appreciation of the Romantic spirit that rushes on even in these unlikely times, in a tempering of the ear to hear the night-herons.

450a _____. "Dionysus Redivivus: The Narrative Intention of Robinson Jeffers' The Women at Point Sur." Masters Thesis, Lehigh University, 1972.

451 KAFKA, Robert M. "Jeffers' Preface to Brides of the South Wind." Robinson Jeffers Newsletter, 34 (February, 1973), 9-11.
     Article is based on an item in Sidney Alberts' bibliography in which he notes two prose fragments which Jeffers intended as prefatory material for a volume that was never published, or possibly two volumes that were never published. Alberts contends that the first two titles were variants of the same volume, tentative titles, soon discarded. This author does not believe that the second fragment does not belong with the Brides collection. Article continues with at least five reasons why he thinks this is so. There is no firm conclusion to this matter, but unless more material surfaces it remains questionable that Jeffers had only one book in mind and not two.

452 _____. "The Stone Mason of Tor House: More Corrigenda." Robinson Jeffers Newsletter, 51 (July, 1978), 5-6.
     Intended to serve as a supplement to Donnan Jeffers' list of errors in Melba Bennett's book on Jeffers. Several of these items are related to dates, and others are related to Jeffers' publications.

453 _____. "Robinson Jeffers' Published Writings, 1903-1911."
Robinson Jeffers Newsletter, 53 (June, 1979), 47-68.
       A bibliography, including items Jeffers may have written
pseudonymously with reprintings of poems generally unavaila-
ble. The following categories are covered:

       Poems published, either signed or acknowledged.
       Poems not reprinted in Alberts' Bibliography; with poems
              printed, not just listed.
       Original printings, where they differ from Alberts'.
       List of pseudonymous writings, possibly by Jeffers.
       Poems by "Rob York" and "Edwin Rush," with notes.

454 _____, ed. "Una Kuster's Road Race." Robinson Jeffers
Newsletter, 52 (December, 1978), 7-14.
       This material, for the most part written by Bert C. Smith,
was published in the Los Angeles Times, in May 1911. It
sheds some light on the public activities of Una Jeffers (then
Kuster) during the years before her divorce and subsequent
marriage to Jeffers. The material, in and of itself, is not
very significant.

455 _____, ed. "Una Jeffers Correspondent: Letters to Hazel
Pinkham, 1926-1932." Robinson Jeffers Newsletter, 58 (May
1981), 18-32. Continued in 59 (September, 1981), 6-16.
(1933-1942 Letters)
       Third and fourth segments of Una's letters to Hazel (see
under Jeffers, Una). Continues subjects previously discussed:
trips, the twins, mutual acquaintances, etc.

456 _____, ed. "Una Jeffers, Correspondent: Ellen O'Sullivan
Letters, 1935-1941." Robinson Jeffers Newsletter, 63 (June,
1983), 18-29.
       These letters were transcribed from the Jeffers Collection
at the University of Texas (Austin). The letters are mostly
undated, and, therefore, the editor does not guarantee the
sequence. Ellen O'Sullivan lived within walking distance of
the Jefferses, and they were very good friends. Most of
these letters were written to Ellen when the Jefferses were
in Taos, or Wyoming, or elsewhere. One editorial comment
is that Jeffers least objected to Ellen's visits--her simplicity
and unassuming ways no doubt gave him little to complain of.

457 _____, and Michael Mooney. "Jeffers' Scholarly Materials,
Small and Minor Holdings." Robinson Jeffers Newsletter, 56
(June, 1980), 47-52.
       Editors say that much of this material is of slight impor-
tance in itself. Among locations of these holdings are listed
Middlebury College, Harvard University, Boston University,
Amherst, Wesleyan, New York University, New York Public
Library, Princeton University, University of Pennsylvania,

Temple, Delaware, Maryland, Florida, William Jewell College,
St. John's Seminary, California Historical Society, and Los
Angeles Public Library.

458 KANTOR, MacKinlay. "Plenty of Sex and Plenty of Bible."
     Voices, 7 (February, 1928), 180-183.
     Review of A Miscellany of American Poetry: 1927.

459 KARMAN, James. "The Religion of Robinson Jeffers." Masters
     Thesis, University of Iowa, 1971.

460 _____. "A Note on William Hamilton Jeffers." Robinson Jef-
     fers Newsletter, 42 (August, 1975), 9-11.
        Interesting study of Robinson Jeffers' father, a minister
     and Christian scholar. Some writers have suggested that
     the rebellious prodigal son concept may be central to under-
     standing Jeffers, but the facts do not seem to support this
     theory. Dr. Jeffers, though well-informed and no doubt
     having strong opinions of his own, did not insist that others,
     including members of his own family, have the same opinions.
     Evidence suggests that the environment Robinson grew up in
     was one in which independence of thought was always en-
     couraged. The father was not a stern, doctrinaire believer;
     he was a devout but judicious man, open to change through-
     out his life. In this light, the issue of prodigal rebellion
     loses its significance.

461 _____. "Biographical Sketch." Robinson Jeffers Newsletter,
     43, (December, 1975), 11-12.
        Details in this sketch have been transcribed from the
     General Biographical Catalogue of the Westen Theological
     Seminary of the Presbyterian Church. The excerpt includes
     facts only: date of birth (Cadiz, Ohio, May 11, 1838), dates
     and places of education, ordination dates, travel dates, pro-
     fessor of Greek, date of death, etc. Dr. Jeffers died in
     Pasadena, California, December 20, 1914.

462 _____. "Toward a New Bethlehem: Robinson Jeffers' Pro-
     phetic Re-Vision of LIfe." Ph.D. diss., Syracuse University,
     1976.
        This study takes the epithet "prophet" seriously. Because
     critics have had a difficult time placing Jeffers--his work is
     unlike that of Eliot or Pound and it moves in a direction that
     is different from Stevens and Williams--they have devoted
     most of their energies toward tracking down the sources from
     which he drew. Though this approach has met with some
     success and has revealed Jeffers' grasp of world history and
     literature, it has served to fragment rather than to unify our
     understanding of his vision.

463 _____, ed. "The Writings of Dr. William Hamilton Jeffers,

1838-1914." Robinson Jeffers Newsletter, 43 (December, 1975), 11.

This item is an announcement, or notice, that such writings have been forwarded to the Newsletter, the author having made copies of them at the University of Syracuse. There are three of these documents: Dr. Jeffers' Inaugural Address in 1877 at Western Theological Seminary; a Memorial Sermon for Reverend Samuel Jennings Wilson, preached before the Synod of Pennsylvania, October 18, 1883; and an expanded version of that sermon, included as a memoir in Occasional Addresses and Sermons by Reverend Samuel J. Wilson (Dodd, Mead & Co., 1895).

464 KARO, Leila M. "Robinson Jeffers." Present Day American Literature (Montgomery, W. V.), 4 (March, 1931), 160-165.

465 KELLER, Karl A. "Robinson Jeffers and 'The Beauty of Things': A Concept of Nature." Masters Thesis, University of Utah, 1959.

466 _____. "California, Yankees, and the Death of God: Allegory in Jeffers' Roan Stallion." Texas Studies in Language and Literature, 12 (Spring, 1970), 111-120.

This work has been of critical interest mainly because of its classical form, but when read primarily as an allegory built on a personal mythology rather than as complex symbolism, the poem yields substantial meaning under the pressure of critical analysis. The wooden characters take on mythic significance, the offensive plot assumes an archetypal shape, and the argument becomes a lively part of the plot. Through allegory, the literal issues of Jeffers' didactic system become poetry.... The cast of Jeffers' poem is identified by an allegory that assigns to each character a place in the structure of Jeffers' social philosophy.... The death of God is a necessary metaphor for Jeffers' schematized explanation for the depravity of contemporary western man. In nature, as the identity of the stallion shows, transcendence is transmuted into immanence, but the opposites of existence are in bitter conflict and cannot endure each other. The tragedy of man is that he is forever alienated from nature; the divine, power, beauty, and significance. This is the loss of God that is presumed by human experience.

467 _____. "Jeffers' Pace." Robinson Jeffers Newsletter, 32 (July, 1972), 7-17.

During Jeffers' lifetime his prosody was generally dismissed as free verse, and, since his death, it has been more accurately identified as accentual verse of a fairly traditional variety, but the effect has been the same: because it could be labeled, it was thought to be understood and could be ignored. But of all the features of Jeffers' poetic form, his work with

rhythm remains the most interesting and the least explored.
Article is a carefully illustrated study of this aspect of Jeffers, with due recognition to the few studies which have previously been published.

468 KIEL, Fred O. "Robinson Jeffers' Prescriptions for Man." Fer-
ment: A Quarterly of Poetry and Poetic Comment, 3 (July-
September, 1963), 8-18. (Published by Transient Press,
Chapel Hill, North Carolina).
Article is a general introduction to and review of Jeffers'
poetry.

469 KILEY, George B. "Robinson Jeffers: The Short Poems."
Ph.D. diss., Pittsburgh University, 1957. DA, 18 (1958),
2210A.
This study is based on the poet's methods, his prosody,
his diction, his philosophical ideas--primarily polarities to be
resolved--and his conflicts (personal longings for death, but
commitment to life). Concludes with a discussion of the universality of Jeffers' themes and with a study of the poem
"Night."

470 KING, Alexander. "Terrors of Tamar." San Francisco Chronicle,
September 26, 1926.

471 KLEIN, Herbert Arthur. "A Study of the Prosody of Robinson
Jeffers." Masters Thesis, Occidental College, 1930.

472 _____. "The Poet Who Spoke of It." Robinson Jeffers Newsletter, 11 (August, 1965), 2-6.
Article covers briefly the concepts of science that Jeffers
wove into his poetry "with such power and understanding."
In discussing these concepts Klein quotes intelligently and
accurately from Jeffers' works, thus illustrating that the poet
did indeed understand the "quantum theory" and "relativity
theory." Article concludes with passages from Jeffers' last
book in which he talks about "a third war ... fought with
what weapons?" He thinks it is logical that nuclear war will
come, but somehow he still rebels "against this conviction of
self-genocide."

473 _____. "The Cleft Axeman." Robinson Jeffers Newsletter, 17
(April, 1967), 4-6.
Long poem written to Jeffers in 1948 after reading The
Double Axe.

474 _____. "Czech Poet, Jeffers Translator: Kamil Bednar, A
Memoir and a Tribute." Robinson Jeffers Newsletter, 35 (May,
1973), 10-19.
Bednar died May 23, 1972, not yet 60 years old. In 1966
Bednar had said, "I intend to devote my future to his [Jef-
fers'] work," and from that time forward he did work tirelessly

in translating, publishing, and in general creating interest
in Jeffers in Czechoslovakia. This article is a rather lengthy
review of Bednar against the background of his native country, Hitler, World War II, followed by the Soviet domination.
It was in 1950 that he discovered Jeffers, in the volume Be
Angry at the Sun (originally published in 1941). Almost at
once he began translating some of the shorter Jeffers' lyrics,
gradually feeling his ability to undertake the longer works.
A poet in his own right, Bednar and Jeffers shared much in
common in their works, and it is perhaps because of this that
Bednar was able to render such accurate and moving translations of Jeffers.

475 _____, ed. "Jeffers Observed: A Memoir." Robinson Jeffers
   Newsletter, 61 (July, 1982), 7-18.
      This article is derived from 1931 letters of Mina Cooper,
   later Mrs. Herbert Arthur Klein. Gives a background of
   Miss Cooper who started writing to Klein as early as 1928
   and eventually married him in March of 1932. They were
   married until her death from cancer in November 1979.
   These letters, not heretofore published, addressed to Her-
   bert Klein, are of interest to Jeffers' scholars because Mina
   Cooper was a lifelong admirer of Jeffers, and her letters to
   Klein contain numerous references to Una and Robin Jeffers.

476 KNIGHT, Grant C. American Literature and Culture. New York:
   Long and Smith, 1932. Robinson Jeffers, pp. 476-477.
      At the present moment many critics are willing to call
   Robinson Jeffers the most impressive poet that America has
   produced. Although he sets the scene of most of his narrative poems in California, he introduces crimes and perversions
   which we are prone to associate with Greek drama. Certainly
   Jeffers is the most tragic, the most desperate, and within
   his range the most passionate and powerful of all our poets.
   Jeffers is our supreme poetic pessimist and futilitarian. What
   the future will say of him cannot be predicted; it may be that
   his mood suits too well that of the present and so misleads
   our judgment.

477 KRAFT, Stephanie. No Castles on Main Street: American Authors and Their Homes. Chicago: Rand McNally, 1979.
      Consists of 240 pages with 90 photographs, presenting a
   cross-country and cross-section pilgrimage to homes of 30
   important American writers. Among these is Robinson Jeffers and Tor House, pp. 220-224.

478 KRESENSKY, Raymond. "Fire Burning Cross." Christian Century, 47 (June 11, 1930), 757-758.
      Review of Dear Judas, etc.

479 _____. "Beloved Judas." The World Tomorrow, 13 (February,

1930), 90.
Review of <u>Dear Judas</u>, etc.

480 KREYMBORD, Alfred. <u>Our Singing Strength: An Outline of</u>
     <u>American Poetry, 1620-1930</u>. New York: Coward-McCann,
     1929. Jeffers, pp. 624-630.
          Compares Whitman and Jeffers who "afford parallels and
     antithesis to the student of the American race. Both men
     are prophets; both write in the grand manner; and each re-
     flects his own period." So far as one can limit any age to
     its leading characteristics, one might say that Whitman's age
     was all for love, Jeffers' all for hatred. The Whitman period,
     stemming from Emerson, believed in the virtues of the race;
     the Jeffers' period believes in its evil and vices. The roman-
     tic Manhattanite and tragic Californian, democrat and aristo-
     crat, worldling and hermit, require an epic figure somewhere
     between, or inclusive of both.

481 _____, ed. <u>An Anthology of American Poetry: Lyric America</u>,
     <u>1630-1930</u>. New York: Tudor Publishing Co., 1930. Prints
     five selections by Robinson Jeffers, pp. 489-495.
          Prints "Part III from 'Tamar,'" "Granite and Cypress,"
     "Wise Men in Their Bad Hours," "Tor House," and "Shine,
     Perishing Republic," without biographical or critical introduc-
     tion. Of all poets to select for an anthology, perhaps Jeffers
     least lends himself to the task. His best poetry is in long
     forms, and the short poems are overly familiar. "Tor House"
     is as excellent as any of the shorter works and is totally
     representative of Jeffers.

482 KRUTCH, Joseph Wood. "Understanding a Poet." <u>Robinson Jef-</u>
     <u>fers Newsletter</u>, 29 (August, 1971), 6-11.
          This essay is the text of a talk given by Krutch at Occi-
     dental College in 1955, on the 50th anniversary of Robinson
     Jeffers' graduation. The manuscript is unfinished, a type-
     script, hand-corrected and altered. After Krutch's death,
     May 22, 1970, Mrs. Krutch gave the manuscript to Occidental
     College. The article given here has been edited slightly by
     Professor Brophy.

483 KUNITZ, Stanley J. "The Day Is a Poem." <u>Poetry</u>, 59 (Decem-
     ber, 1941), 148-154.
          Review of <u>Be Angry at the Sun</u>.
          Continuing his "epic" Jeffers opens this volume with a long
     narrative poem which does no more than restate, with a new
     cast of incestuous phantoms, the allegory he has been writing
     for some twenty years. He flicks his long whip-like lines;
     the rhythms are beautifully controlled; the story leaps from
     one explosion of emotion to another. Perhaps a certain con-
     fusion has developed in Jeffers' mind between the non-human
     and the in-human. His pursuit of the one endowed him with

a ferocity and grandeur of spirit that made him a legend in
his time, as if he summed up, in a gesture of unappeasable
nihilism, man's distaste for his own corruptibility.

484 _____. A Kind of Order: A Kind of Folly. Boston: Little,
Brown, 1975. "Barbaric Omens," pp. 198-203.
Article basically the same as item listed above.

485 _____, and Howard Haycraft. Twentieth Century Authors.
New York: H. W. Wilson, 1942. Jeffers, pp. 722-723.
Biographical sketch with a list of his principal works and
a highly selective list of works about Jeffers. Although
mainly objective, the sketch concludes with an evaluation:
"Jeffers is a unique phenomenon in American and indeed in
world literature. Sometimes he is grandiose rather than
grand, sometimes his unremitting monotony of doom grows
wearying, but of his fierce and original genius there can be
no doubt."

486 KURRIK, Maire J. "Robinson Jeffers' Negations: The Dialectics
of 'Not' in 'The Bloody Sire.'" Psycho-cultural Review, 1
(Spring, 1977), 195-201.

487 LAGUNA, Frederica de. "Robinson Jeffers: The Poets' Poet."
The Ebell, 1 (November, 1927), 30-31.

488 LAL, C. B. "Revie of Cawdor and Other Poems." San Francisco
Examiner, January 27, 1929.

489 LAMONT, Joyce H. "Jeffers Scholarly Materials: University of
Alabama." Robinson Jeffers Newsletter, 46 (September, 1976),
42-43.
Article is a letter from the librarian of Special Collections
at the University of Alabama, in which she admits that the
Jeffers material there is in disarray. A catalog was planned
but never completed. They would like to publish a catalog
but have no plans for doing so. She names two items (which
her correspondent, Robert Kafka had asked for): "Promise
of Peace" and "The Resurrection of Achilles." The papers
at Alabama are restricted, the donation of Dr. Wallace Bruce
Smith in honor of Hudsson Strode.

490 LANZ, Henry. The Physical Basis of Rime: An Essay on the
Aesthetics of Sound. Stanford: Stanford University Press,
1931. Reprinted New York: Greenwood Press, 1968. Jeffers, p. 351.
Shows a photographic record of a fragment from Robinson
Jeffers, "Humanity is needless...." etc. Fragment is highly
interesting to see the effect of unusual consonantal environ-

ment, consisting largely of $\underline{M}$, $\underline{N}$, and $\underline{L}$, upon the unaccented vowels. Such environment evidently tends to equalize the distribution of energy among the syllables.

491   LAWLESS, Ray M. "Robinson Jeffers, Poet." Present Day Amer-
      ican Literature (Montgomery, W. V.), 4 (March, 1931), 154-
      160.

492   LAWRYNOWICZ, Zygmunt. "John Robinson Jeffers: A Bibliogra-
      phy of Poems in Polish Translation." Robinson Jeffers News-
      letter, 50 (March, 1978), 7-11.
         Contains some letters addressed to the Jeffers' Committee
      and Mrs. Bennett (long after her death). Main objective,
      however, is to list poems in Polish by Jeffers. The several
      categories are: poems in anthologies, poems in periodicals,
      and books of poems. Most of the translations are by Lawryn-
      owicz, but there are other translators, some of whom have
      published in journals no longer available. The list does not
      presume to be complete, and many of the translators not men-
      tioned had only a marginal interest in Jeffers.

493   LEHMAN, Benjamin H. "The Most Significant Tendency in Mod-
      ern Poetry: Lectures on Significant Tendencies in Contempo-
      rary Letters." Scripps College Papers, 2 (March-April,
      1930), 1-12. Reprinted in Saturday Review of Literature, 8
      (September 5, 1931), 97-99.
         Mentions Jeffers as a poet not completely able to cope with
      modern science. Thinks he is too negative and has not real-
      ized that the highest calling of the artist is to trace the uni-
      verse in its human and nonhuman manifestations.

493a   _____. "Review of Roan Stallion, etc." California Monthly,
       2 (September, 1926), 37.

493b   _____. "Recollections and Reminiscences." Robinson Jeffers
       Newsletter, 63 (June, 1983), 12-18.
          This excerpt is printed from an oral history of life in the
       Bay Area, 1920-1969. The tapes are in the Bancroft Library,
       University of California (Berkeley), and the interviewer was
       Amelia Fry. Most of Ms. Fry's questions were directed at
       getting a better "inside" understanding of Jeffers: did he
       live like a hermit at Tor House? What has been the influence
       of the Catholic religion on Jeffers? What role did Una play
       in his life? Professor Lehman attempted an answer to most
       of these questions, but to some of them he said he did not
       know, could not go very far into that. On the subject of
       Una, he said rather succinctly that she was the motivating
       force in his life. "He was completely committed to her, no
       matter what other things may have happened. She was his
       life."

494   LEITCH, Mary S. "Review of Roan Stallion, Tamar, and Other
      Poems." Virginian Pilot (Norfolk), March 3, 1926.

495 LeMASTER, J. R. "Lorca, Jeffers, and the Myth of Tamar."
     New Laurel Review, 1 (1971), 44-51.
          Jeffers in his poem "Tamar" and Lorca in "Thamar and
     Amnon" both look for a way to express the essense of man's
     existence today through old modes. Both retell the story
     found in II Samuel, trying to capture the essence of modern
     man through incest. In Lorca the conflict is between primi-
     tivism and civilization. Jeffers uses the biblical narrative
     and Greek myth. For him the incestuous relationship, result-
     ing in jealousy, indicates radical introversion--the sickness
     of modern man. Lorca and Jeffers bring the old story of
     man the animal versus man the civilized being up to date,
     and both are on the side of nature rather than civilization.

496 LENHART, C. S. Musical Influence on American Poetry. Ath-
     ens: University of Georgia Press, 1956. Jeffers, passim.

497 LEVY, William T. "Notes on the Prophetic Element in the Poetry
     of Robinson Jeffers." Masters Thesis, Columbia University,
     1947.

498 _____. "Review of The Beginning and the End and Other
     Poems." New York Times Book Review, May 5, 1963.
          Once again Jeffers writes those wonderfully unexpected
     poems of personal record. But for the most part his focus
     remains cosmic, and he sees the universe as a great heart
     through which pulsate all the energies that exist. In old
     age Jeffers remains constant to the youthful vision which
     served for a lifetime to keep him at one with the splendor
     of a world he found so beautiful that man alone seemed un-
     worthy of his Creator. His answer will not be ours, but he
     instructs us how our minds might be exalted in beauty--and
     so share in the divine quality and fabric of all creation.

499 LEWIS, Sinclair. The American Fear of Literature. New York:
     Harcourt, Brace, 1931. 23-page pamphlet.
          Work contains "Why Sinclair Lewis Got the Nobel Prize,"
     by Erik Axel Karlfeldt (Permanent Secretary of the Swedish
     Academy), December 10, 1930; and "Address by Sinclair
     Lewis," before the Swedish Academy, December 12, 1930.
     Lewis' address, "The American Fear of Literature," is an
     appraisal of the American scene in literature, and at times
     a bitter denouncement of the literary climate in America
     which belabors such writers as Theodore Dreiser, Sherwood
     Anderson, Eugene O'Neill, James Branch Cabell, etc. What
     Lewis is really appalled at is the American rejection of real-
     ism and honest artistry in the telling of truth. Our nation
     will not accept anything that is not romantically inflated,
     idealistic, and sentimentally idiotic. The speech is a bitter
     indictment of America.

500 LEWISOHN, Ludwig. Expression in America. New York: Har-
       per & Brothers, 1932. Jeffers, p. 583.
       Brief comments on Jeffers in closing chapter as he pre-
       pares to leave the subject of creative expression in America.
       Among others he "leaves the real power as well as the uncon-
       vincing Titanism of Robinson Jeffers" to the judgment of the
       future.

501 LILIENTHAL, T. M. "The Robinson Jeffers Committee." Quar-
       terly News Letter (Book Club of California), 28 (1963), 81.

502 LIND, L. Robert. "The Crisis in Literature Today." Sewanee
       Review, 47 (January-March, 1939), 35-51. Parts II, III, and
       IV of article in Sewanee Review, 47, pp. 184-203; 345-364;
       524-551. Jeffers, passim.
       At one point Lind says: "Power and the poetry of Robin-
       son Jeffers are almost synonymous terms. Seldom has a poet
       written in our country with so much terrible force of utter-
       ance, such Hebraic thunder; for one must realize that Jeffers
       stands in the old tradition of the poet as preacher and that
       his chief motive in writing is moral and didactic.... In hu-
       man pain Jeffers finds his most satisfactory symbol; it is in
       the will to endure all the malignities of Nature and human
       nature that he sees one small spark of nobility in man. The
       contrast between the complete unfeeling of Nature and man's
       suffering (feebly noble in a creature otherwise wholly vile)
       is relentlessly and frequently drawn. If only men were hawks
       or stones or other instinctive or unfeeling or utterly uncon-
       scionable things, it seems that the universe of Jeffers' imagi-
       nation would be complete in its admirable bleakness.

503 LINN, Robert. "Robinson Jeffers and William Faulkner," in
       American Spectator Year Book, November, 1934. Edited by
       George Jean Nathan. N.Y.: Stokes, 1934. Pp. 304-307.

504 LIPSON, Benjamin H. "Robinson Jeffers and the Paradox of
       Humanism." Masters Thesis, Columbia University, 1951.

505 LITTLEJOHN, David. "Cassandra Grown Tired." Commonweal,
       77 (December 7, 1962), 276-278.
       Reprinted in Littlejohn, Interruptions (1970), discussed
       below.

506 _____. Interruptions. New York: Grossman Publishers,
       1970. Jeffers, pp. 109-113.
       Comments on Jeffers' death, which occurred early in 1962,
       and continues with a brief review of the poet's career. "Even
       to the tiny world that pays attention to poets, Jeffers had
       been dead for years. Critics who had hailed him twenty or
       thirty years ago had nothing to say when Jeffers died. They
       had perhaps changed their minds." Jeffers, however, has

been forgotten not so much by the style he chose as by what
he had to say: Man is vile and valueless, a chance bit of
cosmic dust caught between spectral epochs. Soon he will be
dissolved and scattered again so that primeval Beauty can
reign, eternally undisfigured by his excremental acts....
The shock of this message may have helped assure him an
audience on first appearance, but Jeffers said the same things
over and over, from one generation to another, no new paths
were taken, no change, no self-renewal occurred. This has
probably been one of the most devastating causes of Jeffers'
own "perishing."

507 LOCKARD, E. N. "A Visit to Robinson Jeffers in 1945." Eng-
     lish Language Notes, 12 (December, 1974), 120-123.
          Brief article is based upon an experience the author and
     a friend had in June 1945. At the time they were stationed
     at Monterey, where they and other officers were being trained
     in military government for the occupation of Japan. On this
     occasion Jeffers was hospitable and showed the soliders about
     his house and "hawk tower," both of which Jeffers had built
     himself out of stones from the region. The soliders were im-
     pressed and in turn asked Jeffers to come see them in Mon-
     terey and have lunch. He said he would like to. They left
     happy and looking forward to a further visit. In the mean-
     time came August of that year, and the atomic bomb suddenly
     ended the war in Japan. They left without any further oppor-
     tunity to return to Tor House or invite Jeffers to visit them.

508 LOGGINS, V. I Hear America ... Literature in the United
     States Since 1900. New York: Crowell, 1937. "Questioning
     Despair," pp. 33-70, refers to Jeffers.
          No image appears more frequently in Jeffers' poetry than
     cold, indifferent, beautiful granite. It is a symbol for philo-
     sophic detachment, for the peace of death, for the scientist's
     God. The hawk, usually standing for man's restless, praying
     energy is also a favorite image. Jeffers is the supreme mod-
     ern poet of despair. He has said the last word on pessimism
     as the twentieth century feels it. Jeffers' utterances are like
     the wailings of violent winds sweeping upon land from the
     sea. There can be heard in them also the mustering cry for
     rebellion. Jeffers is a Titan as well as a "tower beyond
     tragedy."

509 LOVING, Pierre. "An American Poet." Paris Times, September
     4, 1927.

510 LUCCOCK, Halford E. Contemporary American Literature and
     Religion. Chicago: Willett, Clark, 1934. Jeffers, p. 28 et
     passim.
          Of far-reaching moral influence has been the effect of
     Freud on the idea of sin. Freud says that the most bitter

blow to human vanity is "the discovery by the psychoanalysts
that the ego is not master in his own house." Similar expres-
sions of determinism have led to the substitution, by many,
of environmental conditions and influences for moral choices
as the source of evil. The result has been the weakening of
the sense of moral responsibility and the feeling of guilt.
This has filtered down into the thinking of many who have
never been directly influenced by the new psychology....
Among such American authors is Robinson Jeffers.

511 LUDWIG, Richard M., ed. Aspects of American Poetry: Essays
Presented to Howard Mumford Jones. Columbus: Ohio State
University Press, 1962. Jeffers, passim.
    Does not discuss Jeffers; is referred to in essay on Robert
Frost, pp. 121, etc.

512 LUHAN, Mabel Dodge. Lorenzo in Taos. New York: Knopf,
1932.
    Addressed to Jeffers, it explains Mrs. Luhan's disappoint-
ment in D. H. Lawrence and why she hopes Jeffers will become the great creative spirit of Taos.

513 _____. Una and Robin, edited with a Foreword by Mark
Schorer. Berkeley: Friends of the Bancroft Library, 1976.
36-page booklet. Review by Robert Brophy, Robinson Jeffers
Newsletter, 46 (September, 1976), 5-6.
    An interesting and useful little work, although it is only
one of the manuscript versions extant. Another longer version is still restricted at Yale. On three counts it is unique:
its insights about Una's first husband, the vivid sense of the
daily routine at Tor House, and its analysis of Una's forma-
tive relationship with Jeffers.

514 LYMAN, W. W. "Robinson Jeffers: A Memoir." Robinson Jeffers Newsletter, 34 (February, 1973), 19-24.
    Article begins in 1924 when the author and his wife rented
a house in Carmel for three months. For the next five or six
years they saw little of the Jeffers family, but for twenty
years after 1931 they saw a good deal of them. Feels that a
great deal is misunderstood about Jeffers, and that some of
his dominant characteristics served as defense mechanism.
Una Jeffers was not seen as a stimulating personality, but it
seemed her function to keep things running smoothly for her
husband. Article is accompanied by the facsimile of a letter
which Jeffers wrote to Lyman in 1934.

515 LYON, Horace D. "Jeffers as a Subject for Horace Lyon's
'Camera.'" Robinson Jeffers Newsletter, 18 (June, 1967),
2-5.
    Article is a recollection by the photographer of the years
1936 to early 1938 during which time he took a remarkable set

of pictures of the Jeffers family and the Jeffers country, intended for publication. Jeffers wrote a Foreword, but the
book was never published. In this informal essay "an invaluable and sensitively understanding portrait of Jeffers" emerges.

516 _____, photographer. Jeffers Country: The Seed Plots of
Robinson Jeffers' Poetry. Poetry by Jeffers; photographs by
Horace Lyon. San Francisco: Scrimshaw Press, 1971.
    Review by Robert Brophy, Robinson Jeffers Newsletter,
30 (January, 1972), 9-10. This is the long-awaited volume
of the Carmel-Big Sur photographs selected in the 1930's for
the purpose of relating the poet's work to the landscape from
which it grew. A Foreword gives the history of the project
from its inception to its completion, nearly forty years later.
The book contains forty photos, thirty related to passages of
poems. The frontispiece is a full length photo of Jeffers.
The photographs are in black and white, capturing the essential ruggedness and violence of the coast.

517 _____. "The Little People of Santa Lucias." Robinson Jeffers
Newsletter, 48 (March, 1977), 7-9. Article has been reprinted
from The Echoes, May 1966: Words, Words, Words, A Literary Supplement.
    Article is valuable for biographical information on Robinson
and Una Jeffers, their friendship, and the role this famous
photographer played in their lives.

518 LYON, Thomas J. "Western Poetry." Journal of the West, 19
(January, 1980), 45-53.

519 McALLISTER, Mick. "Meaning and Paradox in Jeffers' 'Return.'"
Robinson Jeffers Newsletter, 42 (December, 1975), 12-15.
    Refers to a sonnet which is one of Jeffers' most successful
workings of the rock-hawk polarity central to his thought.
In this poem Jeffers makes a statement about the duality and
essential unity of man and the natural world. We must return
to that world, reexperience it, to free ourselves from our
crippling obsession with the life of the mind. Article is a
close examination of the imagery and structure of the poem,
to illustrate the relationship of language and meaning in the
poem. The irony or paradox resides in the fact that although
the poem urges a release from "the life of the mind," it is
only through contemplation or the process of thought that
the poem has meaning.

520 MacDONALD, E. Dwight. "Robinson Jeffers," Parts I and II.
Miscellany, 1 (August and September, 1930), 1-10, 1-24.
    "Alone among his contemporaries has Jeffers written poetry
to which the adjective great can at times be applied. Not

only is he the most brilliant master of verse among contemporaries, but his is the broadest and most powerful personality. The elevation of style, the dignity without pomposity, the grandeur without bombast, is not more than the reflection of a corresponding moral and intellectual elevation in the author."

521   _____. "Robinson Jeffers' New Work a Moving Search for Peace." Philadelphia Record, March 27, 1932.
        Review of Thurso's Landing, etc.

522 McGINTY, Brian. "The View from Hawk's Tower: Poet Robinson Jeffers and the Rugged Coast That Shaped Him." American West, 10 (1973), 4-9.
        Article is illustrated with several impressive photographs of Jeffers and his Carmel coastline. Writing is descriptive not critical. Ten years have passed since Jeffers' death, but the walls of Tor House and Hawk Tower, built by the poet, still stand on their rocky knoll. From the road above the house, the tower seems almost to float on the sea. The appearance is deceptive, for its walls are firmly anchored in bedrock. The house in which the poet lived for nearly fifty years sits quietly in the shadows of the tower and a dense growth of eucalyptus and Monterey cypress. Modern homes have crowded near the place in the decade since Jeffers' death, but the stones he laid have not changed, and their cool, gray strength still casts a spell over Carmel Point.

523 McHANEY, Thomas L. "Robinson Jeffers, 'Tamar' and The Sound and the Fury." Mississippi Quarterly, 22 (Summer, 1969), 261-263.
        A prime analogue for the incest theme, which Faulkner used in several novels, is the story of Absalom and Tamar, the children of David. Faulkner's source is not only the version in II Samuel, however, but also Jeffers' long poem "Tamar." He drew from it especially for The Sound and the Fury. He also used it again in Absalom! Absalom! and in The Wild Palms.

524   _____. "Jeffers' 'Tamar' and Faulkner's The Wild Palms." Robinson Jeffers Newsletter, 29 (August, 1971), 16-18.
        Article is a continuation of study above. Jeffers' poem certainly provided themes, images, and phrases of dialogue for the two earlier novels, and it may have inspired several scenes of The Wild Palms. In the context of this last novel, it may also have suggested an elaboration of his theme of endurance. The similarities of the two works center mainly about the characters of the women and in the manner with which they meet their ultimately tragic ends.

525 MACKSEY, Richard A. "The Old Poets." Johns Hopkins Magazine, 19 (1968), 42-48.

Does not discuss Jeffers but mentions him as one of "the old poets" in an age when all emphasis is on youth. Also includes a good picture of Jeffers sitting at a table looking out over the Bay. Article mostly discusses William Carlos Williams and Wallace Stevens.

526 McMURTRIE, B. "Review of The Women at Point Sur." Pittsburgh Press, December 17, 1927.

527 McWILLIAMS, Carey. "When the Big Boys Were Small." San Franciscan, 3 (January, 1929), 31-32.

528 _____. "Robinson Jeffers: An Antitoxin." Los Angeles Saturday Night, 9 (August 3, 1929), 5.

529 _____. The New Regionalism in American Literature. Seattle: University of Washington Book Store, 1930. Jeffers, pp. 20-27.
      Does not discuss Jeffers except to say he is not at all similar to most writers who would be listed as "Middle to Far West." In fact this author thinks that most generalizations about regional writers are inaccurate, particularly of the greater writers.

530 _____. "Review of Dear Judas and Other Poems." Los Angeles Saturday Night, 10 (January 25, 1930), 16.

531 MACY, John, ed. American Writers on American Literature. New York: Horace Liveright, 1931. "Literature on the Pacific Coast," by Charles Caldwell Dobie, pp. 414-425.
      From San Francisco's literary Bohemia sprang the Carmel colony. There was a great deal in the Carmel tradition that was empty sound and fury, but much that was fine sprang from it. George Sterling became one of the strongest assets, to be succeeded by Robinson Jeffers.
      If the Pacific Coast in the future achieves a striking literature it will be in the drama. All of Jeffers' narrative poems are drama in their essence--even the term Greek has been applied to them. Jeffers relies on exaggerated force. Tides, headlands, elemental rocks, are hurled upon each other, while Jeffers, treading the vicious circle like a tragic Greek chorus, sings an endless Dies Irae. Superficially, Jeffers' pessimism seems to possess the enduring strength to which it is dedicated. When it fails, it fails on no mean level; its aim is of the highest. Though his works are indubitably poetic, they miss the deepest element of major poetry. They have force, but they lack final power; they have force in lieu of a faith.

532 MANLY, J. M. and Edith Rickert. Contemporary American Literature. New York: Harcourt, Brace, 1929. Pp. 204-205, Guide to reading Jeffers' poetry.

533 MARCHAND, L. A. "Robinson Jeffers: Poet Extraordinary."
     Manuscript (MS), 3 (October, 1931), 3, 9.

534 _____. "A Viewpoint on Jeffers." Carmelite, 4 (November
     19, 1931), 11.

535 MARKHAM, Edwin, ed. The Book of Poetry, 2 vols. New York:
     William H. Wise, 1927. Jeffers, Vol. I, pp. 705-706.

536 _____, ed. Songs and Stories. Los Angeles: Powell Publish-
     ing Co., 1931. Jeffers, p. 395.

537 MARONE, F. B. "The Freedom of Purity." San Francisco Wasp,
     March 27, 1926.
          Review of Roan Stallion, etc.

537a MARY NORMA, SISTER. "The Many Faces of Medea." Classi-
     cal Bulletin, 45 (December, 1968), 17-20.
          Reviews some of the compositions which have been based
     on the Jason and Medea story, beginning with Euripides,
     followed by Ovid and Seneca. In the eighteenth century the
     French dramatist Corneille wrote Médée. Within the last cen-
     tury three modern versions of the story have appeared: by
     William Morris, T. Sturge Moore, and Maxwell Anderson in
     the play The Wingless Victory. Jean Anouilh and Robinson
     Jeffers created stories which more closely resemble the classi-
     cal tragedies. In Jeffers' work, sex and lust are the chief
     motivations, closely linked with the urge to kill. This woman
     is so obsessed by jealousy and a fear of rejection that she
     passes from the normal world into the regions of insanity.

538 MASTERS, Edgar Lee. "The Poetry Revival of 1914." American
     Mercury, 26 (July, 1932), 272-280.
          He brought out Tamar in 1924.... If the latter was not
     a carry-on of the 1914 Revival, there was no Revival. In
     Jeffers' book of that year he abandoned rhymes and old
     forms, in which he had had much practice, and adopted a
     long rhythmical line of great beauty, and one which is organ-
     ically suited to his genius.... As time goes on the difference
     between 1914 and 1924 will lessen as the parallax draws to-
     gether. But in a deeper sense than that, Jeffers belongs to
     the Revival of 1914. He has great imagination, motivated by
     a thinking mind of subtlety, courage, and power. Being still
     in the heyday of his creativeness, the success to which he
     may go is beyond prediction.

539 MAUTHE, Andrew K. "The Significance of Point Lobos in
     'Tamar.'" Robinson Jeffers Newsletter, 25 (February, 1970),
     8-10.
          Like Egdon Heath in Hardy's novel, Point Lobos functions
     as more than merely a fitting place to set a story already

conceived. In the Foreword to his Selected Poetry, Jeffers
credits this particular place with being one of the main inspi-
rations for the poem, the strange, introverted and storm-
twisted beauty of Point Lobos. This beauty pervades the
entire poem and influences the action and the characters.
The Point functions symbolically as the permanence against
which the insignificance and transience of human affairs may
be contrasted, though, in a larger sense, even this permanence is somewhat diminished by comparison to the ultimate
cycle of the universe that it symbolizes.

540 _____. "Jeffers' Inhumanism and Its Poetic Significance."
Robinson Jeffers Newsletter, 26 (July, 1970), 8-10.
   The doctrine of "Inhumanism" that underlies Jeffers' poetry
is based upon the belief that the universe is organized around
an inevitable cyclical process. This process, a kind of cosmic law of conservation of matter, moves endlessly through
the life, death, and renewal of all forms of existence. In
terms of this process, man's relationship to the cosmos is
similar to that of any other particle of matter, except that
it is possible for him to go "beyond tragedy." In either role,
however, man can never be the center of the universe; unless
he is able to transcend the human milieu, as Orestes does in
The Tower Beyond Tragedy, man must act out his own part
within the limitations of the larger process.

541 MAYFIELD, John S. "Robinson Jeffers Receives a Convert."
Overland Monthly, 86 (August, 1928), 279-280..

542 MAZZARO, Jerome, ed. Modern American Poetry. New York:
David McKay Company, 1970. Reprints "A Sovereign Voice:
The Poetry of Robinson Jeffers," pp. 183-203, by Robert
Boyers (see under Boyers).

543 MENCKEN, H. L. "Books of Verse." American Mercury, 8
(June, 1926), 251-254.
   Review of Roan Stallion, etc. Makes a list of some sixty
volumes of verse and says: "I offer this appalling list as
proof beyond cavil that the art and mystery of the poet still
flourishes among us, despite Coolidgism and Rotary, despite
even the collapse of the New Poetry Movement." Among his
listing is Roan Stallion, Tamar, and Other Poems by Robinson
Jeffers, of which he says: "Something of first-hand air is in
the book, though the actual matter lies far from the poet's
own experience. There is a fine and stately dignity in him,
and the rare virtue of simplicity. His publishers announce
that twenty years of striving lie behind him. Now that success has come to him at last, it seems to be solid and prom-
ises to be enduring."

544 _____. "Market Report: Poetry." American Mercury, 24
(October, 1931), 151-153.

"The poets of America, like the farmers, are suffering
from hard times, but it is not because of a dull market: their
trouble is that they seem to be unable to make a crop. Fif-
teen or so years ago they did a very brisk business, and
scarcely a month went by without a new one horning into it
to great applause.... Since Robinson Jeffers I can recall
but one debutant who has really got any serious notice: to
wit, Hart Crane."

545 MESSER, Richard. "Jeffers' Inhumanism: A Vision of the Self,"
in Essays on California Writers, edited by Charles L. Crow.
Bowling Green, Ky.: Bowling Green University Press, 1978.
Pp. 11-19.
At first glance Inhumanism does not sound like an affirmation of human existence, and many of Jeffers' critics see it
as nihilistic at worst and somewhat noble but joyless stoicism
at best. Yet if one examines the doctrine closely and in con-
junction with the insights provided by depth psychology concerning the nature of the self, Inhumanism can be seen as
profoundly positive. Simply defined, it is a bitter protest
against mankind's narcissism. It contends that man's misery
stems mainly from his obsessive preoccupation with his own
emotions. It demands that the inward gaze of the Christian
Humanist tradition be redirected to Nature, to processes outside the Self.

546 MILLER, Benjamin T. "Toward a Religious Philosophy of the
Theatre." Personalist, 20 (October, 1939), 361-376.
Article is based upon the premise that the theatre is essentially religious in its origin and in its high function as a
distinctive human expression which persists hopefully in the
midst of a crisis of culture and passes into the fully conscious,
individual mystical recognition of the religious experience....
Several poet-dramatists are discussed--Maxwell Anderson,
Conrad Aiken, Robinson Jeffers. In the foreward to his
Selected Poetry, Jeffers says: "poetry is bound to concern
itself with permanent aspects of life. This excludes much of
the circumstance of modern life; they exist but will never
exist again. The permanent has poetic value; the ephemeral
has only news value."

547 _____. "A Study in Aesthetic Naturalism." Masters Thesis,
Pacific School of Religion, 1938.

548 _____. "Review of Be Angry at the Sun." Chrisitan Century,
59 (June 3, 1942), 729.
In this ninth volume Jeffers has written what will in all
probability stand as the strongest and most profound verses
to come out of this war. With extraordinary sensibility to
poetic tragedy and with the paradoxical strength of a passionate disinterestedness, he allows the monstrous decay and

violence of these times to speak themselves out and refuses
to have any part in them, except to christen each poem, in
dutiful hope of burning off at least the top layer of the
time's uncleanness.

549 MILLETT, Fred B. Contemporary American Authors: A Critical
     Survey and 219 Biographies and Bibliographies. New York:
     Harcourt, 1940. Jeffers, pp. 149-150; 406-409.
        To Jeffers, modern man and his works are, without equiv-
     ocation, abominable, and the thing most worthy of admiration
     is the unconsciousness of nature. Such views underlie most
     of the narrative and lyrical writing of Jeffers.... His tech-
     nical powers, however, are impressive. No other American
     poet of our time is his equal in imaginative magnitude or emo-
     tional violence. But most of the time Jeffers' poetry is over-
     violent; the coloring is barbaric, and the giant figures are
     discovered to be facades of hollow plaster and not of marble.
     Courageous as Jeffers is, the solution he proposes is as neu-
     rotic as the characters that deserve it.
        Article concludes with biographical sketch and a short
     bibliography of articles and studies.

550 MILOSZ, Czeslaw. "To Robinson Jeffers." Kult, 192 (October,
     1963), 21-24. Reprinted in Robinson Jeffers Newsletter, 58
     (May, 1981), 16-17.
        Free-verse adaptation of a tribute to Jeffers. Author was
     Nobel Prize recipient for Literature in 1980. Poem is stream-
     of-consciousness imagery, all of which, in one way or another,
     relates to Jeffers' life or his poetry.

551 MINER, Priscilla. "A Note on Literary Influences of The Alpine
     Christ." Robinson Jeffers Newsletter, 40 (January, 1974),
     3-4.
        Article consists of less than a page, with listing of parts
     of Goethe's Faust (original in German and Bayard Taylor
     translation), which directly or indirectly influenced Jeffers
     in his composition The Alpine Christ. These passages are
     found in Part I, Prologue in Heaven; Part II, Act IV, cho-
     ruses with generals, etc.; and Part III, Act V, Scene vii,
     mountain scenery, dead spirits, deities, etc.
        It is known that Jeffers studied the work, and the author
     thinks that "part of the plot and a little of the text could
     stem from that early period."

552 MINOT, J. C. "Review of The Women at Point Sur." Boston
     Herald, July 13, 1927.

553 MINSHALL, Herb, edited with illustrations. Yonder the Sea:
     An Anthology of Sea Prose and Poetry. San Diego: Sea
     World Incorporated, 1973. Jeffers, pp. 19, 99.
        Prints two poems by Jeffers, "Continent's End, "opposite

a full-page illustration of a lone observer by the shore, and "Evening Ebb."

554 MIURA, Tokuhiro. "Ideas and Symbols in 'Give Your Heart to the Hawks.'" Studies in English Literature, 8 (1965), 109-128. (Printed by the English Society of Hosei University, Tokyo.)

555 _____. "A Vision in Robinson Jeffers' 'Tamar.'" Kiyo 11 (April, 1967), 115-129. (Printed by Research Journal, School of Liberal Arts, Hosei University, Tokyo.)

556 _____. "Poetics of Robinson Jeffers: Disclaimer of Modernism." Bungaku-bu-Kiyo, 23 (September, 1977), 1-29. In Japanese; abstract in English. (Printed at Hosei University, Tokyo.)

557 MOLL, Ernest G. "Poet in Stone," and "Builder of Tor House." Robinson Jeffers Newsletter, 17 (April, 1967), 2-3.
Two poems dedicated to the memory of Jeffers.

558 MONJIAN, Mercedes Cunningham. Robinson Jeffers: A Study in Inhumanism. Pittsburgh: University of Pittsburgh Press, 1958.
Consists of 103 pages, with short bibliography. In three chapters: The Philosopher-Poet; The Poet-Philosopher; and The Achievement.
"Inhumanism" has nothing to do with "inhumanity." Jeffers' inhumanism would deny man's interests and development, "subduing them in the interests of something greater--or a shifting of emphasis and significance from Man to Not-Man." Man is contrasted against the magnificent beauty and immense worth in the natural world. These are the basic principles on which Jeffers' philosophy is founded.

559 _____. "Robinson Jeffers: A Study in Inhumanism." Masters Thesis, University of Pittsburgh, 1958.

560 MONROE, Harriet. "Power and Pomp." Poetry, 28 (January, 1926), 160-164.
Review of Roan Stallion, Tamar, etc. Refers to the review of this book by Mr. James Daly (Poetry, August 1925) and thinks there is no need for another exhaustive review. Mentions "the revolting subject" of the title poem and hopes that Jeffers has gone as far as he will in a direction so repellent to modern taste. Most of this article discusses "The Tower Beyond Tragedy" and Jeffers' relationship to the Greeks. Jeffers' version of the Clytemnestra story has passages of splendid eloquence, and, while too expansive, is done in huge pounding rhythms like the Pacific at Carmel.

Remarks on several of the shorter poems, which she considers in many respects superior to the longer ones. For instance, "Shine, Perishing Republic" is of immediate interest, and representative of his art not in the grand manner.

561 _____, and Alice Corbin Henderson, eds. The New Poetry. New York: Macmillan, 1932. Jeffers, pp. 719-720.
Jeffers was not represented in earlier editions of this work, 1917, 1923, 1925.

562 MOORE, Virginia. "Two Books." Voices, 5 (November, 1925), 70-72.
Review of Tamar, etc., and Continent's End.

563 MORE, Paul Elmer. "A Revival of Humanism." Bookman, 71 (March, 1930), 1-11.
A review of Humanism and America, edited by Norman Foerster (New York: Farrar & Rinehart, 1930). Does not discuss Jeffers but does deal with "The Dilemma of Modern Tragedy" by Alan Reynolds Thompson, which treats of problems in the tragic narratives of Robinson Jeffers. Article by Thompson is favorably regarded by reviewer. "Though concerned primarily with tragedy, may be extended to the whole range of literature."

564 MORRIS, Lawrence S. "Robinson Jeffers: The Tragedy of a Modern Mystic." New Republic, 54 (May 16, 1928), 386-390.
Points out that Jeffers has published three books of poetry of such intensity, passion, and scope of thought that American readers have not yet been able to assimilate them, nor even to realize with any precision their intent. Sometimes his meanings are thought to be obscure. His questions are those which concern all men of thought, all men who have a craving for truth. For the most part, men give up the search, knowing truth cannot be found, but occasionally there are those like Jeffers who refuse to be distracted. Ultimately Jeffers resolves his dilemma by seeking a philosophy of oblivion, utter annihilation in the peace of death.

565 MORRISON, Theodore. "A Critic and Four Poets." Atlantic, 145 (February, 1930), 24-26.
Review of Roan Stallion, and Dear Judas.

566 _____. "Review of Thurso's Landing and Other Poems." Atlantic Bookshelf, September 1932.
Often enough in this work Jeffers reveals the force and vitality of the pure poet; and sometimes, amid the general violence of the story, he reveals the eye and hand of an unusual narrator. But the book is flawed by a central weakness: the degree to which, in story, in temper, in language,

in imagination, it is constructed of purely physical horror
and agony.

567 MORROW, W. A. "Jeffers' Sardonic Smile at Futility of Life Is
     Fanned into Mockery." Daily Oklahoman, October 9, 1927.

568 MOSS, Sidney P. "Robinson Jeffers as a Narrative Poet."
     Masters Thesis, University of Illinois, 1951.

569 _____. "Robinson Jeffers: A Defense." American Book
     Collector, 10 (Summer, 1959), 8-14.
          At the moment, Jeffers' reputation seems to be the most
     precarious of any contemporary poet. Critical studies, books,
     and articles are few and far between, and critics seem to be
     performing a post-mortem study rather than analyzing a living
     body of poetry. Article examines the question of why Jeffers'
     fame has declined almost as meteorically as it arose. Thinks
     the major reason lies in his attitude toward humanity. Thinks
     the fault also lies with the anthologies, which nearly always
     misrepresent Jeffers with excerpts and pieces that are not
     truly a cross-section.

570 MUNSON, Gorham B. "The Young Critics of the Nineteen-
     Twenties." Bookman, 70 (December, 1929), 369-373.
          Points up that no one need argue that fresh impulses did
     arise in American literary life during the 1920's, and cites
     numerous critical works to prove it. These critics, however,
     did not find themselves more quickly, blossom, and rearrange
     their literary scene all within a few years. As a matter of
     fact by the end of the decade there does not appear a very
     sharp demarcation between the young, younger, and older
     critics. Perhaps one of the chief differences in criticism of
     this period was not the age of the critics but rather the
     authors they wrote about: Sherwood Anderson, Upton Sinclair
     Robinson Jeffers, etc.

571 NADEL, Barbara S. "The Religious Vision of Robinson Jeffers:
     The Human Problem and the Transhuman Solution." Ph.D.
     diss., University of Chicago (Divinity School), 1976.

572 _____. "Robinson Jeffers' 'Cawdor': The Emergence of Man's
     Tragic Beauty." Journal of the American Academy of Religion,
     (1976).

573 NATHAN, George Jean. Theatre Book of the Year, 1947-1948.
     New York: Knopf, 1948. Jeffers, pp. 77-80; 104-112.
          Review of two dramatic presentations based on works by
     Jeffers. Dear Judas, October 5, 1947, is a dramatization by
     Michael Myerberg with music by Johann Sebastian Bach. It
     had 16 performances at the Mansfield Theatre. Nathan says:

"This suffers from the pox as seriously as have most exhibits of the species. Nor is the play, which views Judas in a more favorable light than the traditional, of sufficient strength to triumph over the gloom imposed upon it. High resolve has gone into it, but the script has been wobbled as theatre by the frequent imposition upon it of a misguided, declamatory, and too sanctimonious staging and directing. Much more simply presented, it would still be very far from a good play, but it would be better than it presently is...."

Medea, October 20, 1947, with Judith Anderson in the title role, played at the National Theatre. In this free, godless rendering of the great tragedy Jeffers presented a more than acceptable performance, much superior theatrically to the Gilbert Murray translation. It is an occasion to be recommended to that share of our audiences whose theatrical stimulation is somehow not accomplished by musical sliding platforms. While commending anew the grace of Jeffers' treatment, the drama vouchsafes him opportunity to indulge himself in the grisly, for which he has ever indicated a quenchless fancy.

574 NATHAN, P. S. "Jeffers' Drama Triumphs in Premiere." Oakland Post Enquirer, November 9, 1932.
       Refers to production of "Tower Beyond Tragedy."

575 NATIONAL ENCYCLOPEDIA OF AMERICAN BIOGRAPHY. New York: James T. White Co., 1930. P. 829.

576 NELSON, John Herbert, and Oscar Cargill, eds. Contemporary Trends: American Literature Since 1900. New York: Macmillan, 1949. Jeffers, pp. 442-466.
       Reprints several poems including "Boats in a Fog," "To the Stone Cutters," and selections from Roan Stallion, without biographical or critical comment.

577 NICHOLL, L. T. "New Poetry." Outlook, 153 (November 27, 1929), 509.
       Review of Dear Judas, etc. The title poem "is all flares and shadows and black blood." "The Loving Shepherdess" is like some low, sweet-smelling bush growing everywhere among the rocks and breaking slowly into incredible white flower; but the roots of the two poems are the same: love of every living creature, terrible consuming pity.

578 NICKERSON, Edward A. "Robinson Jeffers, Poet of Apocalypse." Ph.D. diss., State University of New York (Albany), 1973. DA, 34 (1973), 367.
       This study demonstrates that a sense of apocalypse is present all through Jeffers' poetry and that it grows out of his philosophy of Inhumanism and his concept of "discovery" in the universe. This apocalyptic sense--the feeling that a

catastrophic end is near to human life on earth--manifests
itself both in Jeffers' narratives and in his shorter poems.
It appears vividly in the actual events and images of the
poetry, which remind man of his fragility in the natural
world.   It appears in the tone of the poems, in their symbolic statement and in the author's preoccupation with escha-
tology.   It is bound up with his sense of time.   All of these
factors make Jeffers a modern counterpart of the biblical
apocalyptist.

579   .   "Jeffers Scholarly Materials: Yale University Library."
Robinson Jeffers Newsletter, 36 (October, 1973), 11-14.
       Makes a thorough survey of materials at Yale and for the
most part limits himself to listing them.   There are a few
comments, however.   For instance there is information on
Jeffers' well-known habit of conserving paper.   In addition
to the manuscript collections, Yale also has a number of hard-
to-find editions of Jeffers, both of individual poems and collections.   There is also a large collection of letters from Una
Jeffers to friends.   Most of the unpublished material is not
now available for inspection.   List of manuscripts includes
those "in manuscript only," "in manuscript and typescript,"
"in typescript only," "in galley and page proofs with manuscript corrections."

580   .   "The Return of Rhyme."   Robinson Jeffers Newsletter,
39 (July, 1974), 12-21.
       Some time between the end of World War I and the writing
of "Tamar" in 1922 or 1923, Jeffers eliminated rhyme from his
narratives and from all of his lyrics except a few sonnets
and one twelve-line poem.   He vowed to "shear the rhyme-
tassels from verse," and, many years later, in one of his
last poems, he dismissed rhyme as "tinkling sheep-bells and
a child's game."   With this in mind, it is curious that during
a short period around the beginning of World War II, in six
poems of moderate to substantial length, he put the tassels
back on.   The poems, published in 1941 in Be Angry at the
Sun, have a broad range.   Article continues with analysis
and discussion of each poem, to show the range of rhyming
techniques and to show that his mastery had broadened.
Poems are a partial answer to those who have charged that
all Jeffers could do well was to create heavy-handed dramatic
effects.

581   .   "An Unpublished Poem by Robinson Jeffers."   Yale
University Library Gazette, 49 (October, 1974), 231-233.
       Refers to a poem entitled "Red as I Wouldn't Have You
Red: Una to Langston," written by Jeffers for his wife to
present to Langston Hughes on his 38th birthday.   It consists of three stanzas of four lines each and is pure doggerel
humor.   It was found in a letter from Una to Mr. and Mrs.
Mortimer Clapp, in the Yale Jeffers Collections.

582 _____. "Jeffers Scholarly Materials: Library of Congress."
Robinson Jeffers Newsletter, 40 (November, 1974), 17-20.
    Four folders of materials were given by Una and Robinson
in memory of Albert M. Bender, July 15, 1941. These folders
include the following:

> The original draft of Jeffers' talk at the Library of Con-
>   gress, February 28, 1941.
> Manuscript of a discarded fraft of "Cawdor," in pencil,
>   76 pages.
> Photostats of 20 letters of Jeffers to Sterling (originals
>   at University of California, Berkeley).
> A photograph of George Sterling.
> Also, in papers of W. Orton Tewson (119 items), letter
>   by Jeffers on subject of the critics.

583 _____. "The Una Jeffers Correspondence at Yale: Letters
to the Clapps, Letters to Mabel Dodge Luhan." Robinson
Jeffers Newsletter, 41 (March, 1975), 6-10.
    Article not only lists materials but undertakes to discuss
the personalities of the recipients of these letters. No two
correspondents could be more different. The letters to the
Clapps number 101, from 1927 to 1946, plus numerous miscellaneous clippings and enclosures. There are 150 letters to
Mabel Dodge between 1930 and 1948.

584 _____. "Robinson Jeffers and the Paeon." Western American
Literature, 10 (November, 1975), 189-193.
    In 1942, Brewster Ghiselin concluded that Jeffers' verse
was "rich in paeons" but did not suggest that Jeffers was
using these quadrisyllabic measures consciously. Instead he
speculated that the poet may have scanned his lines in some
more conventional manner. But one of Jeffers' manuscripts
in the Yale Library clearly shows that he was consciously
trying out the ancient Greek paeonic foot. Whether he ever
thought of the foot by this name is unknown, but it is quite
possible that he did, for he knew the classics well and trans-
lated plays from the Greek. The manuscript contains notes
for Tamar in one section, and drafts or fragments of shorter
poems in other parts.

585 _____. "The Holy Light of Jeffers' Poetry." Robinson Jeffers
Newsletter, 47 (December, 1976), 19-28.
    Light, in its many forms, has been a primary symbol of
divinity in the religions of mankind, and so it was with Robinson Jeffers. Hawks, rock, the sea, and other natural things
manifest various aspects of God in his poetry and are often
the subjects of purposely symbolic treatment. While Jeffers
did not treat light in itself with the deliberation with which
he used hawks and rock, it was a central image in the expression of the idea of "discovery," his preferred term for

the dynamic struggle of birth, growth, decay, death, and
rebirth in the universe, eternally yielding new life and new
kinds of life. This act of discovering or uncovering implies
the act of letting light fall on previously hidden forms, a
kind of continuous revelation. The ongoing dynamism which
makes this "lightening" happen is essentially violent--whether
it be dry leaves crackling into flame or wet ones disintegrating into mold. It is also beautiful and divine. Thus, light
epitomizes a whole complex of redemptive values in Jeffers'
poetry.

586 _____. "Robinson Jeffers: Apocalypse and His 'Inevitable
Place.'" Western American Literature, 12 (July, 1977),
112-122.
Even a casual reading leads one to conclude that much of
Jeffers' poetry is profoundly apocalyptic. Fires, deluges,
storms, and earthquakes menace the lives of his major characters and serve as constant reminders of nature's catastrophic potential. There are forebodings of Armageddon and gloomy
speculations about man's fate. A number of narratives result
in the destruction of a small group of people in such a way
as to suggest that they symbolize the human race itself....
The biblical writers, like Jeffers, fixed their gaze on the
coming doom and on the glorious new heaven and earth that
would succeed it. Jeffers looked beyond humanity to find
redemptive splendor. He, too, sought not to reform but only
to write down his gloomy visions. Article continues with analysis of the geographical area in which Jeffers lived, an area
all too familiar with the apocalyptic agents of destruction,
fire, earthquake, wind, and rain, and concludes that it was
this region which largely defined Jeffers' outlook.

587 _____. "A Structure of Opposites." Robinson Jeffers Newsletter, 62 (January, 1983), 6-8.
Begins with a review of the 1950's when the so-called New
Critics made a fetish out of "patterns of opposites in ideas
or actions, and in the very language which expressed these
things." This quality was not often associated with Jeffers,
yet it is present in most of his works. This article takes a
12-line poem, "The Place for No Story," by Jeffers, and does
a line by line examination in terms of patterns of paradox,
opposites, or the element of struggle in Jeffers' poetry.

588 NIMS, J. F. "Greater Grandeur," in Poetry: A Critical Supplement, October 1947. Pp. 5-6.
Explication of Jeffers' poem "Greater Grandeur," which
appeared in the October 1947 issue of Poetry.

589 NOLTE, William H. "Robinson Jeffers as Didactic Poet." Virginia Quarterly Review, 42 (Spring, 1966), 257-271.

It has always been true that the great poet concerns himself with subjects of lasting importance, or universal meaning,
just as it has been necessary for him to interpret his materials from some philosophical viewpoint. Of all major modern
poets, Jeffers came closest to expressing himself in a uniquely
singular style. After his youthful period, he did not embrace
any philosophical or political system, but he persisted in the
belief that man is essentially irrational. In his philosophy of
"Inhumanism" he shifted the emphasis from man to not-man
and rejected the masses of humanity. There can be no doubt,
however, about his concern for the species. If Jeffers found
little in man's confusion to warrant praise, he did increase
our powers of perception; and his stoicism will always befriend
us in the dark days when they come.

590   _____. "Jeffers' 'Fog' and the Gulls in It." Robinson Jeffers
        Newsletter, 16 (December, 1966), 2-5.
        The title of the poem tells us something of the poem's
        meaning. The gulls cry to us from the fog--that is, from
        the realm of illusion and from self-delusion and egocentric
        vanity. The gulls are both the scavengers of earth and the
        deceived ones, the "gulled" humans, the "Worshippers of one-
        ness" in the last line.... Jeffers was the poet of disillusion.
        Unlike many modern artists who insisted on the need for illu-
        sion in a slippery world, Jeffers exhorted man to act ration-
        ally, to cast out his illusions, to love outward rather than
        inward.

591   _____. The Merrill Guide to Robinson Jeffers. Columbus,
        Ohio: Charles E. Merrill, 1970.
        Consists of 45 pages and, like the other Merrill Guides,
        is an introduction to a significant American author, designed
        to give the beginning student perspective and background.
        Reviews Jeffers' life and publication, with a great many quo-
        tations from the works to illustrate general points. Through-
        out, the author makes some critical evaluation, but this is
        not paramount. Much of what is said is oversimplified, but,
        in such a short work for a limited audience, perhaps this is
        to be expected. It has no index, table of contents, notes,
        etc.

592   _____. "Review of Robinson Jeffers: Poet of Inhumanism,"
        by Arthur Coffin. Choice, 8 (September, 1971), 829-830.

593   _____. "Robinson Jeffers, An Uncanny Prophet." The Alter-
        native: An American Spectator (Bloomington, Indiana), 10
        (May, 1976), 11-15.

594   _____. "Robinson Jeffers Redivivus." Georgia Review, 32
        (1978), 429-434.

Article reviews Jeffers' reputation over a period of about
40 years, from 1924 when he published his first volume to
his death in 1962. His first book "seemed to have been still-
born," but when a new and expanded edition of this work
appeared a year later, "few volumes of poetry in our history
have been greeted with such ecstatic praise from important
critics or have met with such demand by the reading public."
During the remainder of the 1920's and in the 1930's his popularity was at its height (he was even featured on the cover
of Time magazine in April 1932). His popularity declined just
before, during, and after World War II. When he died in
1962 his reputation was probably at its lowest ebb in forty
years; by the mid to late 1960's he was once again in favor,
and the 1970's give every indication that he is undergoing a
renaissance greater "than that of any other modern poet.
His cooling period over, Jeffers now occupies a solid niche
in the pantheon of great poets."

594a   . Rock and Hawk: Robinson Jeffers and the Romantic
Agony. Athens: University of Georgia Press, 1978.
Consists of 212 pages with Notes and Index. In six chapters, including "Introduction" and "Coda." Other chapters
are "The Business of Poetry"; "The Sickness Called Self";
"Breaking Out of Humanity"; and "Meditation on Saviors."
In his best poetry, Jeffers provides us with a world that
is beautifully and sometimes terrifyingly real--or real in the
sense that any artistic creation is real; the world of every
artist is, of course, visionary; the degree of his success is
in proportion to the reader's or viewer's or listener's being
convinced that the "world" is real and has meaning. Certainly
no other American poet has approached him in the ability to
endow character with life; his people, tormented and torment-
ing creatures, haunt the memory like grisly phantoms or spectral shapes rising from some atavistic depth of which we were
unaware. Passing before the mind's eye, they reveal those
gulfs over which we daily pass. In their strengths and weaknesses we see ourselves; they reveal to us, above all else,
how slippery is our hold on reason and how tempting are the
lures of irrationality in all its forms. Which is to say, Jeffers did what all great writers have done: He provided insight into the human condition.
Review of book printed in Robinson Jeffers Newsletter, 53
(June, 1979), 6-8, by Bill Hotchkiss, who thinks it is one of
the most important books ever written about Jeffers: "As a
piece of criticism, the work is free of all the usual academic
side-steppings and obfuscations."

595 NUWER, Henry J. "Jeffers' Influence Upon Walter Van Tilburg
Clark." Robinson Jeffers Newsletter, 44 (March, 1976), 11-17.
The influence of Jeffers on Clark has never been explored
satisfactorily and has even been deprecated by critic Max

Westbrook, author of the Twayne critical study of Clark.
The intent of the present article is to demonstrate that, on
the contrary, Jeffers affected Clark's poetry and fiction to
a significant and measurable degree. Article is based on
Clark's Masters Thesis (1934), which was a study on Robinson Jeffers, Clark's early poetry--most of which was later
refined into prose--and on Clark's fiction which makes much
use of the same Western imagery that attracted Jeffers.
Their resemblances are greatest with regard to use of animals, ritualistic themes, and in the use of sexually primitive
forces. Article concludes with a poem by Clark, written
about 1935, as a tribute to Jeffers. It was published in the
Spring 1974 issue of Brushfire (University of Nevada).

596 _____. "The Influence of Henry Adams and Robinson Jeffers
on Walter Van Tilburg Clark." Ph.D. diss., University of
Nevada, 1976.

597 NYREN, Dorothy, ed. A Library of Literary Criticism. New
York: Frederick Ungar, 1964. Jeffers, pp. 257-261.
Reprints a dozen excerpts from well-known works about
Jeffers, including passages from full-length biographies, re-
views of individual books, and commentary from books on
American poetry in general. Offers a limited but extremely
well-chosen introduction to critical material on Jeffers.

598 O'CONNOR, Willian Van. Sense and Sensibility in Modern Poetry.
Chicago: University of Chicago Press, 1948. Jeffers, pp.
25, 50 et passim.
Jeffers not discussed; is referred to several times in con-
nection with poets whose poetry comes very close to prose.
Also mentioned in chapter "Tension and the Structure in
Poetry," as an example of a writer who maintains little or no
direction and creates a poetry of "impulses."

599 O'DAY, E. F. "George Sterling." San Francisco Water, 7
(July, 1928), 9-12.

600 O'NEILL, George R. "Poetry from Four Men." Outlook, 151
(January 16, 1929), 110-111.
Review of Cawdor, etc. There is no man writing poetry
who in any way strives to say what Jeffers endeavors to say
in his strange powerful narratives; his is not to be measured
against any like effort. His world and his speech are his own,
and if he fails in his powers to take others into that world,
it is not to be wondered at. The depth of his passion and
its turbulence is too great for him, as yet.

601 PARKER, Jean Louise. "Robinson Jeffers: A Study of the
     Phenomena of Human Consciousness." Ph.D. diss., Pennsyl-
     vania State University, 1970. DA, 32 (1971), 927A.
         To Jeffers the beauty of the natural world overshadows
     man's imperfect world, and emulation of the patterns of the
     natural world allows human life to assume meaning. His
     poetry presents an intricate exhibition of these contrasting
     principles. This study investigates the idea that while man
     apart from nature is a source of anxiety for Jeffers, human-
     ity or human consciousness, for he uses the terms inter-
     changeably, could be freed from introspection, could achieve
     a heightened perception of experience, if that consciousness
     were reoriented within the wholeness of the universe. Atten-
     tion is concentrated on several sources of self-consciousness
     which distract man from living within the more perfect con-
     text of nature.

602 PASCOE, Stephen E. "Birth-Dues': An Explication." Robinson
     Jeffers Newsletter, 38 (April, 1965), 6-10.
         Begins by noting that "Birth-Dues," a short lyric, is a
     very personal poem, an expression of the poet's most funda-
     mental attitudes and ideas. It is also a theological poem,
     about God being the reality which so far transcends egotisti-
     cal concerns and is such a basic fact of life, that it can
     never be fought or escaped but only loved. He concludes
     that a loving attitude toward reality, which includes both
     pleasure and pain is the stance which will bring peace in
     life. The title indicates that the "dues" that are the price
     of birth depend on accepting the consciousness of both pleas-
     ure and pain.

603 PAYNE, G. M. "Review of The Women at Point Sur." Cincin-
     nati Times-Star, October 15, 1927.

604 PEEVEY, Ron. "Jeffers and the Tao-te-Ching." Robinson Jef-
     fers Newsletter, 55 (December, 1979), 31-36.
         That Jeffers was familiar with Chinese thought in general
     and the Tao-te-Ching in particular is undeniable, if only by
     virtue of four lines from his poem "Theory of Truth." The
     Tao-te-Ching is a collection of 81 short chapters, usually no
     more than a few lines, setting forth the basic Taoist philoso-
     phy. Tao is the Way of the universe and the tendencies that
     characterize it. To date in excess of 70 translations of the
     Tao-te-Ching have been made and released to the English-
     speaking world. By 1924, the publication date of Tamar and
     Other Poems, 16 of these translations had been circulated.
     Jeffers' interest in religious philosophy as well as the eclectic
     quality of his studies would alone indicate that he was aware
     of the text. However, when a comparison is made between
     his philosophical attitude and certain key elements of the
     Tao-te-Ching, the relationship appears quite strong.

605 PETTINGELL, Phoebe. "Robinson Jeffers Revisited." The New
      Leader, May 22, 1977. Pp. 20-21.
          Written on the occasion of three reprints of his books,
      The Women of Point Sur, Dear Judas, and The Double Axe.
      These three volumes illuminate the philosophy of Inhumanism,
      a transcendence devised to explain the discrepancy between
      a god whose terrible beauty and power is manifest in his
      natural order and a fallen and debased humanity. His poetry
      reveres science as the highest form of worship and one calcu-
      lated to force the race's recognition of its own insignificance.

606 PINCKNEY, Josephine. "Jeffers and MacLeish." Virginia Quar-
      terly Review, 8 (July, 1932), 443-447.
          Review of Thurso's Landing and Other Poems. Reviews
      all the so-called Greek qualities of Jeffers' poetry and yet
      thinks "there is something unsatisfactory in the Greek man-
      ner" in this work. It is something like a skeleton, its bony
      reality easily recognized, but its clothing and other trifles
      missing. On the asset side, however, the metrics of Jeffers
      are distinctive and consistent. At times he makes beautiful
      poetry; at others, good prose, as when his characters are
      analyzing, defining, explaining their motives. He is marvel-
      ously apt at describing action, and the strongest part of his
      contexture is his use of imaginative verbs. They explode all
      through the poem and always effectively.
          Remainder of article is a review of Archibald MacLeish's
      Conquistador, also published in 1932.

607 POLLARD, Lancaster. "Jeffers as Example of Modernism."
      Seattle Post-Intelligencer, August 14, 1927.
          Review of Roan Stallion and The Women at Point Sur.

608 POTTS, Lawrence K. "A Spirit for the Stone: The Crisis of
      Hope in the Short Poems of Robinson Jeffers." Masters
      Thesis, Graduate Theological Union (Berkeley), 1975.

609 POWELL, Lawrence Clark. "Leaves of Grass and Granite Boul-
      ders." Carmelite, 4 (October 22, 1931), 8-9.

610 _____. "An Introduction to Robinson Jeffers." Ph.D. diss.,
      Dijon University (France), 1932. Published, Dijon: Imprim-
      erie Bernigaud and Privat, 1932.

611 _____. Robinson Jeffers: The Man and His Work. Foreword
      by Robinson Jeffers; Decorations by Rockwell Kent. Los
      Angeles: Primavere Press, 1934. Revised edition edited by
      James Hawkins, Pasadena, Calif.: San Pasqual Press, 1940.
      Reprinted New York: Haskell House, 1969.
          Consists of 215 pages with brief bibliography and index.
      In nine chapters: Jeffers on Carmel; Volumes and Contents;
      The Narratives; A Poet's Land; The Lyrics; Some Elements

of Style; A Poet's Universe; Jeffersian Values; and Critical
Conclusions.

In concluding chapter, author seems to express a rather
complete understanding of Jeffers: "Preferring the beautiful
inhuman universe of the stars, sea-granite, hawks and herons,
to humanity, led by his own unsocial nature to dislike and
distrust the thickening social centers, morbidly sensitive to
the pain which flesh is heir to, this poet has faced with frank-
ness and honesty the problem which confronts the man whose
vision leads him beyond humanity, but who is drawn back by
a wish to lend a hand to his fellows, for the most part lost
and blindly groping in a labyrinth of pain and suffering."

612   _____. Alchemy of Books. Los Angeles: Ward Ritchie Press,
       1954. Jeffers, pp. 175-196.

Article is based on a lecture which the author gave to a
class in Narrative Poetry at UCLA, 1949. In general the article is an assessment of Jeffers' poetry and why this critic
has responded to it: "My first and strongest conviction
about Jeffers' greatness is deep and instinctive, yet on ex-
amining my intellectual response to his poetry, I find that my
feelings and my beliefs are not in conflict. The more I think
about and analyze my primary response to Jeffers' verse, the
more I am convinced that it is a sound and lasting one, and
that I have not been carried away by emotional reactions to
the admittedly sensational elements in Jeffers' poetry....
Jeffers is not presently in fashion. The bright young men
of the quarterly reviews have no use for him because he does
not fit into their pre-conceived patterns. Confronted by the
bulk of Jeffers, they are like the blind man describing the
elephant. The timid are shocked by his themes. The ortho-
dox are outraged by his analysis of the origin of religions.
And of course the great majority are simply indifferent to
him."

613   _____. "The Double Marriage of Robinson Jeffers." South-
       west Review, 41 (Summer, 1956), 278-282. Reprinted in
       Books, West Southwest. Los Angeles: Ward Ritchie Press,
       1957. Pp. 110-120.

The double marriage refers to Jeffers' marriage to Una
Jeffers, in 1913, and his marriage to the environment of
Carmel, California, where he built Tor House and lived until
his death. Una Jeffers died in 1950, thus ending a union
which was one of the most creative in all literature. In sum-
mation, Powell says: "His view of mankind and of life developed slowly, ripened gradually, and his work was founded
as true and unswerving as a Roman road; it is strong stuff,
not for babes or shallow optimists--for those who would have
the Oedipus Rex in Technicolor."

614   _____. "Homage to the Big Sur," in Books, West Southwest.

Los Angeles: Ward Ritchie Press, 1957. Pp. 93-100. Jeffers, passim.
  Is not principally about Jeffers but interesting in that it
treats the region to which Jeffers attached himself with so
much admiration and devotion.

615 _____. Books in My Baggage. Cleveland, Ohio: World Publishing Co., 1960. "Making of a Poet," pp. 139-147.
  Essentially the same article as listed above (1956), in
which Powell undertakes to account for the change in Jeffers
from around 1912 to twelve years later. What turned the inward eye from his own emotional preoccupations outward to
the external world of rock and stars and cyclical history?
Thinks two factors entered into the change: Una Jeffers and
a new environment. They were married in 1913 (after six
years of separation while she divorced her first husband),
and they moved to Carmel in 1914. Here he was fired by the
natural poetry around him; he was ready to deal with it, to
transmute one of the most beautiful places on earth into
literature by the alchemy of art. Una Jeffers died in 1950,
thus ending a forty-year union, one of the most creative in
all literature.

616 _____. "Robinson Jeffers." New York Times, 6 (October,
1968), pp. 2, 26.

617 _____. "Melba Berry Bennett." Robinson Jeffers Newsletter,
23 (April, 1969), 1.
  Notice of the death of Mrs. Bennett, which occurred in the
fall of 1968. Her loss is that of a guiding force in scholarship
and interest in Robinson Jeffers, although she had much help
in her endeavors. The Newsletter will now go under new editorship but will seek to continue and enlarge the direction
and scope she gave it.

618 _____. California Classics: The Creative Literature of the
Golden State. Los Angeles: Ward Ritchie Press, 1971.
"Robinson Jeffers: Give Your Heart to the Hawks," pp. 208-
219. Article first appeared in abbreviated form in Westways,
November 1968, pp. 18-21, 58, as part of the series "California Classics Re-read."
  Reviews the life and works of Jeffers against the background of the country in which the poet lived and wrote his
books. Article is most impressive for its description and analysis of the environment around Carmel. In conclusion he
says: "Time and again I have returned to that enchanged
coast.... His poetry is moving wherever it is read, but
read there in the setting which it exalts, it is supremely so.
However high his soaring vision takes us--and fifty years
ago Jeffers foresaw our colonization in outer space--his poetry
remains rooted in earth. He viewed the coast and the mountains with the eyes of a scientist. His work can be read with

joyful recognition by botanist, ornithologist, geologist, mete-
orologist, and astronomer. Flowers and trees, birds, rocks,
weather, the stars, all are woven into the texture of his
verse, lending it reality."

619 POWER, Sister Mary James. <u>Poets at Prayer</u>. New York: Sheed
     and Ward, 1938. Reprinted Freeport, N.Y.: Books for Li-
     braries Press, 1968. "Robinson Jeffers Takes God to Task,"
     pp. 59-68.
          Robinson Jeffers avows pantheism. To love God for His
     beauty, without hope of requital, is, he maintains, man's pre-
     rogative. Nevertheless Jeffers takes God to task for not bet-
     tering the affairs of mankind. Science, New Russia, and
     poets are all builders: "they serve God, Who is very beauti-
     ful, but hardly a friend of humanity." This is the attitude
     of a Deist: belief in a God as apart from his creations (a
     belief opposed to pantheism) and as a Deity who manifests
     no concern in the functions of his creatures. That Deity he
     finds not only "unkindly all but inhuman," indifferent to
     creatures, but "not moderate enough to trust, and when he
     turns bad, no one can bear him in the end."

620 PYNE, Teresa M. "Minority Group Characters in the Work of
     Robinson Jeffers." Masters Thesis, Washington State Univer-
     sity (Pullman, Wash.), 1972.

621 QUENNELL, Peter. "Recent Verse." <u>Criterion</u> (London), 9
     (January, 1930), 362.

622 QUINN, Arthur Hobson, ed. <u>The Literature of the American
     People</u>. New York: Appleton-Century-Crofts, 1951. Jeffers,
     pp. 878-879.
          After two early volumes, Jeffers began a series of hysteri-
     cally tense narrative poems dwelling with fascinated attention
     on bestiality, incest, blood-lust, and similar violent themes.
     His unorthodox and startling creed is expounded by Jeffers
     with extraordinary technical proficiency and a thorough com-
     mand of the resources of psycho-pathology and folklore....
     For the United States, as typifying the putrefactions of mo-
     dernity, he has only the ironic appreciation which he might
     bestow on the iridescence of dead fish. In revulsion from the
     sickening ways of modern civilization, he prefers the fierce
     keen cruelty of hawks. Only when man yields himself to the
     dark primitive urgings of his being does he partake of the
     grandeur of insentient things and escape from mortal mawkish-
     ness.

623 QUINN, Sister M. B. <u>The Metamorphic Tradition in Modern Po-
     etry</u>. New Brunswick, N.J.: Rutgers University Press,
     1955. Jeffers, passim.

624 RAMSEY, Warren. "The Oresteia Since Hofmannsthal: Images
     and Emphases." Revue de Littérature Comparée, 38 (1964),
     359-375.
         Reviews a number of works since Hofmannsthal's Elektra,
     which was published in 1904 and four years later arranged
     for Richard Strauss's music. The work is interesting in its
     own right, for reasons of style, texture, and construction.
     It further provides a series of familiar plot-positions against
     which versions of the Oresteia as various as those of Jeffers,
     O'Neill, Giraudoux, Sartre, and Eliot may be viewed, a study
     which this article proposes to begin.... No tragic action can
     be expected from Jeffers' characters, no wrestling with an-
     gelic decision, no far-ranging reflections on the nature of
     Justice. There is, on the other hand, conflict between iso-
     lated individual and massed forces of society represented by
     the Argive soldiers. There is also effective contrast between
     pure negation and impure affirmation, expressed mainly in the
     words and attitudes of Orestes and Electra.

625 REDE, Kenneth. "Review of Tamar and Other Poems." Balti-
     more Evening Sun, August 9, 1924.

626 REDINGER, Ellsworth Lee. "An Interview with Dame Judith
     Anderson." Drama and Theatre, 7 (Winter, 1968-1969).
     93-101.

627 _____. "The Poetic Dramas of Robinson Jeffers." Ph.D.
     diss., University of Southern California, 1971. DA, 32
     (1971), 3325A.
         Apparently Jeffers never regarded himself as a practicing
     or expert playwright. However, in spite of his reluctance
     to associate himself with the theater, his skills as a play-
     wright improved, and a greater control of the theatrically
     workable play developed. In his last poetic dramas he had
     almost completely reversed his earlier method of manipulating
     large and unwieldly actions and complicated networks of ideas.
     Instead, he presented tighter, more unified structures and
     thematic thrusts. He condensed action, reduced the size of
     his casts, and simplified his themes, making actions, charac-
     terizations, and incidents dramatically feasible.

628 REDMAN, Ben Ray. "Review of Roan Stallion, etc." The Spur
     (New York), 37 (June 1, 1926), 140.

629 REEVE, Nancy. "Robinson Jeffers: Three Poems of Humanity."
     Masters Thesis, Sacramento State University, 1964.

630 REMSEN, Rem. "Portrait of Robinson Jeffers." Carmel Cymbal,
     2 (September 29, 1926), 1, 9.

631 RICE, Philip Blair. "Jeffers and the Tragic Sense." Nation, 141
     (October 23, 1935), 480-482.

Review of Solstice and Other Poems. Contains some of his best poetry and also makes explicit the ideas and values upon which his work has been based. Jeffers' range is broad but his focus is narrow, and the universality to be found in great poetry is absent. His technical equipment has been overrated, and he often requires shrapnel for an effect that another poet would achieve with a rifle or a dart. His vision of life commands respect for its vigor and its unity. There is a grandeur which is not invalidated by his failure to detect the stirrings of a new culture amid the collapse of the old. And, above all, Jeffers is a superb storyteller.

632   RIDGEWAY, Ann N. "A Study of Inhumanism: Action Symbols in Shorter Poems of Robinson Jeffers." Masters Thesis, Bowling Green State University, 1957.

633   _____. "The Letters of Robinson Jeffers: A Record of Four Friendships--Correspondence with George Sterling, Albert Bender, Benjamin de Casseres, and Mark Van Doren." Ph.D. diss., Bowling Green State University, 1966. DA, 27 (1967), 1834A-1835A.

These letters have been arranged chronologically within each individual's unit of correspondence, and, after a more generalized "Foreword," are preceded by a brief introduction to the addressee and a brief description of his relationship with Jeffers. Problems of editing were few. Dates were frequently difficult to establish but usually at least the year can be supplied. The Jeffers of these letters bears little resemblance to the public image. In his letters, Jeffers' courtesy, mild and gentle manner, and concern for others serve as effective contrast to his usual image of aloof, hard, misanthropist, though the letters affirm his antisocial tendencies.

634   _____, ed. Selected Letters of Robinson Jeffers, 1897-1962. Baltimore: Johns Hopkins Press, 1968. Foreword by Mark Van Doren; photographs by Leigh Wiener.

Contains 407 pages with Index, 413 letters in chronological order. Appendix lists letters and locations and the ones in this collection. There are nearly 500 letters in university and public libraries and in private collections. They provide some interesting details about Jeffers' life and work, as they might be expected to, but what is more important, they declare a personality not commonly known.

Interesting article printed in Robinson Jeffers Newsletter, 12 (November, 1965), 2-5, in which Ms. Ridgeway presents a "Progress Report" on her editorship of the Jeffers' letters. Reviews problems encountered in this age which does not overevaluate letters as a form of literature.

635   RIGGS, Susan F. "A Note on the Stanford Jeffers Holdings." Robinson Jeffers Newsletter, 47 (December, 1976), 28-29.

A simple listing of the materials: Newspaper clippings; autographed pictures of Jeffers; prompt copy of "The Tower Beyond Tragedy"; photostats of letters to George Sterling; two letters to Norman Foerster.

636 RITCHIE, Ward. "Theodore Lilienthal, Robinson Jeffers, and the Quercus Press." Robinson Jeffers Newsletter, 34 (February, 1973), 15-19.
A recollection from the year 1928, when he came to know Theodore Lilienthal, and a history of the Quercus Press which operated from 1937 until 1948. Relates this history to the publication of Jeffers' poems. After 1950 and the death of Una, Jeffers wanted to publish her travel diaries of their trip to Ireland in 1929. He edited it down to a possible size and wrote an introduction, reminiscing about their life together. It was issued under the title Visits to Ireland and was printed in 300 copies. Lilienthal died in 1972. His love of printing made possible the preservation of many of Jeffers' poems in a beautiful format.

637 _____. "Some Recollections of Robinson Jeffers." Robinson Jeffers Newsletter, 52 (December, 1978), 16-27.
Reprinted from pamphlet published in September 1977, which was in fact a revision of a 1963 article. This article is based upon more than fifty years of recollections, during which time the author always knew what Jeffers was doing, what he was writing, how the work was faring, etc. He also knew the Jeffers family on a personal basis, and he knew a great many of the other people who were interested in Jeffers. A portion of this article is given to Una Jeffers and to describing the extraordinary woman she must have been.

638 RIVERS, James Clark Seabrook. "Astronomy and Physics in British and American Poetry: 1920-1960." Ph.D. diss., University of South Carolina, 1967. Jeffers, Chapter 6. DA, 28 (1968), 1826A.
The use of science in British and American poetry of the 17th, 18th, and 19th centuries has been treated in a number of works written since 1930. This dissertation is a continuation of these studies into modern poetry between 1920 and 1960. Five significant poets are studied: Alfred Noyes, Robert Bridges, Archibald MacLeish, Robinson Jeffers, and W.H. Auden. Chapter VI treats of Jeffers' use of astronomy and physics in his poetry and the relationship between Jeffers' philosophy of inhumanism and this usage.

639 ROBERTS, R. E. "Review of Be Angry at the Sun." Saturday Review of Literature, 25 (April 25, 1942), 8.
The most remarkable poem in this book is "The Bowl of Blood." It is a tense, taut piece of work, packed with imaginative understanding and a rare quality of vision. Jeffers'

profound pity for humanity is nobly, sternly expressed. In
some of the other poems there is tenderness and pity with a
dignity and grave beauty he has never exceeded. The long
narrative "Mara" has much of his old skill as a storyteller, but
it has not quite the force he can give to a story. The whole
book confirms a belief that here is one of the few major poets
now writing in English.

640 ROBINSON, A. C. "Jeffers' Mother." Time, 19 (April 25,
     1932), 8.
         A letter to the editor correcting an error which had been
     made in the article of Time, April 4, 1932. It was said that
     Jeffers' father "married an orphan, 23 years his junior."
     Actually his mother was an orphan, age 25, when she mar-
     ried Jeffers. "She was a woman of unusual beauty and char-
     acter, great charm, well-educated, and a good musician."
     Jeffers owed much to her influence, as well as to his able
     father.

641 ROBSON, William J., and Josette Bryson, interviewers. "Looking
     for Giants: An Interview with Charles Bukowski." Southern
     California Literary Scene, 1 (December, 1970), 33 et passim.
         The contemporary poet Charles Bukowski had this to say
     about Jeffers: "All of his figures kind of finally smashed up
     against the landscape. Always fascinating--they are very
     conscious of life. They were blood-filled creatures and they
     finally, usually came to a bad end. He was better on his
     longer narrative poems. When he wrote the short ones he
     tended to preach a little bit. He influenced me a great deal
     with his simple lines--his simple long lines--using the precise
     language, not 'pretty language'--just saying it!"

642 RODDY, Joseph. "View from a Granite Tower." Theatre Arts,
     33 (June, 1949), 32-36.
         Regards Jeffers as a famous dramatist, but feels that he
     has more merit as a poet. He offers only despair and de-
     struction. Although his unusual and unsavory approach has
     for the most part been unsuccessful, he is an outstanding
     phenomenon in poetry.

643 RODGERS, Covington. "A Checklist of Robinson Jeffers' Poeti-
     cal Writings Since 1934." Robinson Jeffers Newsletter, 48
     (March, 1977), 11-24.
         Article undertakes to present a complete record--excluding
     translations and anthology reprints--of works published since
     1934. Has not cited prose works. The first part lists works
     issued as distinct publications in which Jeffers' poems form
     the whole, or at least the majority, of the contents. Any
     poem not originally published in the work is especially noted.
     The second part is a listing of poems originally published in
     journals and in works edited by other authors, including
     poems by Jeffers not previously published.

644 _____. "Notes on the History and Text of Tamar and Other
        Poems." Robinson Jeffers Newsletter, 54 (October, 1979),
        19-29.
        Most of the material has been derived from the letters of
        Peter G. Boyle to Robinson Jeffers (now at the University of
        Texas), and the two publications of "Tamar" (in 1924, and
        in 1925). It was published again in 1935 (Modern Library),
        but Jeffers did not revise the work for this edition. Conclu-
        sion seems to be that no really definitive text of the work
        exists that follows Jeffers' intention as faithfully as possible.
        Article is accompanied by six pages of textual variations.

645 _____. "Jeffers Scholarly Resources: Rare Book and Manu-
        script Library, Columbia University." Robinson Jeffers News-
        letter, 58 (May, 1981), 32-34.
        Begins with statement that numerous items in this library
        are essential to the scholar engaged in biographical or bibli-
        ographical study of the poet. A number of the letters have
        been published, or at least cited. Letters are mostly printed
        or referred to in the Selected Letters. Also of interest to
        Jeffers scholars is the Random House archives. This firm
        published Jeffers' work from 1933 until his death in 1962,
        and its files of correspondence naturally provide a great deal
        of information concerning the long, and not always smooth,
        relationship.

646 RODMAN, Selden. "Review of The Double Axe and Other Po-
        ems." Saturday Review of Literature, 31 (July 31, 1948), 13.
        It is ironic that Jeffers, the rabid spokesman for isolation-
        ism, should be the only contemporary American poet capable
        of communicating with a wide audience in the grand manner.
        It is sad that as the years go by he repeats himself endlessly;
        that he elects to close his eyes to human heroism and good-
        ness and to man-made beauty; and that he feels compelled
        to add more than his quota of hatred and violence to the
        hatred and violence abroad in the world..

647 _____. "Knife in the Flowers." Poetry, 84 (July, 1954),
        226-231.
        Review of Hungerfield, etc. We stand tongue-tied before
        the poetry of Jeffers, not merely in awe of its primitive
        strength but in bewilderment: what is one to think of these
        anachronisms? In an age that has forsworn prophecy, espe-
        cially in art, Jeffers speaks in the accents of Isaiah and
        Jeremiah, albeit invoking no deity. In a time of mutliple
        meanings and ambiguous tropes, Jeffers speaks directly with
        no mistaking his meaning. In a period of harmonic subleties,
        he employs only the whole-tone scale. Among the experi-
        menters with color and textures for their own sakes, Jeffers
        says it in black and white--with a blunt stylus.

648 ROEDDER, Karsten. "Prose Extracts to Test Lyrical Qualities
     of Two Great Modern American Poets." Brooklyn Citizen,
     July 3, 1927.
         Comparison of The Women at Point Sur with Robinson's
     Tristram.

649 ROOT, E. Merrill. "Three Singers Before Sunset." Poetry
     Folio, January-February, 1928.

650 RORTY, James. "Review of Tamar and Other Poems." Sunset
     Magazine (San Francisco), 53 (October, 1924), 51.

651 _____. "In Major Mold: Review of Tamar and Other Poems."
     New York Herald Tribune Books, March 1, 1925.
         "It exhibits the maturity of a remarkable talent, which
     critical opinion will have to take account of and measure at
     leisure. I am convinced that no poet of equal importance has
     appeared on the American scene since Robinson. Nothing so
     good of its kind has been written in America. America has
     a new poet of genius."

652 _____. "Satirist or Metaphysician?" New Masses, 3 (Septem-
     ber, 1927), 26.
         Review of The Women at Point Sur.

653 _____. "World Poetry." Nation, 128 (February 13, 1929),
     197-198.
         Review of An Anthology of World Poetry, edited by Mark
     Van Doren. Books gets high praise, but reviewer cautions
     that it should not be read straight through. Covers 3500
     B. C. to twentieth century A. D. Over four hundred poets
     are represented by more than 1300 poems. Some 274 pages
     are devoted to English and American poetry, all of it good.
     Few of Van Doren's inclusions are likely to be questioned;
     some omissions, of course, may be regretted but are to be
     explained by lack of space. The contemporary Americans
     are E. A. Robinson, Amy Lowell, Robert Frost, Jeffers, Carl
     Sandburg, et al. These are surely the right names and Van
     Doren has made excellent selections from their work.

654 _____. "Symbolic Melodrama." New Republic, 71 (May 18,
     1932), 24-25.
         Review of Descent to the Dead and Thurso's Landing, etc.
     Poetry is an exercise of consciousness and a product of civi-
     lization. But Jeffers' nihilism turns poetry against poetry,
     consciousness against itself. Logically, his steady stream of
     books, increasing in clarity and power, is itself a betrayal
     of his own reiterated allegiance to the retreating drift of the
     remoter star-swirls "fleeing the contagion of consciousness
     that infect this corner of space." Jeffers thinks Thurso's
     Landing his best book; it does express better than earlier

volumes what Jeffers has to express. The shorter volume contains a dozen excellent short pieces which reinforce this theme.

655   _____. "Review of Give Your Heart to the Hawks and Other Poems." Nation, 137 (December 20, 1933), 712.
   As craftsmanship this volume is, in many respects, one of Jeffers' ablest performances. But one starts unconvinced, for the tragedy is frailly premised on drunkenness and chance, and one ends, as too often in Jeffers' terrible stories, racked but unsatisfied.

656   _____. "Review of Such Counsels You Gave To Me and Other Poems." Christian Science Monitor, November 10, 1937.
   Jeffers' poetry is negative and it is doubtful if, in the simple meaning of the word, it can be read for pleasure. But it can be read with profit.

657   _____. "The Ecology of Robinson Jeffers." Quarterly News-letter of the Book Club of California, 32 (1967), 32-36.

658 ROSENHEIM, Ned. "One Tiger on the Road." Poetry, 73 (March, 1949), 351-354.
   Review of The Double Axe, etc. The critics who have re-viewed this volume have been concerned with Jeffers' political doctrine. The book has raised a minor storm, but this re-viewer chooses to deal dispassionately with Jeffers as a poet without reference to attitudes and opinions.... There are parts of The Double Axe which, isolated alike from the actions and convictions which underly the work, possess an enormous power. They are, almost exclusively, those sections in which the sheer violence and magnificence of Jeffers' invective make themselves felt. In patches one is moved, anticipating in the shorter poems opportunities for the appropriate display of skill. Yet when the readers reach these verses, perhaps be-cause of their brevity, we cannot admire their violence; the reader is far too conscious of their source and their direction.

659 ROSENTHAL, M. L. The Modern Poets: A Critical Introduction New York: Oxford University Press, 1960. "Rival Idioms--the Great Generation: Moore, Cummings, Sandburg, Jeffers," pp. 140-159.
   Jeffers is, in his way, overcommitted to his art. That is, he pushes too hard against the limitations of his own formal resources. Having a genuine but hardly overwhelming gift for swift narration, for subtle and evocative description, and for impassioned arguments--all in a basically conventional though loosely manipulated verse-patterning which gives the illusion of being "free," he tries to squeeze out of these tal-ents every drop of symbolic and didactic inference he can.

660 RUDNICK, Lois P. "The Unexpurgated Self: A Critical Biogra-
     phy of Mabel Dodge Luhan." Ph.D. diss., Brown University,
     1977.
         Dissertation is a historical and literary study of the life
     and works of Mabel Dodge Luhan and an examination of her
     most important literary, artistic, and political relationships.
     Throughout her life, 1879 to 1962, Mrs. Luhan served as a
     touchstone for many of the intellectual, aesthetic, political,
     and social movements in America. As a patroness of art and
     politics, she befriended, influenced, and knew many of the
     most important artists, poets, writers, musicians, political
     and social reformers in America and Europe. After two in-
     troductory chapters, which are based primarily on Mrs. Lu-
     han's memoirs, each biographical section is followed by an in-
     depth analysis of her relationship with and influence on one
     of the major writers, and his or her works.

661 _____. "Mabel Dodge Luhan and Robinson Jeffers." Robinson
     Jeffers Newsletter, 49 (June, 1977), 21-26.
         Article is a summary of the forty-page chapter in the
     dissertation listed above, on Robinson Jeffers. He was one
     of the three artists--Gertrude Stein and D. H. Lawrence
     being the other two--with whom Ms. Dodge felt a deep rela-
     tionship. All three worked, in various ways, with a theory
     of symbolism that Mabel seems to have adopted in her mem-
     oirs. The chapter on Robinson Jeffers is largely biographical,
     arranged by an attempt on Mabel's part to separate the
     Jefferses, resulting in an attempted suicide by Una.

662 SALEMSON, H. J. "A Gallery of Americans." Poetry, 33 (De-
     cember, 1928), 165-166.
         A review of an anthology of younger American poets,
     edited and translated into French by Eugène Jolas (Paris,
     1928). Has tried to establish as wide a panorama as possible,
     even though he cannot allow the more important poets much
     more than the others. He has translated the verse of 126
     Americans, representing every school and every movement
     among our contemporaries. Robinson Jeffers is represented
     by "Roan Stallion."

663 SANDERSON, Elizabeth. "Ex-Detective Hammett." Bookman, 74
     (January-February, 1932), 477-487, 518.
         Remarks are based on an interview with this writer who
     contributed a new form of fiction to contemporary literature.
     In the course of the interview it was learned that Hammett
     had written some verse. Also that he thinks Robinson Jeffers
     the best storyteller he has ever read, and the cruellest....

664 SCHARTON, Maurice Alan. "A Contextual Analysis of Prosody

in Selected Narrative Poems of Robinson Jeffers." Ph.D.
diss., Kansas State University, 1978. DA, 39 (1979), 6135A.
    This dissertation develops two mutually dependent theses:
The first is that Jeffers adapted prosody in his narratives
to steadily more intellectual ends as his art and thought developed; the second is that Jeffers' prosody, to be understood accurately, must be read in the context of subject
matter, theme, and style. Though a free verse poet, Jeffers
began with distinctly prosodical inclinations using sound patterns derived from accentual-syllabic, accentual, and quanti-
tative verse to create effects which were mainly aesthetic.

665   _____. "Ascriptive Structures in 'Solstice.'" Robinson Jef-
    fers Newsletter, 54 (October, 1979), 7-14.
    Undertakes a structural analysis of the poem which has
been called Jeffers' worst narrative: "so bad, it is interesting." Reviews some of the criticism which the poem has received but thinks it is largely due to a lack of consideration
for who the narrative persona is at the moment. The other
important consideration is that the story of Madrone is a version of the Medea story, perhaps derived from Egyptian mythology, and the allusive quality of the verse accounts for
much of the outrageous imagery.

666   SCHINDLER, P. G. "Poet on a Tower." Survey Graphic,
    (April, 1930), 46.
    Review of Dear Judas, etc. Agrees with other critical
opinions in saying that "The Loving Shepherdess" a tale of
the California coast, surpasses in quality of feeling and in
the superb simplicity of its utterance, anything that Jeffers
has written.

667   SCHMALHAUSEN, Samuel D. Our Changing Human Nature. New
    York: Macauley, 1929. Jeffers, pp. 165-169 et passim.

668   _____, ed. Our Neurotic Age. New York: Farrar & Rine-
    hart, 1932. Jeffers, pp. 305-306.

669   SCHNEIDER, Duane. "Review of The Selected Letters of Robin-
    son Jeffers." Library Journal, 93 (July, 1968), 2660.
    As might be anticipated, recipients include important liter-
ary figures such as Mark Van Doren, Louis Untermeyer,
Harriet Monroe, George Sterling and many others. The letters,
often dealing strictly with literary matters, may not be of interest to everyone, but the book is a significant one, and
naturally all students of Jeffers will want to see it.

670   SCHWAB, Arnold T. "The Robinson Connection: New Jeffers
    Letters," Robinson Jeffers Newsletter, 57 (November, 1980),
    26-35.

The two poets were on friendly terms, but only slightly,
acquainted. Their correspondence was very brief and is now
at the University of Texas. The two poets never met, but
they had a friend in common, who was something of a letter
writer. This person was Craven Langstroth Betts. Though
Betts' letters have disappeared, fourteen letters to Betts--
four from Jeffers and ten from Una--have survived. They
are printed here for the first time.

671   _____ . "Jeffers and Millay: A Literary Freindship." Robin-
      son Jeffers Newsletter, 59 (September, 1981), 18-33.
           Letters to and from Edna St. Vincent Millay, 1929-1937.
      Students of Jeffers have long known of the mutual admiration
      and friendship between him and Edna St. Vincent Millay. The
      main published and unpublished letters by Jeffers and Una
      contain references to Millay. But until now the association
      between perhaps the most publicized male and female poets
      of the 1920's has not been traced in detail, nor their extant
      letters to each other published. This assocation seems to
      have begun in late 1928. Millay's discovery of Jeffers' work
      can not be dated from published sources, because she pro-
      duced even fewer reviews than he, and her published letters
      do not elucidate the point.

672   SCHWARTZ, Delmore. "The Enigma of Robinson Jeffers: I,
      Sources of Violence." Poetry, 55 (October, 1939), 30-46.
           Includes discussion of poem "Science." Remarks are based
      on a review of The Selected Poetry of Robinson Jeffers (1939).
      The present volume is beautifully printed, contains a hand-
      some photograph of Jeffers, and is furnished with a very in-
      teresting and dignified foreword by the author. Although only
      half of his poetry is here and The Women at Point Sur is
      omitted, because it is the least liked and the least understood
      of his poems, the collection presents a sufficient span of writ-
      ing in 600 pages to give any reader a just view of Jeffers'
      work as a whole. Above all, this selection invites a brief
      consideration with regard to Jeffers' sources.
           Basic sources that are discussed involve Jeffers' use of
      the scientific picture of the universe and the effect of World
      War I.

673   SCOTT, Robert Ian. "Robinson Jeffers' Poetic Use of Post-
      Copernical Science." Ph.D. diss., SUNY (Buffalo), 1964.
      DA, 26 (1965), 1049.
           Among poets writing in English, only Jeffers persistently
      portrays man and the world as seen by post-Copernican
      science. An examination of his poems using science--46 of
      the 81 are analyzed in detail--shows that Jeffers uses three
      very general and basic ideas: post-Copernican astronomy,
      evolution, and atomism, including nuclear reactions and en-
      tropy. With all three, Jeffers expresses man's place in space

and time in terms of such specific discoveries as the expanding universe, the chemical origin of life, and the emptiness within atoms. His multiple similes compare man with stars and atoms; some of his metaphors show the totally interrelated universe as a net, as self-conscious, or as a tragically self-trapped, self-tormenting god.

674 _____. "The World-as-God-as-Net in Jeffers' Unpublished Poem 'Oh Happy Astronomer.'" Robinson Jeffers Newsletter, 38 (April, 1974), 10-17.

Article is based on a one-page undated manuscript in the Jeffers collection at the University of Texas (Austin) Research Center. It is a poem catalogued as "Oh Happy Astronomer." Very few changes have been made on the manuscript, which would indicate that Jeffers had already written the poem when he wrote this copy, but there is no way to date the composition. Article expresses opinion that it may relate to a very early period, on the basis that it was in 1917 in The Alpine Christ that Jeffers first expressed the metaphor of "a world-as-God-as-Net."

675 _____. "Robinson Jeffers' Tragedies as Rediscoveries of the World." Bulletin of the Rocky Mountain Modern Language Association, 29 (1975), 147-165.

676 _____. "Three Unpublished Poems of Robinson Jeffers." Robinson Jeffers Newsletter, 41 (May, 1975), 11-18.

The Jeffers collection at the University of Texas (Austin) includes three unpublished poems about the Second World War, which Jeffers apparently wrote in 1940, 1941, and 1944:
1) The first poem exists as a much-revised but apparently unfinished manuscript in pencil with the title "Belgian Surrender--May--."
2) The second poem exists as an unrevised, apparently finished typescript, with the title "Miching Mallecho," dated May 1941. The title is an allusion, somewhat obscure, to Hamlet.
3) The third unpublished poem exists as an apparently finished typescript marked by only one revision, with the title "An Ordinary Newscaster," dated January 13, 1944.

The poems have some importance because they contribute to a study of Jeffers' relationship to World War II.

677 _____. "Three of Jeffers' Unpublished Second World War Predictions." Robinson Jeffers Newsletter, 44 (March, 1976), 18-21.

Article is based on an undated, typewritten note by Jeffers: "Dearest Blanche, Here are three small pieces of verse that I left out of the book. Two were omitted because they were not good enough poetry; the last because it was written

too late to be included." This note, together with three
short poems, are in Mrs. Blanche Matthias' Jeffers collection.
These three poems are listed as follows: "The Old Gentle-
men," May 1941, is also at the University of Texas, but with
the title "Miching Mallecho"); "The Meddlers," June 1941;
and "Next Armistice Day," no date given.

678   . "Scholarly Materials: Poetry Manuscripts, University
of Texas." Robinson Jeffers Newsletter, 45 (June, 1976),
13-16.
    The size of the Jeffers Collection defies any brief listing.
It includes poems in every stage, from first scribbled notes
to final typescripts.... Possibly no other collection reveals
so much about how he worked and the extent of the writing
which he did not finish or publish during his lifetime. Article does not presume to be complete, but following are examples:
1. Much of "The Alpine Christ," etc.
2. A draft of The Women at Point Sur.
3. Twenty-four short poems, written after 1933, about
World War II, not published during lifetime.
4. An endless number of notes for never-finished narratives.
5. Jeffers also considered writing an autobiography, in
prose, which would include some short poems. One
note suggests he considered a prose autobiography
in 1952 or 1953 because he felt he no longer had the
time or energy that organizing and finishing a narrative poem would take.

679   . "Poet as Prophet: Jeffers' Unpublished Poems about
World War II." North American Review, 15 (Spring, 1978),
82-86.
    Subject previously covered in article listed above [677].
This study, perhaps, is a more complete analysis.

680   . "The Ends of Tragedy: Robinson Jeffers' Satires on
Human Self-Importance." Canadian Review of American Studies, 10 (1979), 231-241.
    Reviews three 1977 reprints of works by Robinson Jeffers:
The Women at Point Sur, Dear Judas, and The Double Axe.
Review also includes a biographical study, Rock and Hawk,
by William H. Nolte, and The Suppressed Poems of Robinson
Jeffers, edited by James M. Shebl.
    Calls these Jeffers' "three most resented books," and thinks it
is time to take another look at his experiments with the structures
and purposes of tragedy. Jeffers wrote tragedies to prevent tragedies in our lives. Tragedies reinterpret history, and the psy-
chologies of characters caught in catastrophes they help cause,
and of course such reinterpretations upset our self-flattering
delusions: if they did not, the tragedies would have no moral

point or purpose. Jeffers' tragedies do, but they also de-
scribe the world beyond, containing human history to let us
see how ultimately unimportant our tragedy-causing concerns
seem by comparison and how lovely is that almost totally nonhuman world.

681 _____. "A Letter by Una Jeffers Discovered." Notable Works
     and Collections (Saskatchewan Library), 9 (December, 1979),
     16-19.

682 _____. "Putting Us in Our Place." Denver Quarterly, 14
     (Summer, 1979), 105-108.
          Review-essay of the 1977 Liveright reprints.

683 _____. "From Berkeley to Barclay's Delusion: Robinson Jef-
     fers vs Modern Narcissism." Mosaic, 15 (September, 1982),
     55-61.
          Article begins by asserting that popularity does not prove
     accuracy, referring specifically to Jsoeph Wood Krutch, who
     "claimed that scientific discoveries of our unimportance have
     made the writing and understanding of such morally meaning-
     ful literature as tragedies almost impossible now, because un-
     less we think the universe exists to serve us, nothing has
     much point or meaning." Article continues with discussion
     of Jeffers' The Women at Point Sur, which is a modern tragedy
     of delusion "evoking a terror that comes from seeing how
     blindly tragic fools make their all-too-human mistakes, and
     how much misery they cause."

684 _____. "Egocentric Versus Ecologically Responsible Poetry."
     Robinson Jeffers Newsletter, 62 (January, 1983), 5-6.
          Review of anthology edited by Robert Bly, News of the
     Universe (1980). Undertakes to present a history of poetry,
     from Milton on, as a struggle between the "Old Position"--
     an assumption that the universe exists to serve a few right-
     thinking individuals--and the less egocentric views of later
     poets, including Jeffers. Presents three of Jeffers' poems,
     which use discoveries that threatened self-esteem to describe
     the universe as enormously beautiful, as what creates human-
     ity and saves it from its egocentric delusions--as God, in
     short, and ultimately Jeffers had no other subject but this
     discovery.

685 _____. "Robinson Jeffers as Anti-Imagist." Robinson Jeffers
     Newsletter, 63 (June, 1983), 8-12.
          In 1908 to 1917, Ezra Pound and other Imagist poets claimed
     poems should concentrate on describing isolated moments,
     precisely and in the fewest possible words. Jeffers did not
     belong to this group, saying on one occasion that he had
     decided to write narrative poems, and poems dealing with phil-
     osophical and scientific ideas. Narratives connect moments
     into sequences of causes and results, and those connections

make the moments more meaningful, a point the Imagists ignored.... In his poems, Jeffers often looks first at some
particular, then at a larger context, which defines that particular moment or subject, more often by a contrast than by
a resemblance.

686 SEAVER, Edwin. "Robinson Jeffers' Poetry." Saturday Review
      of Literature, 2 (January 16, 1926), 492.
            Review of Roan Stallion, etc. Unforgettable as "Tamar"
      might be, "Roan Stallion" is serener, more definite in line
      and more economical in conception, a magnificent achievement.
      Only once does Jeffers depart from the intense objectivity of
      his narrative, and then it is to leap into a characteristically
      frenzied and dancing strophe. It is obvious that Jeffers is
      one of Whitman's "poets to come," whom the earlier primitive
      hailed on the horizon.

687 SEIDLIN, Oskar. "The Oresteia Today: A Myth Dehumanized."
      Thought, 34 (August, 1959), 434-452.
            In the hands of Hauptmann, Sartre, and Jeffers, the cruel
      and violent story of Orestes has become a macabre vision of
      a debased and demoniacal humanity. Jeffers' version of the
      story is "The Tower Beyond Tragedy." In this work Jeffers
      is clearly inhuman, presenting a violent abdication of man as
      man, the reduction of existence to nothingness. His horribly
      blissful vision is the end of all conscious life, the tower be-
      yond tragedy, that stage of numb aloofness and immobility
      where nothing will touch us any more, where we are, indeed,
      beyond tragedy and time, because we are no longer man.

688 SESSIONS, George. "Spinoza and Jeffers: An Environmental
      Perspective." Inquiry, 20 (Fall, 1977), 481-528.
            Long, well-documented article on the subject of man in
      nature. It is preceded by the following abstract, which
      serves as an excellent summary: "Western society has been
      diverted from the goal of spiritual freedom and autonomy as
      expressed in the ancient Pythagorean 'theory of the cosmos'
      ... it can be seen that modern Western society has arrived
      at the opposite pole of 'absolute subjectivism' in which the
      entire non-human world is seen as a material resource to be
      consumed in the satisfaction of our egoistic passive desires.
      Actually Spinozism is a modern version of the theory of
      the cosmos, which, when supplemented by a vision of man's
      identity with the ecological world, provides us with the only
      adequate portrayal of the God-Nature-Man relationship."

689 SEUBERT, Eugene E. "Robinson Jeffers: Poet for an Age of
      Violence." Northwest Missouri Teachers College Studies, 7
      (June, 1943), 3-28.
            Begins with a biographical history and a survey of Jef-
      fers' publications. The article is a close analysis of the plots,

characters, and actions of the narratives with emphasis on
the violence and tragedy they portray. In the conclusion
the critic raises the question, "Is Jeffers correct in his point
of view?" The fact of violence looms larger on our scene than
any other fact. Violence has been increasing. There is a
school of thought, however, that says that violence has not
been the only sire of the world's values. It may have bred
some of them. But love and self-denial have also had their
offspring. Dominant trends have always run their course
and have been superseded by other trends that in their turn
became dominant.

690   SHANE, C. D. "Hamilton Moore Jeffers." Robinson Jeffers
       Newsletter, 46 (September, 1976), 41-42.
          Biographical sketch written for Robinson Jeffers' brother,
       who died in May 1976, at his home in Carmel Highlands. This
       article was originally prepared for the magazine Physics To-
       day. Jeffers, who earned his Ph.D. in astronomy in 1921,
       devoted his life to that science and was highly respected and
       honored in his field. He worked extensively in the field of
       double stars and was also noted for an outstanding series of
       photographs of the planet Mars. He had a natural gift for
       precision, both in his observations and in their analysis. By
       nature he was quiet and reserved. He enjoyed music and
       played the organ until the end of his life.

691   SHAW, Susan. "Elements of Eastern Philosophy in Jeffers."
       Robinson Jeffers Newsletter, 36 (October, 1973), 8-11.
          The poetry of Jeffers reveals an unresolved philosophical
       dichotomy between East and West. Although Jeffers is a
       Western man by birth, his philosophy contains many Eastern
       elements. Author makes a list of tendencies within the two
       cultures and bases discussion on these points:

       1)   As to the nature of reality, Jeffers believed in the
            actuality of the physical, not merely that reality was
            in the mind or the imagination.
       2)   The acceptance of evil is a common ground for Jeffers
            and the Eastern beliefs.
       3)   Jeffers also believes in a cyclic universe, not in a
            linear one.
       4)   The role of artist as prophet is a purely Western idea,
            and Jeffers never abondoned this concept of himself.

       Jeffers is essentially a Western man from a culture of ra-
       tional humanism and he does not succeed in eradicating that
       culture from his work or his philosophy. He suffers the am-
       bivalence of a man caught between opposing poles. He is
       neither entirely Western nor totally Eastern but a patchwork
       of both. His poetry has a fascination born of alienation, and
       the Eastern influence has given it this exotic difference.

692 SHEBL, James Michael. "In This Wild Water: The Biography of
     Some Unpublished Manuscripts by Robinson Jeffers, 1887-
     1962." Ph.D. diss., University of the Pacific, 1974. DA,
     35 (1975), 3009A.
         The biography of The Double Axe and Other Poems, pub-
     lished in 1948, shows that ten poems were expunged from the
     originally submitted manuscript. Notes and letters from this
     period show that Bennett Cerf and Jeffers' editor, Saxe Cum-
     mins, were disconcerted by the fierce intensity and dark
     political ramifications of Jeffers' doctrine. Consequently this
     volume was printed with a disclaimer regarding the "political
     views pronounced by the poet." To the dismay of his pub-
     lishers, Jeffers often uses political persons--Roosevelt, Hitler,
     Mussolini, Truman--to represent the ideas he works with aes-
     thetically. In using these particulars as metaphors, he makes
     contemporary issues and personalities point up his philosophy
     of Inhumanism. These references have the effect of indicting
     them all equally, showing that all leaders and all nations are
     equally capable of distorting the importance and value of hu-
     man endeavor.

693 _____, ed. In This Wild Water: The Suppressed Poems of
     Robinson Jeffers. Pasadena: Ward Ritchie, 1976.
         Describes and prints poems suppressed from The Double
     Axe and Other Poems (1948). Review by Bill Hotchkiss.
     Robinson Jeffers Newsletter, 47 (December, 1976), 7-8.
     Thinks the editorial work is well written, concise, systematic,
     and directly to the point. By drawing together the ten de-
     leted poems, Shebl easily and gracefully constructs his case
     in such a way as to benefit all future Jeffers scholarship--as
     well as to put into the literary record the full parameters of
     The Double Axe issue. In so doing, the critic has performed
     an extremely valuable service for the twin causes of American
     poetry and American poetry criticism.

694 SHIELDS, Jerry Ashburn. "Robinson Jeffers and HIs Savior-
     Inhumanist Dilemma." Masters Thesis, Duke University,
     1966.

695 _____. "The Divided Mind of Robinson Jeffers." Ph.D. diss.,
     Duke University, 1972. DA, 33 (1973), 5199A.
         Based on the belief that Jeffers' problems and much of the
     tension in his poetry stemmed from an Oedipus complex ac-
     quired in early childhood. Applies some of the theories of
     psychoanalysis to the poet's life, works, and correspondence
     and finds a high degree of correlation between his behavior
     and his writings. Concludes that Jeffers suffered from the
     "compulsion neurosis syndrome."

696 SHIPLEY, Joseph T. "Blending of Pity and Horror." New York
     Evening Post Literary Review, April 17, 1926.

697 SHORT, R. W. "The Tower Beyond Tragedy." Southern Re-
     view, 7 (Summer, 1941), 132-144.
         Many critics have testified that Jeffers can employ certain
     of the creative talents with extraordinary ability. Yet some-
     times a poet seems to gain his hearing as much by his faults
     as by his virutes. This is true of Jeffers. He is called phil-
     osophical poet and tragic poet, whereas the philosophic con-
     tent of his poems is bogus, and the kind of art he practices
     with such energy and originality is disqualified as tragic
     art.... In Jeffers' poems the hero is a vividly drawn crea-
     ture of one dimension. The other characters are lesser phan-
     tasms of the same design, who but for impotence, would
     doubtless be glad to sin and suffer just as the hero does.
     They are all of the same somber, muttering stock. When one
     of them goes insane, the author has to inform us that a
     change has taken place in him. This is not tragedy. The
     heroes are too narrow to be truly tragic. The presence of
     didactic materials emphasizes their inadequacy, since they are
     painfully lacking in the universality the didactic materials
     seem to claim for them.

698- SINGLETON, Anne. "A Major Poet." New York Herald Tribune
  9   Books, December 23, 1928. Review of Cawdor, etc.

700 SMALL, H. A. "Review of The Women at Point Sur." San
     Francisco Chronicle, July 3, 1927.

701 SMITH, Chard Powers. Pattern and Variation in Poetry. New
     York: Scribner's Sons, 1932. Jeffers, pp. 387-390 et
     passim.
         In rounding off his discussion, the critic says: "The
     composition and the comprehension of great poetry are among
     the ultimate achievements of the human race, for all the fac-
     ulties are involved...." And in order to appreciate a great
     poem the reader must also have compassed the same horizons
     of thought which the poet has reached. This point is illus-
     trated with passages from several poets, including Jeffers,
     who are radically different from each other but all equally
     great.

702 SMITH, W. J. "Review of The Beginning and the End and Other
     Poems." Harpers, 227 (September, 1963), 112.
         These forty-eight poems are the last works of Jeffers,
     collected from handwritten manuscripts by his sons and sec-
     retary after Jeffers' death in 1962. These are the first poems
     to appear since Hungerfield. The Titanic stance that Jeffers
     assumes in his poetry is often marred by touches of shrillness
     and self-pity. But when he is writing objectively, as he often
     does, of the natural scene--of the wildness of this country,
     the full moon, the Pacific, sea gulls in a storm, the "enormous
     inhuman beauty of things"--no one has ever equalled him.

703   SNOW, Wilbert. "American Poetry--Vintage of 1925." Book
       Notes, 4 (February-March, 1926), 91-92.
              Review of Roan Stallion, etc.

704   SOANES, W. "Student Actors Produce Poetic Drama of Electra."
       Oakland Tribune, November 9, 1932.
              Refers to production of The Tower Beyond Tragedy.

705   _____. "Jeffers Play in Premiere Acclaimed." Carmel Pine
       Cone, 18 (November 18, 1932), 6.

706   SOUTHWORTH, James Granville. Some Modern American Poets.
       Oxford, England: Basil Blackwell, 1950. Jeffers, pp.
       107-121.
              "Being humourless himself he imagines that the characters
       he has created have life. To me they are shadowy creations
       that fade almost as soon as born. The pleasure derived from
       his work is that of immediate excitement. When it is over the
       observer realizes that he has been hoaxed. This judgment
       applies to his long poems. I find his short poems dull. They
       present a point of view of life with which I have little sympa-
       thy. He does not compensate for the uncongeniality of his
       subject-matter by presenting those ideas in a form that in-
       duces a suspension of disbelief. He will undoubtedly continue
       to be popular with a certain type of audience. But it is an
       audience incapable of grasping that Jeffers' reading of life is
       myopic, even pathological."

707   SPIER, Leonard. "Notes on Robinson Jeffers: A Critical View
       of a Noted American Poet." Robinson Jeffers Newsletter, 55
       (December, 1979), 36-42. Reprinted from International Liter-
       ature (Moscow), 6 (1934), 112-117.
              Robinson Jeffers is an Individualist. He as much as tells
       us so. There have been other individuals, and those who
       have not failed to yawp their cherished, if imaginary, self-
       hood, over the rooftops of the world.... Jeffers is and al-
       ways was a member of that class of modern society, each of
       whose members considers himself to be above all classes.
       They toil not.... They constitute the spoiled children of
       today's social family. Jeffers is a great American writer,
       class-conscious and courageous enough to express it. For
       this we can respect him.

708   SPIESE, Richard D. "Robinson Jeffers' Aesthetic Theory and
       Practice." Ph.D. diss., University of New Mexico, 1966.
       DA, 27 (1966), 1840A.
              Influenced by a family background that valued intellectual
       concerns and minimized emotional warmth, Jeffers developed
       an aesthetic theory that set him apart from most other Amer-
       ican poets. These aesthetic views include a distrust of the
       intrinsic value of art that made Jeffers suspicious of the

subtleties of modern poetry, a preoccupation with the "beauty of things," an emphasis on statement and intellectual content, a preference for a long, rhythmic poetic line, and a concept of tragedy that stresses violence and the expression of ideas to the detriment of compassion and fully delineated characters.... Jeffers' aesthetic theory is apparent in his short poems, yet these works often survive the limitations of his views and constitute his most important work. There is often an effective evocation of nature, a cosmic view of existence, and a somber tone, resulting in a poem no other American poet could duplicate.

709 SPILLER, Robert L. Cycle of American Literature. New York: Macmillan, 1955. Jeffers, p. 234. Reprinted with different pagination, New York: Mentor Books, 1957. Also reprinted New York: Free Press Paperback, 1967.
      Jeffers not discussed; is referred to with several other poets as one who helped bring into being the vigorous naturalistic movement.

710 _____, et al, eds. Literary HIstory of the United States. New York: Macmillan, 1946. One-volume reprint edition, 1953. Jeffers, pp. 1347-1348 in "Poetry," Chapter 79 by F. O. Matthiessen.
      He dwelt on the decadence of American society and revealed the extent to which he had been influenced by Spengler. With the depression and the advance of fascism, he merely kept repeating that "civilization is a transient sickness." From his tower retreat at Carmel he averred that he was merely a "neutral" recorder of social decay. But he scorned the city proletariat and insisted on the futility of any radical social reform.

711 SQUIRES, James R. "Robinson Jeffers and the Doctrine of Inhumanism." Ph.D. diss., Harvard, 1952.
      Published in the work below.

712 _____. The Loyalties of Robinson Jeffers. Ann Arbor: University of Michigan Press, 1956; Oxford University Press, 1957; also in paperback.
      Review in Poetry, 104 (July, 1964), 264-265, by Harry Strickhausen. Contains 200 pages with Notes and a short bibliography. In ten chapters as follows:

      1. The Destroying Prodigal
      2. Nietzsche and Schopenhauer
      3. The Broken Balance
      4. The Brain Vault
      5. The Anatomy of Violence
      6. The Eternal Peasant
      7. The Inhumanist

8. The Creed of Permanence
9. The Debate
10. Whitman, Lucretius, and Jeffers

Reviews the stages of recognition and rejection that Jeffers' poetry has undergone. Has ebbed steadily since 1935,
now rather consistently consigned to the ranks of those who
present only "historical" interest. Chapter on "The Inhumanist" is especially clear in illuminating this central doctrine of
Jeffers.

713 _____. "Robinson Jeffers: The Anatomy of Violence," in
Modern American Poetry: Essays in Criticism, edited by Guy
Owens. Deland: Everett/Edwards, 1975. Pp. 117-131.
Printed from Chapter 5, The Loyalties of Robinson Jeffers
(1956). In this excerpt Squires says: "The single most impressive characterstic of Jeffers' mature work is his preoccupation with all manner of violent action. The origins are not
simple, but one can make inroads toward an understanding
by considering the perplexing split between Jeffers' dedica-
tion and its formulation. He arranges his characters so that
they torture each other unbearably and then moralizes that
if this is the human condition, it would be well to 'break out'
of it. He tries thus to solve the problem of passion through
logic, but the effort augments his difficulties if only because
it is man's irrational passions which most readily capture Jeffers' artistic allegiance."

714 STALEY, Gregory A. "'But Ancient Violence Longs to Breed':
Robinson Jeffers' The Bloody Sire and Aeschylus' Oresteia."
Classical and Modern Literature, 4 (Summer, 1983), 193-199.
Jeffers adapted or reworked a number of Greek tragedies,
but his links with the Greek tragedians go beyond his use of
their plays as models for his own work. He turned to them
because he sensed that he was living in an age much like
theirs, an age in which a great civilization had reached its
peak and was just beginning its inevitable decline.... In
The Bloody Sire, a poem which he wrote in the summer of
1940, Jeffers turned to Greek tragedy for precisely this reason. A moment in American history that was so "Greek"
naturally called for poetry that was Greek.

715 STARR, Kevin. "Robinson Jeffers and the Integrity of Nature."
Sierra Club Bulletin, 62 (May, 1977), 36-40.
No twentieth-century artist has done more to demonstrate
an objective regard for natural phenomena, nourishing a new
respect for nature on its own terms, than Robinson Jeffers.
Tor House became an emblem of Jeffers' detachment, his
movement away from human culture toward an identification
with rock and sea and mountains, the grandeur and permanence of God. His environment was his poetry and himself.

He has expanded our consciousness in the matter of inanimate creation. Because of his poetry we are more aware of the otherness of the inanimate (in the fresh and vital respect for the sacred beingness of rocks and rivers and mountains and trees), are the sound beginnings of an environmentalism that is so very much more than a program of protection. It is a philosophy of creation itself.

716 STAUFFER, Donald Barlow. "Review of Medea." New York Times, April 21, 1946.
     The play might act well, for with proper lighting and an ambitious actress, it could explode uncompromising horror in the heart. But it is neither a great tragedy nor a good poem. It is a melodrama that falls between two styles. In the ancient, pottery colors of brick and black and in the decorative motifs, the handsome exterior of this volume evokes the Greek more easily than what the volume contains.

717 _____. A Short History of American Poetry. New York: E. P. Dutton, 1974. Jeffers, pp. 312-314.
     The shocking quality of Jeffers' verse derived from his choice of violent and unusual themes: incest, rape, and murder in long verse narratives full of allegory and symbolism underscoring his love of nature and his hatred of society.... The power of Jeffers' poetry is unmistakable. In its long, sweeping lines, its sharp images of sea-swept cliffs, lonely red woods, and other features of the California landscape, it is arresting and compelling. His supple and forceful free-verse line, alternating between five and ten stresses, is a powerful instrument in his longer narratives.

718 STEPHENS, George D. "The Narrative and Dramatic Poetry of Robinson Jeffers: A Critical Study." Ph.D. diss., Southern California, 1953.

719 STERLING, George. "Rhymes and Reactions." Overland Monthly, 83 (November, 1925), 411.
     Review of Tamar, etc.

720 _____. "A Tower by the Sea." San Francisco Review, 1 (February-March, 1926), 248-249.
     Critical estimate of Robinson Jeffers.

721 _____. Robinson Jeffers: The Man and the Artist. New York: Boni & Liveright, 1926. 40 pages.
     Review of Sterling's work in: The Argonaut, 101 (February 19, 1927), 8; Boston Evening Transcript, February 19, 1927; and American Mercury, 10 (April 1927), 16.
     Sterling concludes his study of Jeffers by saying: "If I have seemed over-enthusiastic in my appreciation of the work of Robinson Jeffers, such enthusiasm is utterly sincere--and

quite shameless.... Few of our great poets have had in their
lifetime the praise and appreciation that were their due. I
am far from sure that that was a good thing for their work;
poets, I imagine, do their best when stimulated by approval,
not when discouraged by inattention. What men will say of
Robinson Jeffers in a hundred years I wish to say now, despite the attitude of the envious, the ungenerous and the
blind."

722 _____. "The Poetry of the Pacific Coast," in Braithwaite,
    ed., Anthology of Magazine Verse... (1926), pp. 91-93.

723 _____; Genevieve Taggard; and James Rorty, eds. Conti-
    nent's End, an Anthology of Contemporary California Poets.
    San Francisco: John Henry Nash, 1926. Printed for the
    Book Club of California.
        Title is derived from poem by Jeffers.

724 STEUDING, Robert F. "Intensification of Meaning in 'Shine,
    Perishing Republic': A Linguistic Analysis," Robinson
    Jeffers Newsletter, 21 (April, 1968), 2-4.
        In his poem Jeffers has bent syntax to his will, turned
    nouns into verbs, and loaded his sentences with assonance,
    consonance, dramatic repetitions, and supra-segmental fea-
    tures. In short, Jeffers has used language to its utmost
    possibilities. One aspect of this poem's greatness lies in Jef-
    fers' artistic control and use of these elements in the creation
    and intensification of the poem's meaning. A close linguistic
    analysis of the poem should reveal this feature and thus
    engender a greater understanding and appreciation of this
    work.

725 STOVALL, Floyd. American Idealism. Norman: University of
    Oklahoma Press, 1943. Jeffers, pp. 205-209.
        He returns to Greek sources for some of his materials, and
    he also adopts the psychology of the subconscious, but his
    style is clear and his rejection of human ideals is too complete
    to allow his acceptance of any institution or any culture cor-
    rupted by man's meddling. He not only repudiates humani-
    tarianism and democracy but all forms of religion, resting his
    hope for man purely on the law of physical nature. His
    poems are rich with beautiful and powerful descriptions, but
    they are also filled with scenes of cruelty, insanity, and hor-
    ror. His philosophy may be called a pantheistic materialism.
    God is represented as unconscious nature, and man's conscious
    separateness is evil. The universe is beautiful in its wholenes
    but not in its parts. Though he rejects idealism, his strong
    love of freedom is the rock on which all idealism must rest. He
    fears and distrusts the tender quality in idealism, and, to off-
    set it, he exaggerates the opposite quality of hardness.

726 STRAUSS, Kate D. "Robinson Jeffers, Poet of the Decline of
     the West." Masters Thesis, Mills College (Oakland, Calif.),
     1935.

727 STRUDWICK, Shepperd. "Paris Premiere of Medea: A Memoir."
     Robinson Jeffers Newsletter, 52 (December, 1978), 15-16.
         Article is an account of the 1955 production of Medea in
     Paris at the Sarah Bernhardt Theatre. Judith Anderson
     played the title role, with a strong supporting cast. Re-
     hearsals for the play had been in New York, and the cast
     stayed in Paris about ten days, for six performances. The
     play was entered in the International Dramatic Arts Festival,
     but although it received honorable mention, Bertolt Brecht's
     "The Caucasion Chalk Circle" was the winner by a consider-
     able margin.

728 STUART, Gloria. "Review of Descent to the Dead." Carmelite,
     4 (1932), 8-9.

729 SWALLOW, Alan. "The Poetry of Robinson Jeffers." Intermoun-
     tain Review, 2 (Fall, 1937), 8-9.

730 SWAN, Addie M. "Review Roan Stallion, etc." Davenport
     [Iowa] Daily Times, January 23, 1926.

731 _____. "Review Cawdor, etc." Ibid., January 12, 1929.

732 _____. "Review Dear Judas, etc." Ibid., November 30, 1929.

733 SWIFT, Arlene R. "Robinson Jeffers: 'The Tower Beyond
     Tragedy': A Critical Study of the Philosophy of Robinson
     Jeffers and his Validity as a Modern Tragedian." Masters
     Thesis, Columbia University, 1950.

734 TAGGARD, Genevieve. "The Deliberate Annihilation." New
     York Herald Tribune Books. August 28, 1927.
         Review of The Women at Point Sur. Calls this volume
     "the annihilation of Robinson Jeffers," and continues by say-
     ing: "After a long search for the secret of his failure I
     come to a very insistent and simple conclusion. An artist
     performs one office only, no matter what his philosophy or
     his feeling--he fulfills his reader. Underlying all that he
     writes, Jeffers has more strongly the desire to withhold ful-
     fillment from his reader, to give him pain only, a desire that
     comes from the same source that compels his preoccupation
     with cruelty."

735 TATE, Allen. "American Poetry Since 1920." Bookman, 68
     (January, 1929), 503-508.

A general review of poetry publications in the 1920's, with
the conclusion that although much had been published and
there had been numerous movements and circles, there was
no center to all this activity, no estimating what the impact
of this decade would be on the future. Of Jeffers he says:
"And there is the far West, where Jeffers stands alone. His
gift for narrative is unequalled in England or America, and
he has invented a new narrative style. He represents, with
his symbols of inversion and sterility, with his anti-intellectu-
alism, the most ambitious reach of the West to erect its disorder and rootless energy into a symbol of the whole American scene."

736 _____. "Poetry as Progress." New Republic, 62 (February
       26, 1930), 51-52.
       A review of Our Singing Strength: An Outline of Ameri-
       can Poetry (1620-1930), by Alfred Kreymborg, a huge volume
       which is "on every page, a labor of love." The book lacks
       objectivity but on the whole deals fairly with contemporary
       poets, still living. This includes Jeffers, whom he sees as
       a descendent of Whitman, in the prophetic vein, and hopes
       "the new Shakespeare may combine the love of Whitman and
       the hate of Jeffers." One may hope that he will not mistake
       the size of his vision for its intelligence and quality.

737 TAYLOR, Frajam. "The Enigma of Robinson Jeffers: II, The
       Hawk and the Stone." Poetry, 55 (October, 1939), 39-44.
       Analysis of "Give Your Heart to the Hawks." The reader
       of Jeffers cannot fail to be impressed by the recurrence in
       his work of two symbols--the hawk and the stone--which,
       though mutually opposed, are equally honored by the poet
       as the tangible representatives of two antipodal ideas. The
       hawk is the image of all that is proud, fierce, and uncon-
       querable. It stands for ruthless force and indomitable cour-
       age. It is a hard, strong, and lonely creature, ready to
       pounce with cruel predatory talons; it bows to no law but
       that of its own being.... Again and again Jeffers exploits
       the ideal of the hawk, but it is in "Give Your Heart to the
       Hawks" that he gives it the fullest, most lucid expression.
       Against all the vitality of the hawk, Jeffers counterpoises
       the quietness, peace, silence, and immobility of the stone.

738 TAYLOR, J. Golden. The Literature of the American West.
       Boston: Houghton Mifflin, 1971. Jeffers, pp. 729-756.

739 _____, and Gerald Haslam, eds. The Literary History of the
       American West. Boston: Houghton Mifflin, 1973. Jeffers,
       passim.

740 TAYLOR, Walter Fuller. A History of American Letters. Boston:
       American Book, 1936. Jeffers, pp. 441-444.

As the naturalism of violence appeared in fiction so it appeared in poetry with the advent of Robinson Jeffers. He is most at home in his treatment of the great, primitive passions and the intense emotions they call forth. Elevation, however, is by no means lacking. Jeffers recognizes that while melodrama may serve as the foundation for great poetry, it must be built upon by something beyond itself. The imaginative lift of Jeffers' poetry is owing in part to his response to the natural grandeur of the California coastal region. His dramas of the emotions are played out under the open sky, against sheer cliffs of world-old granite, beneath huge redwoods, beside turbulent, cool mountain streams, in mountain clefts filled with wildflowers, and on the surf-beaten shore of the Pacific.

741 THOMPSON, Alan Reynolds. "The Cult of Cruelty." Bookman, 74 (January-February, 1932), 477-487.

Begins with a general review of books which are unbelievably graphic and pictorial in their treatment of violence, lust, insanity, and unheard of forms of cruelty. This article focuses on William Faulkner and Robinson Jeffers. In this regard, he says Jeffers is the "final exhibit in our native chamber of horrors, last because most extreme and most powerful." He is unquestionably the most remarkable writer whose gifts have been fostered by the natural scenery, the rugged, beautiful coastal region near Carmel where he lives.... But his themes are horrible. He is obsessed by the thought of death. He imagines the details of physical dissolution with searing vividness and enlarges upon details of the death of the human mind.

742 _____. "The Dilemma of Modern Tragedy," in Humanism in America, edited by Norman Foerster. New York: Farrar & Rinehart, 1930. Pp. 525-527.

The dilemma of modern tragedy remains very real. There is no refuge in obscurantism through return to illusions which science has shattered. Reason denies the objective reality of our dreams; and, so long as the honest man accepts a monism which identifies man with nature, he can find no justification for tragic exaltation.

743 THORP, Willard. American Writing in the 20th-Century. Cambridge: Harvard University Press, 1960. Jeffers, pp. 220-221.

Robinson Jeffers defies the categories of critics and literary historians. He belonged to no school. He made no alliances with other poets and he was as indifferent to criticism as the rocks and surf of the Carmel Coast in California, which the murders and suicides in his long narrative poems should by now have unpeopled. Jeffers believes in his own nihilism, of course, but his violent plots are deliberately chosen because he thinks them appropriate of his time.

744 THURSTON, Lenore. "The Tragic Spirit of Eugene O'Neill,
     Robinson Jeffers, and Theodore Dreiser." Masters Thesis,
     University of Utah, 1933.

745 TOWNE, Charles Hanson. "A Number of Things." New York
     American, April 1, 1932. Also in Chicago Herald and Exam-
     iner, April 8, 1932.
         Review of Thurso's Landing, etc.

746 TREMBLY, Clifford. "A Virile Poet." St. Paul News, November
     29, 1925.
         Review of Roan Stallion, etc.

747 TRENT, Lucia. "Jeffers Dips Pen into Cruel Acid." Philadelphia
     Public Ledger, April 16, 1932.
         Review of Thurso's Landing, etc.

748 TURLISH, Molly Streeter Buffum. "Story Patterns from Greek
     and Biblical Sources in the Poetry of Robinson Jeffers."
     Ph.D. diss., University of Michigan, 1971. DA, 32 (1972),
     6458A.
         Jeffers worked with Greek and biblical sources directly in
     a number of poems. His characteristic theme of inhumanism,
     with its emphasis on a new and vital combination of primitive
     and civilized values, appears in these poems but does not
     usually fit very well with the Greek or Hebraic world pres-
     ented. Only in his narrative poems that parallel mythic ac-
     tions but with modern characters did Jeffers have sufficient
     freedom to present his ideas without destroying the coherence
     of the poem.... The most successful of these poems are
     close enough to the source for the mythic dimension to add
     significance to the modern action and motivation but inde-
     pendent enough to establish their own existence.

749 TURNER, Ethel. "Review of Continent's End." San Francisco
     Review, 2 (July-August, 1926), 40.

750 _____. "George Sterling." Ibid., 2 (November-December,
     1926), 97-98.

751 UNTERMEYER, Louis "Uneasy Death." Saturday Review of Lit-
     erature, 6 (April 19, 1930), 942.
         Review of Dear Judas, etc. Comments on "The Loving
     Shepherdess" as the simplest story Jeffers has written, and
     also the most moving. It holds, in a loose pattern, passages
     of tenderness surpassing the lyrics in which the poet is at
     his best. It seems to mark a new tendency in Jeffers, in
     that for once he allows himself to be kind to his subject.

752 _____. "Five Notable Poets." <u>Yale Review</u>, 21 (June, 1932),
811-817. Includes <u>Thurso's Landing</u>.
"... but between Jeffers the philosopher and Jeffers the
poet there is a significant dichotomy. The philosophy is
negative, repetitious, dismal; the poetry, even when bitterest, is positive as any creative expression must be; it is
varied in movement and color, it vibrates with a nervous
fecundity. It is like nothing else of which we are proud to
boast; it is continually breaking through its own pattern to
dangerous and unfathomed depths. This is not a work to be
enjoyed without sacrificing that sense of ease dear to the
casual reader; I am not sure that, in the common sense, it
can be 'enjoyed' at all. But here is an undeviating, full-
throated poetry, remarkable in sheer drive and harrowing
drama, a poetry we may never love but one we cannot forget."

753 _____. "Review of <u>Such Counsels You Gave To Me</u>, etc."
<u>Saturday Review of Literature</u>, 16 (October 9, 1937), 11.
The sixty pages of the title poem are as emotional as they
are modern, as passionate as they are perverse, as original
in utterance as they are familiar in subject. Once again
Jeffers employs an unhappy family relationship to evoke a
sense of personal tragedy against a background of universal
terror. The other poems are less imposing, but they are
scarcely less interesting. They celebrate strength, the con-
solation of transient beauty, the solidity of sea-granite, and
the will to endure against the horrors of new ways to give
pain, new slaveries. Such elements do not make pretty
verses, but they make impressive monoliths of poetry.

754 _____. "Review of <u>Hungerfield and Other Poems</u>." <u>Saturday
Review</u>, 37 (January 16, 1954), 17.
Here, once more, is Jeffers' approximation of Greek tragedy transferred to the melodramatic coast of California. Here,
too, are Jeffers' familiar similes and symbols: the beauty of
hawks flying, knife-keen winds, plunging promontories,
streams tearing at rocks, the black strength of the flooding
tide. A Jeffers reader will be prepared for all this. But
although he will no longer be either shocked or surprised,
he will not fail to be roused. Jeffers has not lost the gift
of biting language and the ability to communicate the phan-
tasmagoria of terror.

755 _____, ed. <u>A Miscellany of American Poetry</u>. New York:
Harcourt, Brace, 1927. Jeffers, pp. 245-256.

756 _____, ed. <u>Modern American and British Poetry</u>. New York:
Harcourt, Brace, 1928. Jeffers, pp. 221-222. Revised edi-
tion by Untermeyer, Karl Shapiro, and Richard Wilbur. 1955.
Jeffers, pp. 186-198.

Prints 15 of Jeffers' shorter poems, mostly familiar, without biographical or critical comment.

757 _____, ed. Modern American Poetry. New York: Harcourt, Brace, 1942. Jeffers, pp. 402-417.

Prints some twenty of Jeffers' best-known, shorter poems, preceded by Biographical and Critical appraisal. Between Jeffers the philosopher and Jeffers the poet there is a significant dichotomy. The philosophy is negative, repetitious, dismal. The poetry, even when bitterest, is positive as any creative expression must be. It is varied in movement and color; it vibrates with a reckless fecundity; it is continually breaking through its own pattern to dangerous and unfathomed depths. This is not a work to be enjoyed without sacrificing that sense of ease dear to the casual reader; it is doubtful if, in the common sense, it can be enjoyed at all.

758 V., R. L. "Poetic Pictures of California." Syracuse Post-Standard, November 30, 1925.

Review of Roan Stallion, etc.

759 VAN DAM, Denis. "Greek Shadows on the Monterey Coast: Environment in Robinson Jeffers' Poetry." Robinson Jeffers Newsletter, 40 (November, 1974), 9-17.

Begins with a survey of Jeffers' decision to live on the Monterey Coast and not on the Aegean, as he had first planned. Also discusses the poet's background in the Greek classics and the Greek language. Continues by showing how he created the Greek atmosphere on the coast of California, using farmers and other members of the lower social and economic scales. The three narratives of his early period which best illustrate the Greek influence on Jeffers are "Tamar," "The Tower Beyond Tragedy," and "Roan Stallion." Article continues with careful and reasonable discussion of the parallels between the Greek landscape and the one which Jeffers imbued with Greek-like aspects on the coast of California.

760 VAN DOREN, Carl. "Robinson Jeffers," in American and British Literature Since 1890, by Carl and Mark Van Doren. New York: Century, 1939. Pp. 55-57.

The poem called "Tamar" introduced the themes which Jeffers has developed throughout his later work: murder, incest, slaughter, fire, and desperate tenderness. His view of man is as a creature who has perverted himself and his society by too much inward thinking; the theme of incest as Jeffers uses it represents "symbolized racial introversion; man regarding man exclusively--founding his values, desires, a picture of the universe, all on his own humanity." Jeffers is more in love with other creatures--hawks, eagles--who can

love outwardly, and with unconscious entities--mountains, the
sea, the distantly burning stars--whose beautiful existence
does not depend on thought at all.... Jeffers' future reputation will depend upon the intelligibility of his doctrine in a
later age; and upon the ability of his long, loose line to continue impressive as a unit of verse composition.

761 VAN DOREN, Mark. "First Glance: Review of Tamar, etc."
     The Nation, 120 (March 11, 1925), 268.
          "Always with Jeffers, as with other major poets, humanity
     breaks into fire. His way is the way of the great tragic
     poets.... [H]e dredges, as they dredged, too deep in the
     mud of mortality not to come up with images and rhythms
     terrible in their force and beautiful in their strangeness.
     Hence his uniqueness among American poets, and his very
     high rank."

762 _____. "Review of Roan Stallion, Tamar, etc." Nation, 121
     (November 25, 1925), 599.
          All that was said a few months ago about Jeffers will have
     to be said again with greater emphasis. This volume contains
     the poems which then arouses so much concern. It also comes
     forth with several important new poems, one of which, "Roan
     Stallion," ... is a masterpiece.

763 _____. "First Glance: Review of The Women at Point Sur."
     Nation, 125 (July 27, 1927), 88.
          Van Doren says: "I have read it with thrills of pleasure
     at its power and beauty, and I shall read everything else
     Jeffers writes. But I may be brought to wonder whether
     there is need of his trying further in this direction. He
     seems to be knocking his head to pieces against the night."

764 _____. "Bits of Earth and Water." Nation, 128 (January 9,
     1929), 50
          Review of Cawdor, etc. His way is the way of the great
     tragic poets whom Jeffers has been bold enought to take as
     his masters. Imitators are usually ridiculous, but Jeffers is
     not because he is of their company; he dredges, as they
     dredged, too deep in the mud of mortality not to come up
     with images and rhythms terrible in their force and beautiful
     in their explainable strangeness. Hence his uniqueness among
     American poets, and his very high rank.

765 _____. "Judas, Savior of Jesus." Nation, 130 (January 1,
     1930), 20-21.
          Review of Dear Judas, etc. This is far from being one of
     Jeffers' best poems. The setting is somber and fine, and
     utterances of the principal persons often reach a high level
     of rhetoric. But there is significance in the fact that Jeffers'
     long lines frequently forget to be poetry. There is another

long poem in the volume to which these remarks do not apply.
"The Loving Shepherdess" contains some of the best work
that Jeffers has ever done; it is continuously pathetic, exciting and beautiful.

766   _____, ed. American Poets, 1630-1930. Boston: Little,
       Brown, 1932. Jeffers, p. 656.

767   _____; James Rorty; and Richard Eberhart. "Three Memories
       of Robinson Jeffers." Robinson Jeffers Newsletter, 27 (Janu-
       ary, 1970), 3-7.
            Van Doren said, "I respected his reticence, and never
       forced myself upon his attention; I have never ceased to think
       very highly of his poetry, and of him. He was a generous,
       affectionate, faithful, and humorous friend."
            James Rorty said, "Who today can doubt the profundity of
       Jeffers' vision? The machine civilization which he detested is
       in crisis around the world, a crisis which may yet have an
       apocalyptic resolution."
            Richard Eberhart said: "He does not make a poetry which
       depends upon symbol, innuendo, or any kind of double-talk.
       Of its kind there has been nothing successfully like it since
       Whitman. It is direct. It is a man speaking. Granted there
       are other graces and enviable ways of poetry, this way can
       be uniquely powerful in the hands of great talent."

768   VAN WYCK, William. Robinson Jeffers. Los Angeles: Ward
       Ritchie Press, 1938. 17 pages.

769   VARDAMIS, Alexander A. The Critical Reputation of Robinson
       Jeffers: A Bibliographical Study. Hamden, Conn.: Archon
       Books, 1972.
            Based on Ph.D. dissertation. "The Critical Reputation of
       Robinson Jeffers." Columbia University, 1970; review by
       Robert Brophy, Robinson Jeffers Newsletter, 34 (February,
       1973), 3-4.
            Consists of some 300 pages divided into three parts: re-
       views of books by Jeffers; periodical articles; and books and
       portions of books. Under each section, items are arranged
       chronologically by author. Work is very comprehensive in
       scope, omitting only the most trivial newspaper and magazine
       articles. Comments are brief and objective, whenever possi-
       ble quoting key passages in the work. Contains over 1000
       items.
            Book has forty-page introduction, a summary of Jeffers'
       reputation, and an evaluation of his poetry. Does not con-
       tain a subject index. Dissertation is listed in DA, 33 (1973),
       5754A.

770   VAUGHN, Eric. "Dear Judas: Time and Dramatic Structures of
       the Dream." Robinson Jeffers Newsletter, 51 (July, 1978),
       7-22.

Article begins with speculation as to why some poets have been fairly successful in seeing their plays produced while others have enjoyed little or no consideration. Altogether Jeffers wrote seven plays, only one of them, Medea, a successful production. In all truth, this probably was due to the fact that Judith Anderson starred in it. The first five of the plays were written as dramatic poems rather than as plays. The four "Greek" plays are mostly regular in form and structure: Medea, The Cretan Woman, The Tower Beyond Tragedy, At the Fall of an Age; At the Birth of an Age is almost Wagnerian in design; Dear Judas and The Bowl of Blood are alike in being dream-plays, and to that extent seem to be influenced by the Japanese Noh-play. Dear Judas has a three-part structure, whereas The Bowl of Blood has a very standard Greek tragic structure.

Article continues with some discussion of the Japanese Noh-play and the similarity which Jeffers' Judas bears to it. Last part presents a structural-time analysis of Dear Judas as it falls into three distinct parts.

771 VICKERY, John B., ed. Myth and Literature. Lincoln: University of Nebraska Press, 1966. Jeffers, passim.
Discussion similar to study given below. Does not include Jeffers or any of the modern writers.

772 _____. The Literary Impact of the Golden Bough. Princeton: Princeton University Press, 1973. Jeffers, pp. 158-161.
By his own admission, Jeffers has been concerned to explore the sources of contemporary Western civilization. Since this exploration involves attending to the interaction of myth and history in particular cultures, it both resembles and derives in many respects from Frazer's interest in the genesis of society and the reconstruction of the past. Jeffers acts mythopoetically on the Hebrew-Christian, the Greek, and the Teutonic sources of our modern civilization in Dear Judas, The Tower Beyond Tragedy, and At the Birth of an Age, respectively. The last is of particular interest, for it makes extensive use of the symbol of the self-tortured god who hangs himself on a gallows in order to gain wisdom. There are also other themes and figures that attest to the impact of Frazer's work on Jeffers' poetry: the recurrent pattern of existence, the rite of blood-sacrifice, the capacity to bear pain as a test of manhood, the burial ceremonies and the idea of immortality, fetish worship, and the relation of the myths and cultures of the past to those of the present.

773 VIERECK, George S. My Flesh and Blood. New York: Horace Liveright, 1931. Jeffers, p. 2 et passim.
An interesting book of poetry which the author calls "A Lyric Autobiography, with Indiscreet Annotations." In the Introduction which he calls "Confessional," he reviews the

situation of American poetry around the turn of the century
and says "it seemed as if the void left by the passing of the
'great New Englanders' would never be filled." Names a number of emerging poets but thinks they had a far distance to
go before America caught up with them: "George Sterling
was gathering the grapes for his enchanted wine.... Jeffers,
I suspect, was still in the cradle."
    Reference to Jeffers is of little importance; what is per-
haps more important is the similarity in the subject matter of
some of Viereck's poems and Jeffers'.

774 VIVAS, Eliseo. "Robinson Jeffers." New Student, 8 (April,
     1929), 13-15.

775 WAGGONER, Hyatt Howe. "Science and the Poetry of Robinson
     Jeffers." American Literature, 10 (November, 1938), 275-288.
        Quotes a passage from Flagons and Apples (1912) and the
     treatment of the same theme twenty years later in Thurso's
     Landing (1932). Aside from obvious changes in metrics and
     vocabulary, there seems to be one fundamental difference be-
     tween the two passages, a difference that expresses itself in
     three forms: in the twenty-three year period between the two
     passages there had been radical changes in the poet's method,
     his material, and his philosophy. These three approaches are
     not separate, and behind the changes in all of them lies the
     fact that in 1912 the influence of science was not apparent in
     Jeffers' poetry, while in 1932 it was the primary factor to be
     reckoned with. Two changes had taken place in the poet:
     the implications of the science he had learned as a medical
     student had become the dominant elements in his philosophy
     of life, and he had learned to fuse belief, knowledge, and
     experience in creating his poetry.

776 _____. The Heel of Elohim: Science and Values in Modern
     American Poetry. Norman: University of Oklahoma Press,
     1950. "Robinson Jeffers: Here Is Reality," pp. 105-132.
        Includes a discussion of "Margrave." If man and his mind
     are but a momentary disease of matter, how can one trust
     one's judgment about what is real? But it is not, after all,
     nature as experienced by man that is finally real, but nature
     as studied by the natural sciences. The real universe is
     alien to man and cannot be comprehended by man's little
     mind. The size of the universe, the vastness of its time
     scale, and the "inhumanness" of its processes as described
     by the physical sciences make it alien or at best "indifferent."

777 _____. American Poets from the Puritans to the Present.
     Boston: Houghton Mifflin, 1968. Jeffers, pp. 469-476.

What Jeffers finally came to call his "Inhumanism" has
more in common with Emerson's philosophy than we would
suppose, more than would appear if we simply contrasted
idealism and materialism as metaphysical opposites. For both
poets, reality is "overpowering." For both, the universal
beauty is more impressive than the little triumphs of man's
intellect or will. For both, abiding reality is not possessed
and cannot be possessed. Nature, for both, is where we
must look if we are to find reality.

778 WALKER, Charles. "Review of The Women at Point Sur." Independent, October 15, 1927.

779 WALKER, Robert H. "The Lyric Poetry of Robinson Jeffers."
Masters Thesis, Columbia University, 1950.

780 WALTON, Eda Lou. "Dear Judas: A Review." The Symposium,
1 (January, 1930), 135-138.

781 _____. "California's Place in the Literary Firmament." New
York Times Book Review, August 9, 1931.

782 _____. "On the Theme of Time." Nation, 134 (February 3,
1932), 146-147.
    Review of Descent to the Dead. Jeffers is often very
faulty in his narratives, very unpoetic. There are passages
which are in very bad taste. Jeffers can tell a story, despite his symbolism, despite his obsessions; he understands
his characters and presents a well-motivated tale. He has a
perfect sense of human drama. This is a tremendous power
in a narrative poet. But only in his lyrics, as in this volume,
does he show his command of the poetic line.

783 _____. "A Poet at Odds with His Own Civilization." New
York Herald Tribune Books, October 8, 1933.
    Most men, moving with the age, will find in Jeffers no
message and no solace. The poet, entrenched in his personal
religion, will be more and more a voice in the wilderness,
crying out to no purpose whatsoever.

784 _____. "Beauty of Storm Disproportionately." Poetry, 51
(January, 1938), 209-213.
    Review of Such Counsels, etc. As has been said many
times, Jeffers has vigor, dramatic intensity. But he repeats
himself now. And he argues and moralizes where once he
presented beautiful pictures of Nature. Obviously, with his
passion for individualism, Jeffers confronts a most uncongen-
ial world. He would teach this world something, but he has
removed himself too far from his own age to be seriously
listened to as a prophet. The title poem of this volume is a
reenactment of an old Scotch ballad but ends with the would-

be superman son giving himself up to the law of modern
society.

785 WANN, Louis. "Robinson Jeffers: Counterpart of Walt Whit-
     man." Personalist, 19 (July, 1938), 297-308.
          In view of the widespread ingnorance and misunderstand-
     ing that prevail regarding Jeffers, it may be useful to con-
     sider his work as holding up to us the other side of the
     shield from that presented by Whitman. The suggestion has
     been made repeatedly that Jeffers has derived from Whitman,
     both in form and content. This article does not explore the
     relationship of form, but seeks the following: 1) the contrast
     between the mature philosophies of the two; 2) the sources
     of Jeffers' philosophy; and 3) the meaning and value of Jef-
     fers' art and philosophy. Conclusion is that Whitman resolved
     the conflicts of life, but Jeffers has not done so. There are
     many self-contradictions in Jeffers, and it remains to be seen
     if there will be some sort of positive reconciliation, or if we
     must accept his own words: "The discords of our world are
     not resolved but by other discords."

786 WARD, A. C. American Literature, 1880-1930. London: Meth-
     uen, 1932; New York: Dial Press, 1932. Jeffers, pp. 201-
     202.

787 WARREN, Robert Penn. "Jeffers on the Age." Poetry, 49
     (February, 1937), 279-282.
          Review of Solstice, etc. Does not feel that this volume
     will add anything to Jeffers' reputation. Not that the reader
     requires something new every time a poet publishes, but the
     reader may require some new development, extension, or dis-
     covery. This book contains a great deal of self-imitation.
     This is particularly true of the title poem. "At the Birth of
     an Age" is the most interesting long poem, and the short
     poems tend to be fragmentary comments, gnomic utterances
     without adequate context. They do not compare favorably
     with short poems frequently included in some of Jeffers'
     earlier publications.

788 WASSERSTROM, William. "A Discussion of the Criticism of Rob-
     inson Jeffers." Masters Thesis, Columbia University, 1947.

789 WATTS, Harold, H. "Robinson Jeffers and Eating the Serpent."
     Sewanee Review, 49 (January, 1941), 39-55.
          Article begins with a reminder that sexuality was not the
     only instinct which Freud isolated in man. Another equally
     important impulse is theological or that which accounts for
     man's ultimate ends. In Jeffers this motive is largely in-
     verted, because he tries again and again to attain a view of
     man's final destiny without once asking the questions and
     giving the answers of orthodox mysticism and theology.

Having rejected the Christian God, he presses on to the bitter end that awaits alienated man and assigns to his god and
to himself the cosmic tortures recorded in his narratives--
the draining of the bitter poison of the serpent.

790 _____. "Multivalence in Robinson Jeffers." College English,
      3 (November, 1941), 109-120.
         Article is an examination of the violence which occurs in
      the poetry of Jeffers, particularly in the long narratives.
      This violence is often overemphasized by the critics, who do
      not usually ask why the poet seems obsessed with recurrent
      violence, sexual and otherwise. Jeffers maintains that he
      uses it because it is the most tragic of subject matters. In
      the final analysis, however, Jeffers' tragic drama presents
      nothing which informs our spirit. We are unable to rise to
      the occasion of this violence in our own time.

791 WEALES, G. C. American Drama Since World War II. New York:
      Harcourt, Brace & World, 1962. "Poets and Novelists on
      Stage," pp. 182-202.
         Reviews Jeffers' contribution to the stage: an adaptation
      of Medea; The Cretan Woman, the Phaedra story; a dramatic
      version of Dear Judas, written by Michael Myerberg; and
      Jeffers' own adaptation of his poem The Tower Beyond Trag-
      edy.
         Medea became the best known, largely because Judith
      Anderson played the role of Medea. The Cretan Woman, how-
      ever, is probably the best of the Jeffers' plays. Theme is
      a familiar one, although it has its share of Jeffers' poetic
      clichés. Verse is more direct than in Medea, and the play
      as a whole is much more successful in letting the action carry
      the theme.

792 WEEDIN, Everett K., Jr. "Ritualism and Naturalism in the
      Poetry of Robinson Jeffers." Ph.D. diss., Cornell, 1967.
      DA, 28 (1967), 2269A.
         The techniques, concerns, and structures of Jeffers'
      narrative poems have not been fully identified. Until they
      are, these poems, which are usually considered faulty, can
      not be so judged.... Throughout his narratives, Jeffers
      created a compound of realistic, tragic, and epic elements.
      He had done so by submitting all the elements to the control
      of the structure, techniques, and concerns of myth.

793 WEISSTEIN, Judith S. "The Greek Plays of Robinson Jeffers."
      Masters Thesis, Indiana University, 1966.

794 WELLS, Henry W. The American Way of Poetry. New York:
      Columbia University Press, 1943. "Grander Canyons: Jef-
      fers," pp. 148-160. Reprinted New York: Russell & Russell,
      1964.

No American poet has allowed himself to become more profoundly affected by the region where he dwells than Robinson Jeffers. Many ties bind him to the majestic coast of southern California and the mountains towering behind it. In one poem he supposes that his ghost will hover for centuries about his house and ground overlooking the ocean. In another he reflects on the future of the trees which he has planted, the rocks he has loved. Beneath all his imagery lies his fusion of pessimism and stoicism: nature is to him infinitely nobler than man and so far as it deigns to teach him anything, merely teaches him to endure.

795 _____. "A Philosophy of War: The Outlook of Robinson Jeffers." College English, 6 (November, 1944), 81-88.
Begins with a commentary on current written records of the war, many of which are unexcelled for sheer vigor, almost none of which have any literary value, "lacking the inwardness of poetry." From practically the beginning, the war theme has fascinated Jeffers, although he has written no obvious "war poetry" as did Stephen Benet and others. Almost all his long poems are narratives with a military background. Most of them are tales of violent domestic tragedy on the coast of California among persons who have in some way been scarred by war.... Jeffers views war through the eyes of biology and scientific materialism. He sees all matter as engaged in a struggle for existence, and history merely repeats in human terms the struggle demonstrated by the natural sciences. Wars between nations follow from wars within the atom.

796 WEST, Geoffrey. "Seven Poets." Adelphi, 1 (February, 1932), 432-436.
Review of Dear Judas, etc.

797 WEST, George P. "Great New Poet, Jeffers." San Francisco Call, January 2, 1926.

798 WESTON, Edgar, and Brett Weston. "A Robinson Jeffers Memorial." Ramparts, 1 (Summer, 1962), 65-72.

799 WHITE, Kenneth. The Coast Opposite Humanity. Dyfed, England: Unicorn Press, 1975.
Essay on the poetry of Robinson Jeffers, by the British poet.

800 WHITE, William. "Some Unnoticed Jeffers Poems." Papers of the Bibliographical Society of America, 34 (December, 1940), 362-363.

801 _____. "Uncollected Poems of Robinson Jeffers." American Notes and Queries, 1 (January, 1942), 149-151.

802 _____ . "Robinson Jeffers' Space." Personalist, 44 (April,
        1963), 175-179.
        Compare Whitman with this brooding nihilist from Tor
    House, Point Sur, and the rugged Carmel coast. Trained
    in medicine, science, and astronomy, steeped in the Greek
    classics and their Olympian aspect of the world, and having
    little use beyond derision for our earth, Jeffers consistently
    maintains a cosmic viewpoint. This is especially true of the
    short lyrics.... The important point in comparing Whitman
    and Jeffers is that Whitman uses his skills and talents to
    affirm the identity of all men in all places; Whitman embraces
    all humanity, past and present, in sympathy and understand-
    ing. Jeffers, on the other hand, soars into space, not to
    affirm, but to deny and reject humanity.

803 _____ . "Robinson Jeffers: Poet of Black Despair." The
        English Language and Literature, 17 (November, 1965), 91-
        101. (Seoul: English Literary Society of Korea.)

804 _____ . "Robinson Jeffers: A Checklist, 1959-1965." Serif,
        3 (June, 1966), 36-39.

805 _____ . "Robinson Jeffers' 'The Beginning and the End':
        Another Error." Papers of the Bibliographical Society of
        America, 61 (June, 1967), 126.

806 _____ . "Jeffers and Whitman Briefly." Serif, 6 (June, 1969),
        32-33.

807 _____ . "Robinson Jeffers on a Postage Stamp." American
        Book Collector, 24 (1974), 30.

808 _____ , and Robert Brophy. "Not Man Apart." Robinson
        Jeffers Newsletter, 25 (February, 1970), 3-4.
        Review of book, Not Man Apart: Lines from Robinson
    Jeffers, with photographs of the Big Sur Coast by Ansel
    Adams, et al. The editorship and emphasis of this book
    shifted from the original intent of illustrating Jeffers' poetry
    to that of a book of photographs accompanied by Jeffers
    quotations. In any event, the book is superb, and whoever
    matched the lines with the photographs must have known Jef-
    fers, the Big Sur Coast, photography, and poetry. It all
    adds up to a triumph.

809 WILDER, Amos N. Spiritual Aspects of the New Poetry. New
        York: Harper and Brothers, 1940. "Nihilism of Mr. Robinson
        Jeffers," pp. 141-152.
        Apart from the lyrics the work of Jeffers consists of nar-
    rative poems of some length written in a Whitmanesque line
    presenting dramas or rather melodramas of more than usually
    violent and repellent character. Often the characterization

and action is cloudily presented and the style loose.... In the best poems these become sharper and more powerful and one recognizes in any case that the poems are not to be judged first of all as narratives. Continues by suggesting that it is for Jeffers' philosophical and psychological aspects that his work is most valuable: he has created a view of nature, unique in literature, that regards Man as a blight on the face of Nature, a being which maims and kills the creatures of the world.

810 _____. "The Cross: Social Trauma or Redemption," in Symbolism in Religion and Literature, edited by Rollo May, with Introduction. New York: George Braziller, 1960. Pp. 99-117. First published in Daedalus, Vol. 87. Also derived from chapter in Theology and Modern Literature, by Wilder. Cambridge: Harvard University Press, 1958.

   Takes Dear Judas as main text but comments on work as a whole. His affirmation is in terms of a kind of cosmic mysticism, which must be distinguished from all usual forms of pantheism, an attitude which he calls "Inhumanism." The final appeal of his often perplexing narratives lies in their dramatization of triumph, the triumph of some life-principle or world-principle through wounds, mutilation, and agony. This writer's narrative poems are filled with violent actions, with unnatural crimes and with disgust of civilization. He sees the disorder of his characters as a dramatization of our fallen condition. He proclaims his gospel of Inhumanism--the glory of inhuman things which we also may share. In Dear Judas we have a study of Christ and Judas both caught in traps not of their own choosing.

811 WILSON, Don D. "Robinson Jeffers: Poetry Versus Prose in 'Roan Stallion.'" Robinson Jeffers Newsletter, 54 (October, 1979), 14-19.

   Article is accompanied by a passage from the poem, and its arrangement in a prose-like form. Continues by showing that the work is indeed poetry, and any arrangement in prose will destroy more than half of its value. Article is too limited to study the many poetic devices of alliteration and assonance, the rhyme or near-rhyme. Has therefore stressed the rhythmic free verse form in which Jeffers wrote.

812 WILSON, Edmund. Axel's Castle: A Study in the Imaginative Literature of 1870 to 1930. New York: Scribner's, Jeffers, passim.

813 WILSON, James Southall. "Review of The Women at Point Sur." Virginia Quarterly Review, 3 (October, 1927), 611-614.

   For Jeffers, humanity is a seething mass of orgastic frenzy. This work tells a story as complicated as any novel; a story

that, for a reader with a stomach strong enough, has sustained interest and vigor. No one can question the mastery
of sweeping lines, the strength of the phrasing. But it reeks
with the stench of a decadent art. Incest, perversion, sex-
mad humanity have been put to literary uses before but never
in quite the spirit of this work.

814   WINTERS, Yvor. "Robinson Jeffers' Rich but Violent Narrative
      Poems." Philadelphia Public Ledger, July 2, 1927.
      Review of The Women at Point Sur.

815   _____. "Robinson Jeffers." Poetry, 35 (February, 1930),
      279-286.
      Review of Dear Judas and Other Poems. The poem shares
      the structural principles, or lack of them, with other narra-
      tives by Jeffers. It has no quotable lines except possibly
      the last three, which are, however, heavy with dross. The
      other long poem, "The Loving Shepherdess" succeeds in being
      no more than a very Wordsworthian embodiment of a kind of
      maudlin humanitarianism--which is a curious, but not unex-
      pected outcome of Jeffers' sentimental misanthropy.

816   _____. In Defense of Reason. New York: Alan Swallow,
      1947. Jeffers, pp. 31-35.
      This volume is a reprinting of three earlier works: Primi-
      tivism and Decadence (1937), pp. 15-150; Maule's Curse
      (1938), pp. 153-357; and The Anatomy of Nonsense (1943),
      pp. 361-603.
      Jeffers is theologically some kind of monist. He envisages
      Nature as Deity, but his nature is the nature of the textbook
      in physics and astronomy and not that of the rambling bota-
      nist. Nature, or God, is thus a kind of self-sufficient mech-
      anism, of which man is a product, but from which man is cut
      off. God is praised adequately only by the screaming demons
      that make up the atom. Man can choose between two modes
      of action: he may renounce God and rely upon his humanity,
      or he may renounce his humanity and rely upon God.

817   _____. Yvor Winters: Uncollected Essays and Reviews,
      edited with Introduction by Francis Murphy. Chicago: Swal-
      low, 1973. Jeffers, pp. 64-69.
      Reprints review of Dear Judas (Poetry, 35 [February,
      1930], 279-286).

818   _____. "Review of Thurso's Landing, etc." Hound and
      Horn, 5 (July-September, 1932), 681-685.
      Article covers a half-dozen or more books of poetry, of
      which Jeffers' is certainly not the reviewer's favorite. Re-
      fers to his review of Dear Judas and says the same "weak-
      nesses persist though in milder form." There is an attempt
      at some sort of coherent narrative, but the result is merely

dogged and soggy melodrama. Jeffers' verse continues to miss the virtues of prose and verse alike: it is capable neither of the fullness and modulation of fine verse. There is an endless, violent monotony of movement, wholly uninteresting and insensitive, that may have a hypnotic effect upon a good many readers, much as does the jolting of a railroad coach over a bad roadbed.

819 _____. "Robinson Jeffers," in Literary Opinion in America, edited by Morton D. Zabel. New York: Harper and Row, 1962. Pp. 439-443. Reprints review of Dear Judas (Poetry, 25 [February, 1930], 279-286), with minor alterations.

820 WOLFSKILL, George Kenneth. "The 'Modern Temper': The Problem of Rationalism in the Works of Hemingway, MacLeish, and Robinson Jeffers." Ph.D. diss., University of North Carolina, 1980. DA, 41 (1980), 1588A-89A.
Dissertation is built around commentary and analysis of Joseph Wood Krutch's book The Modern Temper. The three writers are representative of their generation and are fitting choices because of the differences in their degree of reaction to the implications of science and rationalism.... Jeffers fully accepted the new world view, finding in it reason for disregarding social as well as individual aspirations that lead, he felt, to meaningless anguish: indeed, the new view gave him cause to rejoice as he realized that man's insignificance made him a part of and therefore reunited him with the larger universe.

821 WOODBRIDGE, Hensley C. "A Bibliographical Note on Jeffers." American Book Collector, 10 (Summer, 1959), 15-18.
Article contains listings that had not appeared in other publications. These include books by Robinson Jeffers, Articles on American Literature, 1900-1950, compiled by Lewis Leary, and chapters or sections of books devoted to Jeffers. These items have all been listed in the present bibliographical work.

822 WRUBEL, David. "Primitivism and Robinson Jeffers: A Survey and a Study." Masters Thesis, Columbia University, 1939.

823 YOUNG, Vernon. "Such Counsels He Gave to Us: Jeffers Revisited." Parnassus, 6 (1977), 178-197.
Principally a review of the four Jeffers books which were published or reissued in 1976-1977: In This Wild Water: Suppressed Poems, edited by Shebl; The Double-Axe; The Women at Point Sur; and Dear Judas.
In the process of commenting on these four volumes, Vernon Young assesses the entire career of Jeffers and concludes

that the poet's chief problem was "that he would not shut up." He does not feel that the suppressed poems were worth publishing, and the others were "monstrous modern works," which reduce everything to absurdity. He finds the shorter poems of Jeffers easier "to assimilate and often achieve a purity of statement that is self-evident." His lengthy, tortured narratives, saturated with symbolism and exploring the nether reaches of abnormal psychology, he has professed to be his best work.

824 ZABEL, Morton D. "The Problem of Tragedy." Poetry, 33 (March, 1929), 336-340.
      Review of Cawdor and Other Poems. Cawdor shares with earlier works those properties of tragic violence and broad dramatic conflict which we have come to regard as this poet's particular marks. The interest is consistent, the movement certain, and the shaping coherent. Details are worked out with a sure touch. The mistake is that instead of writing poetry in the spirit of modern reason and logic, he has endeavored to combine these factors with antique dramaturgy. His obsession for heroic violence and the grand passion of the Greeks furnishes him with themes, but the comments of science in the midst of them seem very weak and puny.

825 _____. "A Prophet in HIs Wilderness." New Republic, 77 (January 3, 1934), 229-230.
      Review of Give Your Heart to the Hawks and Other Poems.

826 ZALLER, Robert. "The Birth of the Hero: Robinson Jeffers' The Tower Beyond Tragedy." Robinson Jeffers Newsletter, 58 (May, 1981), 5-16.
      Article is an excerpt from the work listed below. Critic thinks this poem occupies an anomalous place in the Jeffers canon. Extravagantly praised by early reviewers, it has received scant attention from the more recent critics. There is no consensus even as to its genre. It has generally been considered a verse play and successfully staged as such, but it is best read as a philosophic poem in the form chiefly of dramatic monologues--a not inexact definition of Greek tragedy itself.... Jeffers fused the Aeschylean trilogy into a single narrative structure. The essential plot has been retained, and at least a flavor of the Greek metaphors. But it should not be regarded as an adaptation of Aeschylus. It is rather a reinterpretation of the ancient story in the light of modern consciousness.

827 _____. The Cliffs of Solitude: A Reading of Robinson Jeffers. Cambridge: Cambridge University Press, 1983.
      Reviewed by James Karman, Robinson Jeffers Newsletter, 65 (December, 1984), 4-6.

828 ZORN, Gremin. "Review of Roan Stallion, etc." Brooklyn Daily Eagle, January 16, 1926.

829 _____. A Novel in Verse." Long Island Sunday Press, April 10, 1932.
        Review of Thurso's Landing, etc.

INDEX OF COAUTHORS, EDITORS, TRANSLATORS, AND ILLUSTRATORS

SUBJECT INDEX

"Alpine Christ, The" (by Jeffers) 300c, 551
American literature (histories of, containing discussion of Robinson
     Jeffers) 133, 135, 141, 215, 216, 217, 220, 225, 242, 243,
     286, 325, 329, 388, 401, 476, 477, 500, 502, 508, 510, 511,
     529, 531, 532, 598, 622, 709, 710, 717, 725, 735, 738, 739,
     740, 743, 760, 766, 777, 786, 794, 812
Anderson, Judith 89, 201, 238, 626
Anthologies (containing reprinted poems by Robinson Jeffers) 98,
     126, 137, 142-148, 202, 203, 206, 294, 299, 311, 407, 458,
     481, 535, 536, 553, 561, 562, 576, 653, 662, 684, 722, 723,
     736, 749, 755, 756, 757
"Apology for Bad Dreas" (by Jeffers) 183

"Beginning and the End, The" (by Jeffers) 155, 805
Bender, Albert 190, 441
Bennett, Melba Berry 617
Bible (see also Religion) 181, 458, 748
Bibliographical studies 84, 158, 168, 169, 373, 453, 492, 549, 643,
     769, 804, 821
Biographical comment (short pieces, sketches, anecdotes, reminis-
     cences) 2, 17, 22, 77, 94, 99, 101, 106, 107, 116, 199, 210,
     231, 232, 236, 237, 256, 274, 288, 291, 292, 343, 346, 348,
     364, 365, 383, 384, 399, 411, 425, 426, 427, 428, 464, 485,
     491, 493b, 505, 506, 507, 514, 517, 522, 527, 528, 541, 549,
     550, 575, 609, 610, 616, 630, 637, 649, 767, 774, 797, 798
"Birth Dues" (by Jeffers) 602
"Bloody Sire, The" (by Jeffers) 357, 486
Book-length studies (biographical and critical, including pamphlets;
     also reviews of these works) 92, 127, 129, 157, 184, 224,
     227, 339, 358, 403, 558, 592, 594a, 598, 611, 712, 721, 768
Books (inventory of Jeffers' library) 156
"Brides of the South Wind" (by Jeffers) 300e, 451

Californians, The (by Jeffers) 300b
Carmel 163, 613, 614
Carmelite, The (Special Jeffers Issue) 221
"Cawdor" (by Jeffers) 166, 300a, 572